SEPTUAGINT:

NUMBERS

SEPTUAGINT, VOLUME 4

SCRIPTURAL RESEARCH INSTITUTE
Published by Digital Ink Productions, 2025

COPYRIGHT

Septuagint: Numbers

Third edition. October 30, 2025

Copyright © 2025 Scriptural Research Institute.

ISBN: 978-1998636549

The Septuagint was translated into Greek at the Library of Alexandria between 250 and 132 BCE.

This English translation was created by the Scriptural Research Institute in 2019 through 2025, through the comparison of most published copies of Septuagint manuscripts. Additionally, the Leningrad Codex, Peshitta, Coptic manuscripts, Vetus Latina manuscripts, Targums, Dead Sea Scrolls, and Ketef Hinnom scroll 2 were used for comparative analysis.

The image used for the cover is "Nehushtan" by Raven Mahikan.

Ebook version: ISBN 978-1989852514

Audiobook version: ISBN 978-1990289408

Hard Cover version: ISBN 978-1998636556

TABLE OF CONTENTS

TABLE OF CONTENTS

TABLE OF CONTENTS

FORWARD

In the mid-3rd century BCE, King Ptolemy II Philadelphus of Egypt ordered a translation of the ancient Hebrew scriptures for the Library of Alexandria, which resulted in the creation of the Septuagint. The original version, published circa 250 BCE, only included the Torah, or in Greek terms, the Pentateuch. The Torah is the five books traditionally credited to Moses, circa 1500 BCE: *Cosmic Genesis*, *Exodus*, *Leviticus*, *Numbers*, and *Deuteronomy*.

Since the 1800s, the majority of Biblical scholars have interpreted the books of *Leviticus* and *Numbers* as a later addition to the original laws of Moses found in *Exodus*, with *Deuteronomy* being an even later addition during the Babylonian or Persian eras. *Cosmic Genesis* is either considered to be part of Moses' original work, or a later addition in the Persian era, depending on the scholar. *Leviticus* and *Numbers* contain several amendments to Moses' laws in *Exodus*, as well as establishing the land rights of the various tribes of Israel within historic Canaan, including the assignment of several cities and their environs to the Levitical Priesthood.

The most obvious amendment to Moses' laws, is replacing the sacrifice of the firstborn with the establishment of the Levitical Priesthood. *Exodus* Chapter 13 includes a requirement that the firstborn Israelites must be slaughtered as a sacrifice to the Lord, however, allowed an animal to be

1

substituted. This law would not have been difficult for a group of nomadic shepherds to follow but would have become progressively more difficult as the Israelites became more urbanized in Canaan.

This seems to have resulted in an increase of child sacrifice which the prophet Jeremiah spoke out against during his lifetime, estimated to between 650 BCE and 570 BCE. The practice was officially banned by King Josiah around 630 BCE when the Levites "found" the "original" Torah of Moses during the restoration of Solomon's Temple. According to the books of the Kingdoms, the Temple had previously been restored during the life of Josiah's great grandfather King Hezekiah. Hezekiah led a major anti-Mosaic religious reformation similar to Josiah's later reforms, which included destroying the serpent statue that Moses had created, because the Judahites were worshiping it.

During Hezekiah's reign, between 716 and 687 BCE, the genealogy of nations was added to *Cosmic Genesis*, which appears to have been written in Aramaic, not Judahite. It appears to have been based on Assyrian and Babylonian records, as it includes transliterated Assyrian and Babylonian names. The genealogy of nations in *Cosmic Genesis* and *Bereshít* includes a reference to Kalhu (Χαλαχ / כֶּלַח) being the capital city, which was the capital of the Assyrian empire until 706 BCE, when it was moved to Dur Sharrukin by Sargon II. The genealogy also mentions the Ashkenaz (Ασχαναζ / אַשְׁכְּנַז), the ancestors of the Armenians, who were first recorded in Assyrian records as the Áškuzai (𒀾𒆪𒍝𒀀), a tribe of recent immigrants to the kingdom of Urartu, in 715 BCE, placing the authorship of the genealogy of nations in the early years of Hezekiah.

Both *Cosmic Genesis* and *Numbers* are specifically different from their Leningrad Codex counterparts in regards to the name Shaddai (שַׁדַּי), which is missing from both Greek translations, but found in the Masoretic versions.

In Bereshít, Shaddai was the name of the god of Abraham, Isaac, and Jacob, however, in *Cosmic Genesis*, the god was never named. In *Names*, the Leningrad Codex version of *Exodus*, Moses' god introduces himself as, the god Shaddai (אֵל שַׁדָּי), the god of Abraham, Isaac, and Jacob, while in the Septuagint he introduces himself as the god Ōn (θεὸς Ὤν). As the name Shaddai was transliterated as Saddai (Σαδδαι) in the Septuagint's book of Ezekiel, it is clear the name was in some books of the Aramaic translation. The name Shaddai in the Masoretic text is generally mirrored by 'omnipotent' (παντοκράτορ) in the Septuagint, including 31 times in the book of Job, nevertheless, in *Cosmic Genesis* and *Numbers* it is entirely missing in the Septuagint, indicating it was removed when the Aramaic translations were made, suggesting they were made at the same time, during the religious reformations of King Hezekiah, or shortly thereafter.

King Hezekiah's reforms were anti-Mosaic, however, presented as restoring the Israelite religion, not abandoning it. Therefore, he could not have removed the laws of Moses, and must have added amendments to them that supported the changes he instituted. One of these changes was the removal of the Korahites from administering the temple in Jerusalem, replaced by the Aaronites, later called Kohens. Both the Korahites and Aaronites were viewed as branches of the Levites, the priestly tribe, however, the Korahites had been the priests of the temple in Jerusalem since Solomon built it, while the Aaronites appear to have been mainly operating in Samaria, Edom, and Libnah.

According to the history recorded in the books of the *Kingdoms* (Masoretic *Kings*), Samaria and Judah ended their union in 930 BCE, dividing the kingdoms of Israel. The northern region, where the earlier capitals had been, became the kingdom of Samaria, which before 850 BCE also included most of Aram in modern southern and western Syria. The southern capital of Jerusalem was left in control of Judah and Edom. However, Edom and Libnah revolted over a religious dispute in the 840s BCE. Libnah was a Levitical city in the borderlands of Judah, Edom, Egypt, and the Peleset lands, from which the later Yahwist sect would emerge in the 600s BCE. As the pottery shards discovered in Kuntillet Ajrud in the Sinai desert, which are dated to circa 800 BCE refer to Yahweh as being both the god of Samaria and Teman, the capital of Edom, but not Judah or Jerusalem, it seems apparent that the religious dispute that split the kingdoms was regarding the god Yahweh.

The pottery shards from Kuntillet Ajrud also depict Yahweh as the calf of Asherah, confirming that Yahweh was the calf god worshiped in Samaria, whose priesthood was the Aaronites. The calf god of Aaron was introduced in *Exodus* when it sparked a battle between the followers of Moses and Aaron which resulted in 3000 deaths. Conversely, the book of *Numbers* introduced Moses bronze serpent statue, which was explained as an odd but minor idol that Moses created to protect the Israelites from snakes. The snake idol wasn't otherwise mentioned in the surviving Israelite text, other than possibly being the seraph that Isaiah mentioned as being in the temple before Hezekiah's reforms. If it was created by Moses, then it has to have been carried into Samaria with the tabernacle and ark of the covenant, and ultimately moved into the temple when Solomon built it, which means it was the statue of Ba'al that Solomon erected.

The book of *Numbers* also added the story of Korah, the priest the Korahites were named after, who god killed in *Numbers*. Strangely, even though Korah and everyone who followed him were eaten by Adama, the Elbaite and Hurrian earth-goddess, his sons survived, and founded the Korahites, who Solomon appointed to oversee the temple in Jerusalem. Clearly, this story was not in the Torah until the time of Hezekiah, yet the name Adamah (אֲדָמָה) in the Hebrew version is clearly anachronistic to the culture of Iron Age Israel, suggesting the book of *Numbers* was from the same era as *Exodus*. If Numbers also dates to the bronze age, it must have been used by a priesthood other than the Korahites, suggesting it was an Aaronite text.

The Korahites were a major priesthood before Hezekiah, closely connected to King Solomon, and many of the psalms of David are attributed to the "sons of Korah." Conversely, the

Aaronites were mainly associated with Samaria and Libnah throughout most of Judahite history, with brief exceptions under kings Hezekiah and Josiah. After the fall of Jerusalem to the Babylonians, they continued to operate in Samaria, and Nehemiah recorded they were active among the Samaritans as late as 384 BCE. Nehemiah also reported them as the priesthood who had broken the covenant, indicating that he was a worshiper of Shaddai, the god of Abraham, Isaac, Jacob, and Moses.

According to *4th Kingdoms* (Masoretic *Kings*), King Hezekiah's heir, King Manasseh, reversed all of his religious reforms, and then, according to the *Sanhedrin* (103b) tractate in the Talmud, cut the name of god from the Torah. Given that two versions of the Torah appear to have existed from around the time it was translated into Aramaic, it seems apparent that he was responsible for removing the name from the Aramaic versions of *Cosmic Genesis*, *Exodus*, and *Numbers* which were ultimately translated into Greek.

His son King Amon, was then reported as burning the Torah during his reign, and abandoning the temple, meaning that neither the Korahites nor the Aaronites were active there under his reign. His son King Josiah then ushered in another religious reformation, similar but more extensive than his great-grandfather Hezekiah's, as he sacrificed the priests on their altars before destroying the altars, and then dug up the bones of the dead prophets and kings to defile them. Josiah also restored the temple in Jerusalem, in which was found a copy of the Torah which was reported as being the "original" of Moses.

As this could not have been Moses' original Torah, as Moses had nothing to do with the Temple of Solomon, it was likely when *Leviticus* was added to Hezekiah's Torah. The substitution of the Levitical Priesthood for the firstborn Israelites had already been established in *Numbers* chapter 3, meaning that the Yahwists had already rejected child sacrifice much earlier, likely in the bronze age.

Both *Deuteronomy*, which appears to have originated in Samaria, and *Leviticus*, which originated in Judah during the reign of Josiah, amended the law regarding the sacrifice of the first born, which was reported as happening in Samaria before the Assyrians conquered them, and in Judah before Josiah's reforms. Leviticus appear to be the first of the Israelite texts which was originally written with Yahweh as the one and only god in the text.

The god Yahweh is recorded as Yhwh (𐤀𐤄𐤅𐤆) in Phoenician, Yhw (𐤉𐤄𐤅) in Aramaic, and Yåw (𐤉𐤀𐤅) in Egypto-Aramaic. He is probably the same god the bronze age Canaanites referred to as Yw (𐎊𐎆) in Ugaritic, however, other than a brief passing reference in the Victorious Ba'al, almost nothing is known of the Bronze Age god Yw. He appears again in the archaeological records around 800 BCE, depicted as the calf of Asherah on pottery shards found in Kuntillet Ajrud, near Hashem El Tarif in the Sinai Peninsula near the modern Egyptian-Israeli border. Pottery found in the region also refers to Yhwh as the god of Samaria, confirming

7

that the Yhwh depicted as a calf, was the same Yhwh worshiped by the Israelites at the time.

Åthart (⊶⟨⊨⊷⊸), who later became known as Asherah (אשרה), was originally recorded as an earth and rebirth goddess, worshiped in Canaan by planting oak trees above the graves of important people. However, during the Egyptian New Kingdom era, she was assimilated with Hathor, the mother and sky goddess, resulting in Asherah being viewed as a personification of the starry sky in the Iron Age.

This identification of Asherah with Hathor, was a result of the Egyptian version of Asherah, Iusaaset, being assimilated with Hathor. Like Asherah, Iusaaset was originally associated with earth and rebirth, and worshiped by planting acacia trees. Both goddesses were married to a god associated with the setting sun and great dragon, known today as the galactic great rift. In Egypt, he was Atum, the creator god of Iwnw, later called Heliopolis, while in Canaan, he was Ba'al Shalim, the god Jerusalem was named after. Both Atum and Shalim were accepted as local versions of the South Egyptian sun god Amen during the New Kingdom era, when southern Egypt ruled northern Egypt and Canaan. Therefore, their wives Iusaaset and Asherah were accepted as local variants of Mut, the south Egyptian mother goddess, along with Hathor, the northern Egyptian mother goddess.

In southern Egypt, Amen and Mut's son was Khonsu, the moon god, resulting in Iȯhw the moon god of Iwnw being absorbed into a northern Egyptian trinity. The word Iȯh (⌒) was the Egyptian word for the moon. However, when

8

treated as a god, it was modified to İôhw ( ), mirroring the two pronunciations of the name Yh (𓏺^) and Yhw (𓏺^), indicating that Aaron's calf god Yahweh, originated with İwnw's lunar calf god İôhw.

İwnw (𓊖), later renamed Heliopolis by the Greeks, was the city where Joseph became a priest in *Cosmic Genesis* when the Israelites originally migrated to Egypt. The city was called 'Ôn (אוֹן) in the Leningrad Codex, a transliteration of the Middle Egyptian shortened version of the name İwn (𓊖). In Exodus, the Greek translators transliterated the name of the city as Ōn (Ων), however, the name does not appear in *Names*, suggesting it was removed for some reason, as the Greeks could not have transliterated a name that was not there.

In the Septuagint, the city was one of the three cities the Israelites were referred to as living in within Egypt, the others being Pithom and Ramesses. Both of these other cities have been causes of great debate over the millennia. Pithom, called Pitōm (Πιθωμ) in the Septuagint, and Pitōm (פִּתֹם) in the Leningrad Codex, is generally accepted as the city of Per-Atum (𓉐 𓏤 𓏏𓏤), later called Heroöpolis by the Greeks. The location of both the Egyptian and Greek cities remains unclear, however, several sites have been located that appear to have been known as Per-Atum at various times in Egyptian history. Excavations at the Tel El Maskhuta complex, in the western Nile Delta, show a Hyksos era (15th dynasty) settlement that was likely Per-Atum, although the site was later abandoned until the era of Pharaoh Necho II (26th dynasty, circa 600 BCE).

The location of Ramesses has been a matter of debate since before the Septuagint was translated, and the translators were not sure which ancient Egyptian city the name Ramesses was referring to. The historic city of Ramesses was built in the era of Pharaoh Shoshenq I (943 to 922 BCE) and was still a major city when the stories found in Numbers were most likely compiled into a book under King Hezekiah. The Late-Period city of Ramesses was a rebuilding of the New Kingdom era city of Pi-Ramesses, and as the city of Pi-Ramesses was never called Ramesses during the New Kingdom era, it must be assumed that the name was updated when the stories were compiled under Hezekiah. The city of Pi-Ramesses, which was founded in 1290 BCE, was itself a rebuilding of Avaris, the Hyksos capital, which had been destroyed when the Hyksos were driven from Egypt in circa 1572 BCE, meaning it is not clear if the name Avaris or Pi-Ramesses was updated to Ramesses.

Both Avaris and Pi-Ramesses had served as imperial capital cities when Egypt ruled Canaan, and so either could be the city in the text, however, if one accepts that the city was named Pi-Ramesses when the original story was written, then it dates the events in Exodus to the 1200s BCE, immediately before the Bronze Age Collapse, yet there are already reports from a century earlier of the Šåsw (𓈙𓏤𓂝𓅱), meaning "nomads," of Yhwå (𓇌𓉔𓏲𓄿𓅱) in the Seir Region of modern Jordan, which are generally accepted as a reference to

Yahweh worshipers, meaning the original name was probably Avaris, which had become obscure by Hezekiah's time, and was updated to the contemporary name.

The dating of the exodus from Egypt is different in the Septuagint from the Masoretic text and works out to be a minimum 1547 BCE, when one adds the reigns of Moses, Joshua, and the various judges that ruled the Israelites before Saul became king. This is within decades of when the Hyksos Dynasty was driven from Egypt according to Egyptologists, which, based on the radio-carbon dating of Amenhotep I's mummy, would have been circa 1572 BCE. Given that there was a sizable Hyksos town at Pithom, which was abandoned at the time, and Ramesses was Avaris at the time, the Hyksos capital before it fell and they withdrew to Sharuhen, it does seem to support that the Exodus took place during the expulsion of the Hyksos from Egypt. However, the fact that they were in Heliopolis, suggests that they were not the Hyksos themselves, but remnants of the Canaanite 14th Dynasty, who ruled over the collapsing Egyptian Middle Kingdom before the Hyksos seized control.

Both the books of *Exodus* and *Numbers* tell of the Israelites leaving Egypt, and their travels through the desert, however, the two books appear to have originated with different groups of priests. While both *Exodus* and *Numbers* have specific terms that indicate they are based on older Akkadian Cuneiform texts, the current text of *Numbers* appears to have originated in Edom, as it uses specific words unique to the Edomite dialect of Canaanite. For example, in the *Book of*

Numbers, the earth goddess was referred to in the Leningrad Codex by her Edomite name, Adama, while in Genesis and Exodus she was only referred to as Eretz, her more common Canaanite name.

According to the books of *Kingdoms* and *Paralipomena*, Edom was occupied by the United Kingdom of Samaria and Judah. Then it became a dependency of the kingdom of Judah after the two kingdoms split in 930 BCE, until Edom rebelled sometime between 849 and 842 BCE, along with the town of Libnah, one of the Levite towns in southern Judah. This series of rebellions was reportedly caused by the Judahites worshiping a different god. The town of Libnah was later where the Yahwist priests taught from, including Jeremiah, who was instrumental in enacting Josiah's Yahwist reforms.

Human sacrifice to the Lord is openly discussed in the book of Numbers, indicating that the core texts must have been much older than the time of Hezekiah. The most obvious statement that the Israelites were sacrificing humans is in chapter 31, immediately after the Israelites slaughtered the Midianites, animals were sacrificed to the Lord, and then humans:

> *"Of the people, 16,000, and those sacrificed of them to the Lord were 32."*

This verse about human sacrifice to the Lord is also found in the Leningrad Codex, but not always translated by modern translators. It is sometimes skipped entirely, such as in Tanakh (JPS 1985), which simply has:

"and 16,000 human beings."

While the *Book of Numbers* was likely organized into its current form during the reforms of King Hezekiah, circa 715 , it appears to have been redacted by the Hasmonean Dynasty circa 140 BCE, in an attempt to forge closer ties with Rome, which was still a distant power across the Mediterranean, outside of Greek domination. As the Maccabean Revolt against Greek rule in Judea, between 165 and 140 BCE, the Romans were fighting the final, and bloodiest of their wars against the Carthaginians, the ancient Canaanite colony based in modern Tunisia. The Carthaginians were once the great power of the western Mediterranean, dominating northwest Africa, Iberia, Sicily, Sardinia, and Corsica.

The Romans had been at almost constant war against Carthage for over a century, beginning with the first Punic war in 264 BCE, and in 140 BCE finally defeated them, and effectively exterminated the race. Roman records report that they forced the surviving Carthaginian warriors to fight to the death in arenas, while the civilians were sold as slaves to anyone that would buy them. The population of northwest Africa became a slave-race for centuries and was not freed until the rise of Christianity in the 4th century. In 139 BCE, seven years after the end of the final Punic war, and the year after the Hasmonean dynasty was established in Judea, the Romans evicted all Jews from the republic because the Jews were attempting to promote the idea that the Roman national god Jupiter (Iova) was their national god Yahweh Sabaoth (Jupiter Sabazius). This was recorded by Valerius Maximus:

FORWARD

"Gnaeus Cornelius Hispalus, praetor peregrinus in the year of the consulate of Marcus Popilius Laenas and Lucius Calpurnius, ordered the astrologers by an edict to leave Rome and Italy within ten days, since by a fallacious interpretation of the stars they perturbed fickle and silly minds, thereby making profit out of their lies. The same praetor compelled the Jews, who attempted to infect the Roman custom with the cult of Jupiter Sabazius, to return to their home."

This kingdom had a tenuous alliance with the Roman Republic until General Pompey conquered Syria into the Roman Republic in 69 BCE. Pompey's goal was to liberate Greek-speaking communities in the Middle East that had fallen under the rule of non-Greeks when the Seleucids Syrian Empire had collapsed, and he carved up Judea, and Edom to the east, placing Greek-speaking cities under the protection of the Roman province of Syria. He also liberated several smaller communities that had been occupied by Judea, granting them self-government, including Ashdod, Yavne, Jaffa, Dora, Marissa, and Samaria.

It is generally accepted that there were several versions written in Hebrew or Samaritan before the translation of the Septuagint. Fragments of the Torah have been found in four languages among the dead sea scrolls, generally dated to between 200 BCE and 600 CE. During this time, the land of Judea passed from the rule of the Ptolemys in Egypt to the rule of the Seleucids in Syria around 200 BCE. The Seleucids attempted to Hellenize the Judeans, erecting a statue of Zeus

14

in the Second Temple in Jerusalem, and effectively banning traditional Judaism. This Hellenizing activity was partially successful, creating the Sadducee faction of Judaism, however also led to the Maccabean Revolt in 165 BCE, which itself created the independent Hasmonean Kingdom of Judea.

This kingdom was violently xenophobic and led by a priestly monarchy that combined both the powers of the state and the church. The Hasmonean dynasty attempted to conquer all of the territory that had previously been part of the Persian Province of Judea, and either evicted or exterminated the people that were living there, depending on their ethnicity. When the Edomites were conquered they were allowed to mass-convert to Judaism as they were considered the descendants of Esau, however, most other ethnic groups were not welcome.

While the Hasmoneans ruled Judea, they converted the national script from the old Phoenician script, today called Paleo-Hebrew, to the Aramaic "block script," today called Hebrew. As a result, almost all surviving texts found from the Hasmonean era and later are written in the Aramaic script, and it is unclear how much the Hasmoneans redacted the scriptures when they transcribed them. The scriptures the Hasmoneans left the world were later used as the basis of the Masoretic Text, which are used today by Rabbinical Jews, as well as by Catholic and Protestant Christians.

The differences between the Leningrad Codex and the Septuagint's version of *Numbers*, and several other books in the two collections of scriptures are both minor and startling, as the two sets of scriptures contain the same stories, but different gods. The Leningrad Codex is mostly about the actions of Yahweh, Yahweh Elohim, Yahweh Sabaoth, or Elohim, while the Septuagint contains the Greek translations of various gods' names that appear to have been redacted by the Hasmoneans. The god of the book of *Numbers* in the Septuagint is called Lord the God (Κύριος ὁ Θεὸς) or simplified to Lord (Κύριος), or God (Θεὸς). These terms are mirrored in the Leningrad Codex's Numbers by Yəhōwâ 'ĕlōhêkem (יְהֹוָה אֱלֹהֵיכֶם), meaning "Yahweh your gods," Yəhōwâ (יְהֹוָה), and 'ĕlōhāy (אֱלֹהָי), meaning "god."

One explanation for the difference between the texts is the Christian redaction of the 3rd century CE, when the name Yahweh was removed from the Septuagint, replaced by Lord (Κύριος). Fragments of older Septuagint manuscripts still exist that contain the name Yahweh, transliterated into Greek as Iaō (Ιαω), however, none of the fragments of the Book of Numbers include the name. The name Yhwh (𐤉𐤄𐤅𐤄 / יהוה) is found in a few fragments of the Hebrew Book of Numbers found among the Dead Sea Scrolls, however, none that are believed to date back to before the Hasmonean dynasty.

If the Greeks translated the Septuagint accurately, which everything other than the names of God indicates, then the term God (Θεὸς) would have been ålh (𐤀𐤋𐤄) in the texts they translated. Likewise, Lord the god (Κύριος ὁ Θεὸς) would have been ådny ålhykm (𐤀𐤃𐤍𐤉 𐤀𐤋𐤄𐤉𐤊𐤌), meaning "lord of your gods." This appears to be an older version of the phrase 'ădōnāy hā'ĕlōhîm (אֲדֹנָי הָאֱלֹהִים), meaning "lord of the gods,"

16

found in the Aramaic sections of Daniel. There are a couple of exceptions in Numbers, where the word 'God' (Θεὸς) in the Septuagint is mirrored by El (אל) in the Leningrad Codex, and in both cases appears to be a proper name. These examples are in chapters 12 and 16:

Moses cried to the Lord, "El, I beg you, heal her."

They fell on their faces and asked, "El, god of spirits and all flesh, if one man has sinned, will the anger of the Lord be on the whole community?"

In both cases, the name El survives in the Leningrad Codex, and could only have been used as a proper name in the time of Moses. In other verses where the word God appears in the Septuagint, the Leningrad Codex generally has Elah (אֱלָה), meaning "god" or occasionally Yəhōwâ (יְהֹוָה). As the Greeks transliterated Yahweh as Iaō (Ιαω), and 'ēlâ (אֵלָה) is properly translated as "goddess," it is clear that the source texts they used did not have the same terms used in the Leningrad Codex.

The Canaanite term ålhym (𐤀𐤋𐤄𐤉𐤌), and Aramaic ålhym (𐡀𐡋𐡄𐡉𐡌), are also direct transcriptions of the Neo-Assyrian word elium (𒀭𒈜𒈨), which by the Iron Age meant "god," indicating that text had previously been written in cuneiform, and was translated into Aramaic or Phoenician during the iron age. During the bronze age, the word was Alium (𒀭𒈨𒅋), and referred to a specific god, [deity]An (𒀭𒀭) the highest god, and father of the other gods. His Akkadian name was derived from the word elûm (𒀭𒈨),

17

meaning "higher," as the term was intended to convey the meaning of 'highest.' He was believed to live in the polar region of the sky, where the modern constellation of Draco is located, making him the highest in the sky, around which all the gods (stars) circled.

The term 'ēl 'elyôn (אֵל עֶלְיוֹן), meaning "highest god," was translated into Hebrew in Genesis Chapter 14, where the Greeks translated it as teō tō usistō (θεō τō yψιστω), also meaning 'highest god.' El Elyon is known to have been a major god of the Canaanites, called âl wâlyn (𐤉𐤋𐤏𐤍 𐤋𐤀), meaning "God and Highest" in an Aramaic language Sefire Treaty from circa 750 BCE. The Greek translations of Sanchuniathon's bronze age writing that has survived to the present, referred to the primordial creator god of the Canaanites as Elioun (Ελιουν), which appears to be the same god. According to Sanchuniathon, Elioun was the highest (ὕψιστος) god, who made the sky and the land, and they made the rest of the gods.

During the Old Babylonian and Old Assyrian eras, the gods Marduk and Ashur, the national gods of Babylon and Assyria, replaced the Akkadian Ān as the primary god of the Mesopotamian pantheons, and by the iron age, the word elium had come to mean "god," explaining why the Aramaic term âlhym (𐤉𐤄𐤋𐤀) would have been interpreted as "god," by the Greeks.

Another difference between the two versions of *Numbers* is the word Shaddai, which is missing from the Septuagint's version of *Numbers*. In the Leningrad Codex version of

Numbers, Shaddai is the name of the Prophet Balaam's god, however, in the Septuagint, Balaam's god is simply called God. The Greeks did transliterate the term Shaddai, as Saddai in the book of Ezekiel where it was treated as a proper name, and translated it as pantokratoros (παντοκρατοροσ), meaning "onmipotent" in the *Book of Job*, and therefore had no reason to have skipped it when translating *Numbers*. The definition of Shaddai is different for Christians and Jews. The word Shaddai means "demons" in modern Hebrew, making the meaning of this verse the opposite of the Christian interpretation of Shaddai as "almighty."

In Hebrew, Balaam was receiving his vision from demons, while in Christian translations it was from God. The fact that Shaddai was not in the Greek translation circa 250 BCE, implies the name was added during the Hasmonean redaction between 140 and 37 BCE, likely to devalue Balaam. Balaam son of Beor was revered as a prophet by the Moabites, as proven by the Deir Alla Inscription, (KAI 312), which was found in 1967 during an excavation at Deir 'Alla in Jordan. This inscription, which is dated to circa 800 BCE, records that Balaam son of Beor was a prophet of several gods including Elohin, Shaddaiin, Ashter, and Shugr. This word has not survived among the Dead Sea Scrolls fragments of Numbers, however, Dead Sea Scroll 4QNum[b] does have a partial copy of this verse which is significantly shorter than the Leningrad Codex, indicating that the verse was still being rewritten during the Hasmonean Dynasty.

FORWARD

A series of wars including both of Julius Caesar's campaigns and a Parthian invasion led to the weakening of the Hasmonean dynasty and in 37 CE the Roman Senate appointed the Edomite King Herod the Great, as "King of the Judeans." Herod's rule wasn't particularly popular, as he allowed the Romans to establish themselves within Judea, however, he did expand Judea, reintegrating the Greek and Samaritan cities, and annexing Galilee and Edom. When he died, his kingdom was divided between four successors, a situation that ended in 66 CE when the Romans conquered the region. An uprising in 120 CE led to the Jews being exiled from Judea, and the region became a Greco-Roman colony. In the wake of the Jews, the Samaritans rose in numbers, along with the Christians after Christianity was legalized. Between 529 and 555 CE, the Samaritans revolted and were effectively annihilated, by the Byzantine Empire.

The modern Samaritan religion is similar to Judaism, in that they have versions of the Torah and the book of Joshua, however, they do not trace their ancestry to ancient Judah, but rather to ancient Samaria also called the Northern Kingdom of Israel. According to the Samaritans, they were the original Israelites, and the Temple of the Lord was not Solomon's Temple in Jerusalem, but rather a Temple of Mount Gerizim, in Samaria. These "other Israelites" also contributed to the creation of the Septuagint, as the Book of Tobit, was the story of a Samaritan that had been taken to Nineveh, the capital of the Assyrian Empire after the Kingdom of Israel was conquered by the Assyrians. This book and several others were not considered important to Simon the Zealot, and not translated into Hebrew.

Outside of Judea, the Septuagint was the dominant form of Israelite scriptures across the Greek-speaking world, which at the beginning of the Christian era extended from the Roman Empire in the west, to the Indo-Greek Kingdom in the east. Judean traders had established small colonies along the trade routes of the Red Sea and the Indian Ocean, reaching as far south as Eritrea, and as far east as southern India, and these Judeans spoke Aramaic and Greek and used the Septuagint. The earliest Christians used the Septuagint exclusively, as far as the Israelite scriptures were concerned, and as a result, it is impossible to even understand the chronology of the world they described unless using the Septuagint. It is unclear why the Septuagint, Masoretic texts, and Samaritan Asatir each contain a different chronology of the world. Adding the Book of Jubilees, and various variations of the Torah found within the Dead Sea Scrolls, there are no less than six ancient Israelite chronologies.

The Septuagint's *Cosmic Genesis* includes an additional millennium of human history that was dropped from the Proto-Masoretic Text in order to align the creation of the world with the beginning of the age of El, when the constellation Taurus became the marker of the northern vernal equinox, in 3760 BCE. The Bull El was the dominant God of the Canaanite pantheon until circa 1700 BCE, when Attar the Goat (Aries) and Yam the Sea-Monster (Cetus) fought for domination of the world beneath the sky, ultimately both being replaced by the god of thunder Ba'al Hadad, in the Canaanite Ba'al Cyle. Traditional Jewish interpretations of the timeline within the Masoretic Text, is further hampered by the so-called 'missing years' of Rabbinical Time, in which hundreds of years of the Persian Empire are skipped over in order to make the timeline fit into the era since 3760 BCE, a problem Christian chronologists have never had as Christianity developed after the astrology of Babylonian-era Judaism had been forgotten.

The earliest Bibles, all used the Septuagint, however, by the 4th century some Christian scholars were debating whether they should retranslate the Old Testament from the version the Jews were using, and some even suggested using the Samaritan version. Both suggestions were generally dismissed as heretical, as Jesus and the Apostles had quoted from the Septuagint, even though they had access to the Hebrew version then in use. This argument held in the west until the Middle Ages, when Catholic Bibles switched to the Masoretic Text. In the east, Orthodox Bibles continued to use the Septuagint, as they do today. To the south, the Ethiopian Tewahedo Church continued to use the Septuagint, and across Asia, the Thomas Christians and Nestorians continued to use the Septuagint. Only in Western Europe were the later Masoretic Text adopted, abandoning the more ancient Septuagint, on the assumption that the Jews had copied their texts more faithfully than the Greeks had translated them. This assumption was carried forward into the Protestant Churches that broke off from the Catholic Church, and therefore almost all Protestant Bibles use the Masoretic Text for the basis of the Old Testament.

Unfortunately, this means that the earliest Christian writing is generally confusing and ignored by Protestants and Catholics. The earliest Christians of the first and second centuries quoted books that are no longer in the Bible, and as such, their writings are not always understood. *Septuagint: Numbers* is the fourth in a series of 21st century translations aimed at correcting this problem.

One of the problems with academic translations of the Septuagint, is the use of unfamiliar names or terms, as the Septuagint was written in Greek, and therefore many names are unrecognizable to modern readers who are used to Hebrew-derived names. This project uses the more commonly understood Hebrew-derived names instead of their Greek translations, such as Canaan instead of Chanaan, and Melchizedek instead of Melchisedec. Common modern names are also used instead of either Greek or Hebrew terms when geographical locations are known, such as the archaeological name Uruk instead of the Greek Orech, or the Hebrew Erech, and the archaeological term Sumer instead of Shinar or Senar. While this could be argued as not being a correct academic procedure, it does fulfill the goal of making the translation easy to read and understand.

CHAPTER 1

The Lord[1] spoke to Moses[2] in the Wilderness of Sinai,[3] at the tabernacle of witness, on the first day of the second month, in the second year after they departed from the land of Egypt, saying, "Count all the community of Israel according to their families, and according to the houses of their fathers' families, and according to their number by their names, and according to their heads. Every male twenty years old and up, everyone that went out in the army of Israel, count them with their strength, you and Aaron go count them. With you, there will be each one of the rulers according to the tribe of each, and they will be according to the houses of their families."

"These are the names of the men who will be present with you:"

"From the tribe of Reuben: Elizur the son of Shedeur."

"From the tribe of Simeon: Shelumiel the son of Zurishaddai."

"From the tribe of Judah: Nahshon the son of Amminadab."

"From the tribe of Issachar: Nethanel the son of Zuar."

"From the tribe of Zebulun: Eliab the son of Helon."

"From the tribe of the sons of Joseph: from Ephraim: Elishama the son of Ammihud, and from Manasseh: Gamaliel the son of Pedahzur."

CHAPTER 1

"From the tribe of Benjamin: Abidan the son of Gideoni."

"From the tribe of Dan: Ahiezer the son of Ammishaddai."

"From the tribe of Asher: Pagiel the son of Ochran."

"From the tribe of Gad: Eliasaph the son of Deuel."

"From the tribe of Naphtali: Ahira the son of Enan."

These were famous men of the community, heads of the tribes according to their families. These are heads of thousands in Israel. Moses and Aaron took these men who were called by name. They assembled all the community on the first day of the month in the second year, and they record them after their lineage, after their families, after the number of their names, from twenty years old and upwards, every male according to their number, and as the Lord commanded Moses, so they were counted in the Wilderness of Sinai.

The sons of Reuben the firstborn of Israel according to their families, according to their divisions, according to the houses of their families, according to the number of their names, according to their heads, all males from twenty years old and upward, everyone who went out with the army, the count of the tribe of Reuben was 46,400.

For the children of Simeon according to their families, according to their divisions, according to the houses of their families, according to the number of their names, according to their polls, all males from twenty years old and upward, everyone who went out with the army, the count of the tribe of Simeon was 59,300.

CHAPTER 1

For the sons of Judah according to their families, according to their divisions, according to the houses of their families, according to the number of their names, according to their polls, all males from twenty years old and upward, everyone who went out with the army, the count of the tribe of Judah was 74,600.

For the sons of Issachar according to their families, according to their divisions, according to the houses of their families, according to the number of their names, according to their polls, all males from twenty years old and upward, everyone who went out with the army, the count of the tribe of Issachar was 54,400.

For the sons of Zebulun according to their families, according to their divisions, according to the houses of their families, according to the number of their names, according to their polls, all males from twenty years old and upward, everyone who went out with the army, the count of the tribe of Zebulun was 57,400.

For the sons of Joseph, the sons of Ephraim, according to their families, according to their divisions, according to the houses of their families, according to the number of their names, according to their polls, all males from twenty years old and upward, everyone who went out with the army, the count of the tribe of Ephraim was 40,500.

For the sons of Manasseh according to their families, according to their divisions, according to the houses of their families, according to the number of their names, according to their polls, all males from twenty years old and upward, everyone who went out with the army, the count of the tribe of Manasseh was 32,200.

For the sons of Benjamin according to their families, according to their divisions, according to the houses of their families, according to the number of their names, according to their polls, every male from twenty years old and upward, everyone who went out with the army, the count of the tribe of Benjamin was 35,400.

For the sons of Gad according to their families, according to their divisions, according to the houses of their families, according to the number of their names, according to their polls, all males from twenty years old and upward, everyone who went out with the army, the count of the tribe of Gad was 45,600.

For the sons of Dan according to their families, according to their divisions, according to the houses of their families, according to the number of their names, according to their polls, all males from twenty years old and upward, everyone who went out with the army, the count of the tribe of Dan was 62,700.

For the sons of Asher according to their families, according to their divisions, according to the houses of their families, according to the number of their names, according to their polls, every male from twenty years old and upward, everyone who went out with the army, the count of the tribe of Asher was 41,500.

CHAPTER 1

For the sons of Naphtali according to their families, according to their divisions, according to the houses of their families, according to the number of their names, according to their polls, every male from twenty years old and upward, everyone who went out with the army, the count of the tribe of Naphtali was 53,400.

This is the count which Moses and Aaron and the rulers of Israel, being twelve men, conducted. There was a man for each tribe, they were according to the tribe of the houses of their family. The whole count of the children of Israel with their army from twenty years old and upward, everyone that went out to set himself in battle formation for Israel came to 603,550. But the Levites of the tribe of their family were not counted among the children of Israel.

The Lord said to Moses, "See, you will not muster the tribe of Levi, and you will not count their numbers, among the children of Israel. Set the Levites over the tabernacle of witness, and over all its furniture, and over all things that are in it. They will do service in it, and they will camp around the tabernacle. When moving the tabernacle, the Levites will take it down, and in pitching the tabernacle they will set it up, and let the stranger that advances to touch it die. The children of Israel will camp, every man in his own order, and every man according to his captain, with their army. But let the Levites camp round about the tabernacle of witness neighboring it, and so there will be no sin among the children of Israel. The Levites themselves will keep the guard of the tabernacle of witness."

CHAPTER 1

The children of Israel did according to all that the Lord commanded Moses and Aaron, so did they.

CHAPTER 1 NOTES

1 Codex Vaticanus: KS (κ̄c̄). Translation: lord

• Dead Sea Scroll 4QLXXNum (LXX 803): Yhwh (𐤉𐤄𐤅𐤄) in later chapters. LXX 803 was a copy of Numbers in which the name Yhwh had been inserted in Judahite script.

• Leningrad Codex: Yəhōwâ (יְהֹוָה)

This verse has not survived among the Dead Sea Scrolls, however, the name Yhwh is used later in the Dead Sea fragments of Numbers where the Leningrad Codex used Yəhōwâ and Septuagint used "Lord."

• Dead Sea Scroll 4QLev-Num^a: Yhwh (יהוה)

• Dead Sea Scroll 2QNum^a: Yhwh (יהוה)

• Dead Sea Scroll 4QNum^b: Yhwh (יהוה)

• Peshitta: mryå (ܡܪܝܐ). Translation: master

• Targum Onkelos: Yəyā (??). Translation: Yahweh

• Targum Pseudo-Jonathan: Yəyā (??). Translation: Yahweh

• Ketef Hinnom scroll 2: Yhwh (𐤉𐤄𐤅𐤄). KH2 is a silver scroll engraved with Judahite text similar to three verses in Chapter 6. It is generally dated to between the 7th and 4th centuries BCE, although some scholars have stated it could be as recent as the 2nd century BCE. The text is similar to verses in *Numbers* Chapter 6, but not identical, as it refers to Yhwh as "the warrior."

• Sahidic manuscripts 2044: pJoeis (ⲡϪⲟⲉⲓⲥ). Translation: the master

There are no early surviving copies of the Septuagint's version of Numbers which have the Greek translation of the name in them,

Iaō (Ιαω), like the early fragments of the Septuagint's Leviticus known as 4QpapLXXLev[b], and therefore it cannot be known conclusively if the name was ever in the Septuagint's Numbers or not. There are fragments of a copy of the Septuagint's version of Numbers known as 4QLXXNum which include the name, however, it is copied into the Greek text in the Judahite script (𐤀𐤅𐤄𐤆), indicating it was a kaige redaction from the 1st or 2nd century CE.

The original Phoenician script version of Numbers likely used the word Adon (𐤀𐤃𐤀) which meant "Lord." The Aramaic sections of Masoretic Daniel that were not translated into Hebrew maintain the term 'ădōnāy hā'ĕlōhîm (אֲדֹנָי הָאֱלֹהִים), meaning the "Lord of the gods" where the Septuagint has "Lord the god" (Κύριον τὸν θεόν). As most books of the Septuagint were translated from Aramaic texts, the Aramaic text almost certainly used the term 'ădōnāy where the Septuagint has "Lord." The name Yahweh appears to have been added to most of the Hebrew books when the texts were translated to Hebrew during the Hasmonean Dynasty of Judea, between 140 and 37 BCE. According to the Talmud, this was to repair the damage King Manasseh had done 600 years earlier when he removed the name Yahweh from the Israelite texts.

The name Yhwh (𐤉𐤄𐤅𐤄) does appear to have originally been in some of the books of the Septuagint, such as Leviticus, which originated under the rule of King Josiah, and Yhw (𐤉𐤄𐤅) was a popular god among Judeans and Israelites under Persian and Greek rule. The translators at the Library of Alexandria transliterated this name as Iaō (Ιαω) in the books it was originally in, however, under the Hasmonean Dynasty it seems to have been added to all the books translated into Hebrew, creating some confusion among early Christians. There were debates in the early Christian era about which version of the Israelite scriptures to use, the Greek, Hebrew, Samaritan, or Syriac translations, resulting in different versions of the scriptures being used by different churches. This created a great deal of confusion among Christians, and ultimately the books of the Septuagint that had the name Iaō in them were redacted so all the books used the term Lord (Κύριοσ). Most Christian translations, as well as Jewish translations, have continued to use the term "Lord" in place of the name Yahweh, due to the prohibition on using any names of God that was introduced during the Hasmonean dynasty.

2 Codex Vaticanus: Mōusēn (ⲘⲱⲨⳭⲎⲚ)
- Septuagint manuscript 318: Mōusē (Ⲙⲟⲟⲩⲟⳑ)
- Septuagint manuscript 58: Mōsēn (Ⲙⲟⲟⳑⲱ)
- Septuagint manuscript 72: Mōsei (Ⲙⲟⲟⲟ⳩)
- Leningrad Codex: Mōšeh (מֹשֶׁה)
- Peshitta: Mwšå (ܡܘܫܐ)
- Targum Onkelos: Mšeh (מֹשֶׁה)
- Targum Pseudo-Jonathan: Mšeh (מֹשֶׁה)
- Sahidic manuscripts 2044: Mōusēs (ⲘⲱⲨⳭⲎⲤ)

It is generally accepted that at some point before the Septuagint was translated, half of Moses' name was redacted from the text. This theory is based on the similarity of the Egyptian term msî (𓄟𓋴), meaning "give birth to," or "created by," which was a common element of Egyptian names. Many kings of Egypt were known as the "msî" of a god, including Ramses (𓇳 𓄟𓋴), Ahmose (𓇍𓄟𓋴), Thutmose (𓅝𓄟𓋴), Amenmose (𓇋𓏠𓈖 𓄟𓋴), and Ptahmose (𓎗𓏤𓄟𓋴𓐰). A theory that has been circulating since at least the time of Josephus in the 1st century CE, is that Moses' original name was Hapymoses, meaning the "Nile created him." If this is the origin of the name, the name of the god that created Moses was likely dropped from the name very early in Israelite history, as there are no known surviving texts with the full name. The latest this is likely to have happened would have been during the Aramaic translation of King Hezekiah, however, it may have happened much earlier.

An alternate interpretation is that the name is complete, and is derived from the Egyptian term mw-šåỏ (𓈗𓃾𓂝𓏤), meaning "beginning on water," which appears to be what the princess stated in Exodus, when she found Moses and named him.

3 Codex Vaticanus: Seina (ϲⲉⲓⲛⲁ)
- Septuagint manuscript 18: Sinae (Σιναι)
- Septuagint manuscript 30: Sēna (Σωλ)
- Septuagint manuscript 46: Sina (Σινλ)
- Septuagint manuscript 126: Sin (Σιν)
- Leningrad Codex: Sînay (סִינַי)
- Peshitta: Syny (ܣܝܢܝ)
- Targum Onkelos: Sînay (סִינַי)
- Targum Pseudo-Jonathan: Sînay (סִינַי)
- Sahidic manuscript 2044: Sina (ⲥⲓⲛⲁ)

The Wilderness of Sin (Σιν) is the translation in the Septuagint for both the Masoretic Wilderness of Sîn (סִין) in Exodus, and the Wilderness of Sin (צִן) in Numbers, which was followed by Jerome in the Latin Vulgate as the Wilderness of Sin. This suggests that the early Aramaic version of the Torah did not differentiate between the two. As the book of Numbers was likely organized into its current state during the era of King Hezekiah's reforms, and it was almost certainly written in the Phoenician script that was in use in Judah at the time, it is likely that it more accurately records the two locations as separate places. In Numbers Chapter 33, they are both listed in the long sequence of stops the Israelites made as they traveled from Egypt, confirming that the Hebrew translator, and probably the Judahite or Moabite compiler of the original book of Numbers viewed them as separate places.

Conversely, Exodus shows clear signs of having been written in Middle Babylonian cuneiform, which is likely where the pronunciation of Sin is derived, ultimately from the Akkadian spelling of Sīn (░▓▓), which was spelled in Aramaic as Syn (𐤎𐤉𐤍), the direct transliteration of the Hebrew Syn (סין). While the Aramaic spelling would have been standardized by the common spelling of the name of the moon god, there was nothing to standardize the spelling of the toponym in the Phoenician script, resulting in both toponyms being rendered phonetically by the scribes that unified the stories found in Numbers into a book circa 700 BCE. The locations of these wildernesses have been a matter of debate for more than 2000 years, and early Christians era scholars widely debated this issue, with the majority favoring the region around Petra, in Jordan, or the Midian Mountains in northwestern Saudi Arabia. The Wilderness of Sin is identified within the Torah, as being between Elim and Mount Sinai, however, both locations are debated today. The Wilderness of Sinai is identified as including the site of Kadesh Barne, however, this location is also debated. Emperor Constantine's mother, Helena Augusta, renamed the Sinai Peninsula and Mount Sinai in Egypt in the 330s CE to resolve this issue, however, few scholars agree with this location today, as other references indicate the Israelites were wandering in northwest Saudi Arabia, Jordan, southern Syria.

Currently, Christian and Islamic scholars treating the Exodus as history, prefer Petra in Jordan, as the site of Kadesh, and Jebel al-Madhbah near Petra as Mount Sinai. This mountain has the Valley of Moses, called Wadi Musa in Arabic, which has an ancient staircase leading to the top of the mountain. It was clearly an ancient religious site, housing rain-fed cisterns, and two gigantic obelisks. At the entrance to the Valley of Moses is the Spring of Moses, which is believed to be the location that Moses struck the rock with his wand and caused water to flow. Based on the 1st century Josephus' claim that Kadesh Barnea was at Petra, the Wilderness of Sinai appears to be another name for the southern Arabah, the mostly dry valley running north from the Gulf of Aqaba to the Dead Sea. By extension, if Sinai and Sin are not two different spellings of the same place, then the location of the Wilderness of Sin would have to be the Sinai Desert, between An-Nekhel (Elim), and Hashem El Tarif (Rephidim).

CHAPTER 4

CHAPTER 2

The Lord said to Moses and Aaron, "Let the children of Israel camp near each other, every man keeping his rank, according to their standards, according to the houses of their families. The children of Israel will camp around the tabernacle of witness. Those that camp closest to the east will be the order of the camp of Judah with their army, and the prince of the sons of Judah, Nahshon the son of Amminadab. His forces were counted at 74,600."

"Those who camp next are from the tribe of Issachar, and the prince of the sons of Issachar will be Nethanel the son of Zuar. His forces were counted at 54,400."

"Those who camp next are from the tribe of Zebulun, and the prince of the sons of Zebulun will be Eliab the son of Helon. His forces were counted at 57,400. All that were counted of the camp of Judah were 186,400. They will move first with their forces."

"This is the order of the camp of Reuben, their forces will be towards the south, and the prince of the children of Reuben will be Elizur the son of Shedeur. His forces were counted at 64,500."

"Those who camp next to him are from the tribe of Simeon, and the prince of the sons of Simeon will be Shelumiel the son of Zurishaddai. His forces were counted at 59,300."

CHAPTER 2

"Those who camp next to them is the tribe of Gad, and the prince of the sons of Gad, Eliasaph the son of Deuel. His forces were counted at 45,650. All who were counted of the camp of Reuben were 151,450. They with their forces will proceed in the second place."

"Then the tabernacle of witness will be set forward, and the camp of the Levites will be between the camps, as they will camp, so also will they commence their march, each one next in order to his fellow according to their companies. The station of the camp of Ephraim will be by the sea with their forces, and the head of the children of Ephraim will be Elishama the son of Ammihud. His forces were counted at 40,500. Those who camp next is from the tribe of Manasseh, and the prince of the sons of Manasseh, Gamaliel the son of Pedahzur. His forces were counted at 32,200."

"Those who camp next is from the tribe of Benjamin, and the prince of the sons of Benjamin, Abidan the son of Gideoni. His forces were counted at 35,400. All that were counted of the camp of Ephraim were 108,100. They with their forces will set out third."

"The order of the camp of Dan will be towards the north with their forces, and the prince of the sons of Dan, Ahiezer the son of Ammishaddai. His forces were counted at 62,700."

"Those who camp next to him will be the tribe of Asher, and the prince of the sons of Asher, Phagiel the son of Ochran. His forces were counted at 41,500.

CHAPTER 2

"Those who camp next are from the tribe of Naphtali, and the prince of the children of Naphtali, Ahira the son of Enan. His forces were counted at 53,400.

"All that were counted of the camp of Dan were 157,600. They will set out last according to their order."

This is the number of the children of Israel according to the houses of their families. All the number in the camps with their forces was 603,550. However, the Levites were not counted with them, as the Lord commanded Moses. The children of Israel did all things that the Lord commanded Moses, and they camped in their order, and so they began their march in succession each according to their divisions, according to the houses of their families.

CHAPTER 3

These are the generations of Aaron and Moses, on the day that the Lord spoke to Moses at Mount Sinai. These are the names of the sons of Aaron: Nadab the firstborn, and Abihu, Eleazar, and Ithamar. These are the names of the sons of Aaron, the anointed priests whom they consecrated to the priesthood. Nadab and Abihu died before the Lord, when they offered strange fire before the Lord, in the Wilderness of Sinai. They had no children. Eleazar and Ithamar ministered in the priests' office with Aaron their father.

The Lord said to Moses, "Take the tribe of Levi and set them before Aaron the priest, and they will minister for him and will keep his orders, and the orders of the children of Israel, before the tabernacle of witness, to do the works of the tabernacle. They will keep all the furniture of the tabernacle of witness, and the orders of the children of Israel conducting all the works of the tabernacle. You will give the Levites to Aaron, and his sons the priests. They are given as a gift to me from the children of Israel. You will appoint Aaron and his sons over the tabernacle of witness, and they will keep their order of priesthood, and all things belonging to the altar, and within the veil, and the stranger that touches them will die."

The Lord said to Moses, "Look, I have taken the Levites from among the children of Israel, instead of every male that opens the womb from among the children of Israel, they will be their price, and the Levites will be mine, as every

41

firstborn is mine. In the day in which I struck every firstborn in the land of Egypt, I sanctified to myself every firstborn in Israel, both of man and beast, they will be mine. I am the Lord."

The Lord said to Moses in the Wilderness of Sinai, "Count the sons of Levi, according to the houses of their families, according to their divisions, count every male from a month old and upwards."

Moses and Aaron counted them by the word of the Lord, as the Lord commanded them. These were the names of the sons of Levi: Gershon, Kohath, and Merari. These are the names of the sons of Gershon according to their families; Libni and Shimei: and the sons of Kohath according to their families; Amram and Jezer, Hebron, and Uzziel. The sons of Merari according to their families, Mahali and Musi. These are the families of the Levites according to the houses of their families. To Gershon belongs the family of Libni, and the family of Shimei: these are the families of Gershon. The counting of them according to the number, every male a month old and up, their count was 7,500."

"The sons of Gershon will camp westward behind the tabernacle. The ruler of the household of the family of Gershon was Eliasaph the son of Lael. The order of the sons of Gershon in the tabernacle of witness was the tent and the veil, and the covering of the door of the tabernacle of witness, and the curtains of the court, and the veil of the door of the court, which is by the tabernacle, and the remainder of all its works. To Kohath belonged one division, that of Amram, and another division, that of Jezer, and another division, that of Hebron, and another division, that of Uzziel: these are the divisions of Kohath, according to number. Every male from a month old and upward, 8,600, keeping the orders of the holy things."

"The families of the sons of Kohath will camp beside the tabernacle towards the south. The chief of the house of the families of the divisions of Kohath was Elizaphan the son of Uzziel. Their order was the ark, and the table, and the candlestick, and the altars, and all the vessels of the sanctuary where they do holy service, and the veil, and all their works. The chief over the heads of the Levites was Eleazar the son of Aaron the priest, appointed to keep the orders of the holy things. To Merari belonged the family of Mahali, and the family of Musi: these are the families of Merari.

"The mustering of them according to number, every male from a month old and upwards, was 6,050. The head of the house of the families of the division of Merari was Zuriel the son of Abihail, and they will camp by the side of the tabernacle northward. The oversight of the order of the sons of Merari included the chapiters of the tabernacle, and its bars, and its pillars, and its sockets, and all their furniture, and their works, and the pillars of the court round about, and their bases, and their pins, and their cords. Those who camp before the tabernacle of witness on the east will be Moses and Aaron and his sons, keeping the orders of the sanctuary according to the orders of the children of Israel, and the stranger that touches them will die. All the numbering of the Levites, whom Moses and Aaron counted by the word of the Lord, according to their families, every male from a month old and upwards, were 22,000."

The Lord said to Moses, "Count every firstborn male of the children of Israel a month old and up and record the number by name. You will take the Levites for me, I am the Lord, instead of all the firstborn of the sons of Israel, and the livestock of the Levites instead of all the firstborn among the livestock of the children of Israel."

Moses counted, as the Lord commanded him, every firstborn among the children of Israel. All the male firstborn in number by name, from a month old and upwards, were according to their numbering 22,273.

The Lord said to Moses, "Take the Levites instead of all the firstborn of the sons of Israel, and the livestock of the Levites instead of their livestock, and the Levites will be mine. I am the Lord! For the ransoms of the 273 which exceed the Levites in number of the firstborn of the sons of Israel, you will even take five shekels[1] per head. You will take them according to the holy shekel,[2] twenty gerahs[3] to the shekel. You will give the money to Aaron and to his sons, the ransom of those who exceed in number among them. Moses took the silver, the ransom of those that exceeded in number the redemption of the Levites. He took the silver from the firstborn of the sons of Israel, 1,365 shekels, according to the holy shekel. Moses gave the ransom of them that were over to Aaron and his sons, by the word of the Lord, as the Lord commanded Moses.

CHAPTER 3

CHAPTER 3 NOTES

1 Codex Vaticanus: siklous (ϲικλογϲ). Translation: shekels

• Leningrad Codex: šəqālîm (שְׁקָלִים). Translation: shekels

• Peshitta: mtqlyn (ܡܬܩܠܝܢ). Translation: scales (or weights, shekels, or gerahs)

• Targum Onkelos: sil'în (סִלְעִין). Translation: selas (or rocks)

• Targum Pseudo-Jonathan: sil'în (סִלְעִין). Translation: selas (or rocks)

• Sahidic manuscript 2006: siklos (ϲικλοϲ). Translation: shekels

The shekel was a unit of weight used throughout the Middle East for thousands of years, weighing approximately 8.6 grams of silver. The Greek drachma was a coin weighing approximately half a shekel, and therefore under Greek rule of the Middle East, a two-drachma coin was used. As the Greeks clearly translated shekel into didrachma, the term shekel is restored in this translation. The sela, mentioned in the Targums, was a weight and coin although the value varied depending on the metal it was made of.

2 Codex Vaticanus: didrakmon (ΔιΔρΑχΜΟΝ). Translation: two drachmas

• Codex Ambrosiano A 147: didragmon (ΔιΔρΑΓΜΟΝ)

• Septuagint manuscript 30: didrakma (διδραχμα)

• Septuagint manuscript 130: didagmon (διδαγμω)

• Septuagint manuscript 320: didragman (διδραγμαν)

• Septuagint manuscript 246: dēdragmon (δηδραγμω)

• Septuagint manuscript 767: didragma (διδραγμα)

• Septuagint manuscript 321: didrankmon (διδραγχμω)

• Leningrad Codex: šəqālîm (שְׁקָלִים). Translation: shekels

CHAPTER 3

- Peshitta: mtqlyn (ܡܬܩܠܝܢ). Translation: scales (or weights, shekels, or gerahs)
  - Targum Onkelos: sil'în (סִלְעִין). Translation: rocks
  - Targum Pseudo-Jonathan: sil'î (סִלְעִי). Translation: sela (or rocky)
  - Sahidic manuscript 2006: kite (ⲕⲓⲧⲉ). Translation: qite
  - Sahidic manuscript 2045: siklos (ⲥⲓⲕⲗⲟⲥ). Translation: shekels

The shekel was a unit of weight used throughout the Middle East for thousands of years, weighing approximately 8.6 grams of silver. The Greek drachma was a coin weighing approximately half a shekel, and therefore under Greek rule of the Middle East, a two-drachma coin was used. In this verse, the Greek translators used by the transliteration of siklous (σίκλους) and the Greek translation of didrakmon (διδραχμον), while the Hebrew, Aramaic, and Coptic manuscripts consistently used the same term. As the Greeks clearly translated shekel into didrachma, the term shekel is restored in this translation.

The qite mentioned in Sahidic manuscript 2006, was a translation of the ancient Egyptian unit of measurement equal to a Greek drachma. The measurement was in use in the New Kingdom era, as the qdt (𓏲𓎼), and in the early Iron Age as the qt (𓈎𓏏). The Egyptian term was antiquated by the time the Coptic translation was made, yet it is used in come Sahidic manuscripts of the Torah, such as 2006, 2069, 2002, and 2020, ranging from the 6th century to the 11th century CE. This could indicate that Sahidic translation was partially based on a demotic Egyptian translation. There were some Israelite texts translated into demotic in the 7th and 6th centuries BCE; however, translations of the Torah have not been found. References to Abraham, Isaac, and Jacob are common in Egypto-Israelite texts, suggesting that a version of Cosmic Genesis did exist in Demotic. As "drachma" was the Greek translation of beka, the term beka is restored in this translation.

CHAPTER 3

3 Codex Vaticanus: obolous (ΟΒΟΛΟΥϹ). Translation: obols

- Septuagint manuscript 833: oboloi (ουο/ϐι)
- Septuagint manuscript 72: obolois (ουο/ϐιϲ)
- Leningrad Codex: gērâ (גֵּרָה). Translation: gerah
- Peshitta: mȯyn (ܡܥܝܢ). Translations: mahs
- Targum Onkelos: mā'în (מְעִין). Translations: mahs
- Targum Pseudo-Jonathan: mā'în (מְעִין). Translations: mahs
- Sahidic manuscript 2006: siklos (ϹΙΚΛΟϹ). Translation: shekels

The obol was a Greek coin used from around 1100 BCE, worth ⅙ of a drachma, approximately 0.72 grams of silver. The gerah was a measurement equaling one-twentieth of a shekel. The mah mentioned in the Targums was the Phoenician coin equivalent to the obol, suggesting it is the term in the Aramaic text that the Greeks translated. As the Greek translators substituted the obol, the name gerah is restored.

CHAPTER 4

The Lord said to Moses and Aaron, "Take the number of the children of Kohath from among of the sons of Levi, after their families, according to the houses of their fathers' households, twenty-five years up until fifty years, everyone that goes in to administer, to do all the works in the tabernacle of witness. These are the works of the sons of Kohath in the tabernacle of witness. It is sacred. Aaron and his sons will go in, when the camp is about to move and will take down the shadowing veil, and will cover with it the ark of the testimony. They will put on it a cover, even a blue skin, and put on it above a garment all of blue, and will put the staffs through the rings.

They will put on the table set out for show-bread a purple cloth, and the dishes, and the censers, and the cups, and the vessels with which one offers drink offerings, and the continual loaves will be on it. They will put on it a scarlet cloth, and they will cover it with a blue covering of skin, and they will put the staffs into it. They will take a blue covering, and cover the candlestick that gives light, and its lamps, and its snuffers, and its funnels, and all the vessels of oil with which they minister. They will put it, and all its vessels, into a blue skin cover, and they will put it on bearers. They will put a blue cloth for a cover on the golden altar and will cover it with a blue skin cover, and put in its staffs. They will take all the instruments of service, with which they minister in the sanctuary: and will place them in a cloth of blue, and will cover them with blue skin covering, and put them on staffs."

"He will put the covering on the altar, and they will cover it with a purple cloth. They will put on it all the vessels with which they minister on it, and the fire-pans, and the flesh-hooks, and the cups, and the cover, and all the vessels of the altar, and they will put on it a blue cover of skins and will put in its staffs, and they will take a purple cloth, and cover the laver and its foot, and they will put it into a blue cover of skin, and put it on bars. Aaron and his sons will finish covering the holy things, and all the holy vessels, when the camp begins to move, and afterward the sons of Kohath will go in to take up the furniture, but will not touch the holy things, or else they'll die. Then the sons of Kohath will carry in the tabernacle of witness. Eleazar the son of Aaron the priest is overseer, the oil of the light, and the incense of composition, and the daily sacrifice and the anointing oil, are his order. Even the oversight of the whole tabernacle, and all things that are in it in the holy place, in all the works."

The Lord said to Moses and Aaron, "You will not destroy the family of Kohath from the tribe of the Levites. This you do to them, and they will live and not die when they approach the holy of holies: Let Aaron and his sons advance, and they will place them each in his post for carrying. So they will by no means go in to look suddenly on the holy things, and die."

The Lord said to Moses, "Take the number of the children of Gershon, and these according to the houses of their lineage, according to their families. Take the number of them from twenty-five years old up until the age of fifty, everyone that goes in to minister, to do his business in the tabernacle of witness. This is the public service of the family of Gershon, to minister and to carry. The family will carry the skins of the tabernacle, and the tabernacle of witness, and its veil, and the blue cover that was on it above, and the cover of the door of the tabernacle of witness. All the curtains of the court which were on the tabernacle of witness, and the appendages, and all the vessels of service that they minister with they will attend to. According to the direction of Aaron and his sons will be the ministry of the sons of Gershon, in all their ministries, and all their works. You will take account of them by name in all things borne by them. This is the service of the sons of Gershon in the tabernacle of witness, and their order by the hand of Ithamar the son of Aaron the priest. The sons of Merari according to their families, according to the houses of their lineage, take the count of them. Take the count of them from twenty-five years old up until fifty years old, everyone that goes in to perform the services of the tabernacle of witness."

"These are the orders of the things done by them according to all their works in the tabernacle of witness: they will carry the chapiters of the tabernacle, and the bars, and its pillars, and its sockets, and the veil, and there will be their sockets, and their pillars, and the curtain of the door of the tabernacle. They will carry the pillars of the court round about, and there will be their sockets, and they will carry the pillars of the veil of the door of the court, and their sockets and their pins, and their cords, and all their furniture, and all their instruments of service, record their number by name and all the articles of the order of the things borne by them. This is the ministration of the family of the sons of Merari in all their works in the tabernacle of witness, by the hand of Ithamar the son of Aaron the priest. Moses and Aaron and the rulers of Israel took the number of the sons of Kohath according to their families, according to the houses of their lineage, from twenty-five years old and up to the age of fifty years, everyone that goes in to minister and do service in the tabernacle of witness. Their count according to their families was 2,750."

This is the numbering of the family of Kohath, everyone that ministers in the tabernacle of witness, as Moses and Aaron counted them by the word of the Lord, by the hand of Moses. The sons of Gershon were counted according to their families, according to the houses of their lineage, from twenty-five years old and upward until fifty years old, everyone that goes in to minister and to do the services in the tabernacle of witness. Their count according to their families, according to the houses of their lineage was 2,630. This is the numbering of the family of the sons of Gershon, everyone who ministers in the tabernacle of witness, whom Moses and Aaron counted by the word of the Lord, by the hand of Moses. Also, the family of the sons of Merari were counted according to their divisions, according to the house of their fathers; from twenty-five years old and upward until fifty years old, everyone that goes in to minister in the services of the tabernacle of witness. Their count according to their families, according to the houses of their lineage was 3,200.

CHAPTER 4

This is the numbering of the family of the sons of Merari, whom Moses and Aaron counted by the word of the Lord, by the hand of Moses. All that were counted, whom Moses and Aaron and the rulers of Israel counted, namely, the Levites, according to their families and according to the houses of their lineage, from twenty-five years old and upward until fifty years old, everyone that goes in for the service of the works, and the order of the things that are carried in the tabernacle of witness. They who were counted were 8,580. He reviewed them according to the word of the Lord by the hand of Moses, appointing each man over their respective work, and their burdens. They were counted, as the Lord commanded Moses.

CHAPTER 5

The Lord said to Moses, "Order the children of Israel, to send out of the camp every leper, and everyone who has gonorrhea, and everyone who is unclean in the mind.[1] Whether male or female, send them out of the camp, so they will not defile their camp in which I live among them."

The children of Israel did so and sent them out of the camp as the Lord said to Moses, so did the children of Israel. The Lord said to Moses, "Tell the children of Israel, "Every man or woman who will commit any sin that is common to man, or if that mind will in any way have neglected the commandment and transgressed, that person will confess the sin which he has committed and will make satisfaction for his trespass. He will pay the principal, and will add to it the fifth part, and will make restoration to him against whom he has trespassed. But if a man has no near relative to make satisfaction for his trespass to him, the trespass-offering paid to the Lord will be for the priest, besides the ram of atonement, by which he will make an atonement with it for him. Every first fruits in all the sanctified things among the children of Israel, whatever they will offer to the Lord, will be for the priest himself. The sacred things of every man will be his, and whatever a man will give to the priest, the gift will be his."

The Lord said to Moses, "Tell the children of Israel, "Whoever's wife transgresses against him, and slight and despise him, and supposing anyone will lie with her carnally,

55

and it is hidden from the eyes of her husband, and she should
conceal it and be herself defiled, and there be no witness with
her. Should there come on him a spirit of jealousy, and he
should be jealous of his wife, and she is defiled, or, there
should come on him a spirit of jealousy, and he should be
jealous of his wife, and she should not be defiled, then, will
the man bring his wife to the priest, and will bring his gift for
her, a tenth of an ephah[2] of barley. He will not pour oil on it,
nor will he put frankincense on it, as it is a sacrifice of
jealousy, a sacrifice of memorial reminding of sin."

"The priest will bring her, and make her stand before the
Lord. The priest will take pure running water in an earthen
vessel, and he will take from the dust that is on the floor of
the tabernacle of witness, and the priest having taken it will
cast it into the water. The priest will cause the woman to
stand before the Lord, and will uncover the head of the
woman, and will put into her hands the sacrifice of memorial,
the sacrifice of jealousy, and in the hand of the priest will be
the water of this conviction that brings the curse. The priest
will adjure her, and will say to the woman, 'If no one has lain
with you, and if you have not transgressed to be polluted,
being under the authority of your husband, be free from this
water of the conviction that causes the curse.' But if being a
married woman you have transgressed, or been polluted, and
anyone has lain with you, besides your husband.' Then the
priest will adjure the woman by the oaths of this curse, and
the priest will say to the woman, 'The Lord curse you under
an oath among your people, in that the Lord should cause
your thigh to rot and your belly to swell, and this water

bringing the curse will enter into your womb to cause your belly to swell, and your thigh to rot.' The woman will say, 'Amen, Amen!'"[3]

"The priest will write these curses in a book and will write them in with the water of the conviction that brings the curse. He will cause the woman to drink the water of the conviction that brings the curse, and the water of the conviction that brings the curse will enter into her. The priest will take from the hand of the woman the sacrifice of jealousy, and will present the sacrifice before the Lord, and will bring it to the altar. The priest will take a handful of the sacrifice as a memorial of it and will offer it up on the altar, and afterward, he will cause the woman to drink the water. It will happen, if she is defiled, and have altogether escaped the notice of her husband, then the water of the conviction that brings the curse will enter into her, and she will swell in her belly, and her thigh will rot, and the woman will be cursed among her people. But if the woman has not been polluted, and is clean, then will she be guiltless and will conceive seed."

This is the law of jealousy, in which a married woman should happen to transgress and be defiled, or in the case of a man on whoever the spirit of jealousy should come, and he should be jealous of his wife, and he should place his wife before the Lord, and the priest will execute towards her all this law. Then the man will be clear from sin, and that woman will carry her sin.

CHAPTER 5

CHAPTER 5 NOTES

1 Codex Vaticanus: akaṯarton epi ṡyǩē (ΑΚΑΘΑΡΤΟΝΕΠΙϯΥΧΗ). Translation: foul (or unclean, impure) in psyche (or mind, personality)

• Septuagint manuscript 318: akaṯarton epi ṡyǩēn (ΔΙιαɴθαρτⲱ ϭπι Ψυχⲱ). Translation: foul (or unclean, impure) in psyche (or mind, personality)

• Septuagint manuscript 319: akaṯarton apo ṡyǩē (ΔΙιαɴθαρτⲱ Δπο Ψυχⲗ). Translation: foul (or unclean, impure) from psyche (or mind, personality)

• Septuagint manuscript 16: akaṯarton tē ṡyǩē (ΔΙιαɴθαρτⲱ τⲗ Ψυχⲗ). Translation: foul (or unclean, impure) the psyche (or mind, personality)

• Septuagint manuscript 426: akaṯarton epi tyǩē (ΔΙιαɴθαρτⲱ ϭπι τυχⲗ). Translation: foul (or unclean, impure) in action (or fate, providence)

• Septuagint manuscript 54: akaṯarton epi ṡyǩēs (ΔΙιαɴθαρτⲱ ϭπι Ψυχⲗc). Translation: foul (or unclean, impure) in psyche (or mind, personality)

• Septuagint manuscript 72: akaṯarton en tē ṡyǩē (ΔΙιαɴθαρτⲱ ⲟⲩ τⲗ Ψυχⲗ). Translation: foul (or unclean, impure) in the psyche (or mind, personality)

• Leningrad Codex: ṯāmē' lānāpeš (טָמֵא לְנֶפֶשׁ). Translation: ritually unclean to (or of) soul (or psyche, life, person, will)

• Peshitta: tmȧ bnpšh (ܛܡܐ ܒܢܦܫ). Translations: ritually unclean of ego (or breath, psyche)

• Targum Onkelos: təmê napšā' de'ĕnāšā' (טְמֵי נַפְשָׁא דֶּאֱנָשָׁא). Translations: ritually unclean of ego (or breath, psyche) of man (or human, mortal)

CHAPTER 5

- Targum Pseudo-Jonathan: təmê napšā' dəmît (טְמֵי נַפְשָׁא דְמִית). Translations: ritually unclean of ego (or breath, psyche) of man (or human, mortal)

- Sahidic manuscript 2006: etjahm ejn ouśuḱē (ⲉⲧϫⲁϨⲙ ⲉϪⲛ ⲟⲩⲯⲨⲭⲎ). Translation: defiled (or poluted, impure) of the soul (or ka, life force)

- Sahidic manuscript 2019: eto nakaṭartos ejn ouśuḱē (ⲉⲧⲟ ⲚⲀⲔⲀⲐⲀⲢⲦⲞⲤ ⲉϪⲛ ⲟⲩⲯⲨⲭⲎ). Translation: greatly impure of the soul (or ka, life force)

2 Codex Vaticanus: oifi (ⲟⲓϥⲓ)

- Leningrad Codex: 'êpâ (אֵיפָה). Translation: ephah

- Peshitta: såtå (ܣܐܬܐ). Translations: bowls (or measurements)

- Targum Onkelos: bitlat sə'în (בִּתְלָת סָאִין). Translations: in three sahs

- Targum Pseudo-Jonathan: bitlat sə'în (בִּתְלָת סָאִין). Translations: in three sahs

- Sahidic manuscript 2006: ši (Ϣⲓ). Translation: weight (or measurement)

The Septuagint includes a Greek transliteration of the Hebrew term åyph (איפה). The ephah was a unit of measurement adopted by the Canaanites and Arabs from the Egyptian oipe (𓏺𓈇𓄿𓅓). It continued to be used in Egypt during the classical era, where the word was spelled in Coptic as aeipe (ⲁⲉⲓⲡⲉ) in Akhmimic, aipi (ⲁⲓⲡⲓ) in Fayyumic, oeipe (ⲟⲉⲓⲡⲉ) in Sahidic, and ōipi (ⲱⲓⲡⲓ) in Bohairic, depending on dialect. The ephah was a dry measurement equalling 432 eggs, meaning the measurement in the text was the equivalent or 43.2 eggs.

59

CHAPTER 5

3 Codex Vaticanus: genoito genoito (ΓΕΝΟΙΤΟΓΕΝΟΙΤΟ).
Translation: Earth forbid Earth forbid

- Leningrad Codex: 'āmēn | 'āmēn (אָמֵן \ אָמֵן). Translation: "I agree" (or artist, master, craftsmen, creator, expert, foster parent, Amen) "I agree"

- Peshitta: åmyn åmyn (ܐܡܝܢ ܐܡܝܢ)

- Targum Onkelos: 'āmēn 'āmēn (אָמֵן אָמֵן)

- Targum Jerusalem: 'āmēn dəlā' 'ista'ăbît 'āmēn 'în 'ănā' 'ătîdâ ləmista'ābā' (אָמֵן דְּלָא אִסְתְּאָבִית אָמֵן אִין אֲנָא עֲתִידָה לְמִסְתְּאָבָא). Translations: Amen if not unclean Amen not will become unclean

- Targum Pseudo-Jonathan: 'āmēn 'în 'ista'ābît kad mē'arsā' 'āmēn 'în 'ista'ābît kad nəsîbətā' (אָמֵן אִין אִסְתְּאָבִית כַּד מֵאַרְסָא אָמֵן אִין אִסְתְּאָבִית כַּד נְסִיבְתָּא). Translations: Amen not unclean when married Amen not unclean when offered [in marriage]

- Sahidic manuscript 2006: esešōpe esešōpe (ⲉⲥⲉϣⲱⲡⲉ ⲉⲥⲉϣⲱⲡⲉ). Translation: may it be, may it be

As the original text could not have used the Greek expression, the term amen is imported from the Masoretic Text. If the Canaanite expression amen was not derived from the name of the supreme Egyptian god Amen's name during the Egyptian rule of Canaan when the Book of Numbers is set, it's possible it was based on the Akkadian word for artist, ummānu (𒌝𒈠𒉡), however, this seems less likely than the name of the Egyptian creator god. According to Egyptologists, during the New Kingdom era, Amen (𓇋𓏠𓈖) is believed to have been pronounced as Åman. Earlier, during the Middle Kingdom the name was pronounced as Jaman, explaining the pronunciation of Benjamin, and later during the Nubian dynasty, the name was pronounced as Åmon, explaining the pronunciation of King Amon's name.

CHAPTER 6

The Lord said to Moses, tell the children of Israel, "Whatever man or woman should specially vow a vow to separate oneself with purity to the Lord, he will purely abstain from wine and strong drink. He will drink no wine or strong alcoholic drink. Whatever is made from grapes he will not drink, neither will he eat fresh grapes or raisins. All the days of his vow: he will eat none of all the things that come from the vine, wine from the grape-stones to the grape-stone. All the days of his separation, a razor will not come on his head, until the days are completed which he vowed to the Lord."

"He will be holy, cherishing a head of hair, even long hair, all the days of his vow to the Lord. He will not come near to any dead body, to his father or his mother, or his brother or his sister. He will not defile himself for them when they have died, because the vow of God is on him on his head. All the days of his vow he will be holy to the Lord. If anyone should die suddenly by him, immediately the head of his vow will be defiled, and he will shave his head in whatever day he will be purified. On the seventh day, he will be shaved. On the eighth day, he will bring two turtledoves, or two young pigeons, to the priest, to the doors of the tabernacle of witness."

"The priest will offer one as a sin offering, and the other as a whole burnt offering. The priest will make atonement for

61

him in the things in which he sinned respecting the dead body, and he will sanctify his head in that day in which he was consecrated to the Lord, the days of his vow being interrupted, he will bring a year-old lamb for a trespass-offering, and the former days will not be counted, because the head of his vow was polluted. This is the law of he who has vowed. On whichever day he has fulfilled the days of his vow, he will himself bring his gift to the doors of the tabernacle of witness. He will bring his gift to the Lord, one year-old male lamb without imperfection for a whole burnt offering, and one year-old female lamb without imperfection for a sin offering, and one ram without imperfection for a peace offering, and a basket of unleavened bread of fine flour, including loaves kneaded with oil, and unleavened cakes covered with oil, and their sacrifice, and their drink offering."

"The priest will bring them before the Lord and will offer his sin offering, and his whole burnt offering. He will offer the ram as a sacrifice of peace offering to the Lord with the basket of unleavened bread, and the priest will offer its sacrifice and its drink offering. He that has vowed will shave the head of his consecration by the doors of the tabernacle of witness and will put the hairs on the fire which is under the sacrifice of peace offering. The priest will take the sodden shoulder of the ram, and one unleavened loaf from the basket, and one unleavened cake, and will put them in the hands of the Nazarene[1] after he has shaved off his vow. The priest will present them as an offering before the Lord, it will be the holy portion for the priest beside the breast of the heave-offering and beside the shoulder of the wave-offering, and afterward, the Nazarene will drink wine."

This is the law of the Nazarene who has vowed to the Lord his gift to the Lord, concerning his vow, besides what he may be able to afford according to the value of his vow, which he may have vowed according to the law of separation.

The Lord said to Moses, "Tell Aaron and to his sons, 'You will bless the children of Israel, saying them, 'The Lord bless you and keep you. The Lord make his face shine on you, and have mercy on you. The Lord lift his face on you and give you peace.'² They will put my name on the children of Israel, and I, the Lord will bless them."

CHAPTER 6 NOTES

1 Septuagint manuscript 963: eugmenou (ⲈⲨⲄⲘⲈⲚⲞⲨ)

• Codex Vaticanus: eugmenou (ⲎⲨⲄⲘⲈⲚⲞⲨ). Translation: devotee (or vower, prayer)

• Codex Colberto-Sarravianus: euǩomenou (ⲈⲨⲭⲞⲘⲈⲚⲞⲨ)

• Codex Ambrosiano A 147: euxamenou (ⲈⲨⲌⲀⲘⲈⲚⲞⲨ)

• Septuagint manuscript 407: ēgmenou (ⲏⲅⲙⲁⲩⲟⲩ)

• Septuagint manuscript 458: egmenou (ⲟⲅⲅⲙⲁⲩⲟⲩ)

• Septuagint manuscript 72: ēgnismenou (ⲏⲅⲛⲓⲥⲙⲁⲩⲟⲩ)

• Septuagint manuscript 799: ēēgmenou (ⲏⲏⲅⲙⲁⲩⲟⲩ)

• Leningrad Codex: nāzîr (נָזִיר). Translation: separated (or monk)

• Peshitta: nzyrwtå (ܢܙܝܪܘܬܐ)

• Targum Onkelos: nəzîrû (נְזִירוּ)

CHAPTER 6

- Targum Pseudo-Jonathan: nəzîrā' (נְזִירָא)
- Sahidic manuscript 2006: etbbof (ⲉⲧⲃⲃⲟϥ). Translation: purified

The Greeks translated this term was 'devotee' in Numbers, suggesting the term was obscure when the Torah was translated circa 250 BCE. In Judges, the same term was used for Sampson, who was described as being a nəzîr (נְזִיר) from birth in the Masoretic text, which was transliterated as nazir (ναζιρ) in the Codex Vaticanus and naziraion (ναζιραιον) in the Codex Alexandrinus. *1ˢᵗ Maccabees* records that there was a community of naziraeous (ναζιραίους) in Judea during the revolt, which was between 165 and 140 BCE. The word used in *1ˢᵗ Maccabees* can be translated several ways, including Nazirites, Nazarenes, and Nasoreans, depending on the religious views of the translator, however, all would have been spelled as nzyr (נזיר) in Hebrew.

The Jewish interpretation, as defined in the Talmud, was a Jew that took vows to abstain from wine, not cut their hair, and not touch corpses, as described in *Numbers*. The Nazarene community in *1ˢᵗ Maccabees* is sometimes theorized to be an early reference to the Essenes. The term Nazarene was used in the Christian gospels as a title of Jesus, and therefore became the Arabic and Hebrew term for "Christian," however, the Mandaeans claimed the term referred to their priesthood, which had once been led by John the Baptist, who had baptized Jesus.

In the case of Sampson, he judges the Israelites between approximately 1130 and 1110 BCE, under the rule of the Pelesets, who the Egyptians had surrendered Canaan to. This means that the concept of the Nazir was already established by that era, supporting the antiquity of this section of Numbers. As the Greeks appear to have translated the term Nazir as 'devotee,' the most common English translation is used.

2 A similar phrase is found in Ketef Hinnom scroll 2, which is generally reconstructed as: "-hbrw. May be blessed he by Yhw[h], the warrior and the rebuker of [E]vil, may bless you, Yhwh keep you. May shine, Yh[w]h, his face [on] you and grant you p[ea]ce."

KH2 is a silver scroll inscribed in Judahite, that was found in an archaeological site near Jerusalem dating to the 4th century BCE. It is generally considered a magical amulet to have been created sometime between the 7th and 4th century BCE. It is unclear if it was a paraphrase of this verse in *Numbers*, or simply a similar phase, however, if it was a paraphrase from *Numbers*, it would mean the text of *Numbers* was different at the time, as Yhwh is not referred to as "the warrior," in *Numbers*.

CHAPTER 7

It came to pass on the day in which Moses finished setting up the tabernacle, that he anointed it, and consecrated it, and all its furniture, and the altar and all its furniture, he even anointed them and consecrated them. The princes of Israel brought gifts, twelve princes of their fathers' houses: these were the heads of tribes, these are they that presided over the numbering. They brought their gift before the Lord, six covered wagons, and twelve oxen, a wagon from two princes, and a calf from each, and they brought them before the tabernacle.

The Lord said to Moses, "Take from them, and they will be for the works of the services of the tabernacle of witness. You will give them to the Levites, to each one according to his administration. Moses took the wagons and the oxen and gave them to the Levites. He gave two wagons and four oxen to the sons of Gershon, according to their administrations. Four wagons and eight oxen he gave to the sons of Merari according to their administrations, by Ithamar the son of Aaron the priest. But to the sons of Kohath, he did not give, because they have the administrations of the sacred things. They will carry them on their shoulders.

The rulers brought gifts for the dedication of the altar on the day that he anointed it, and the rulers brought their gifts before the altar. The Lord said to Moses, "One chief each day, will offer their gifts a chief each day for the dedication of the altar."

On the first day Nahshon the son of Amminadab, prince of the tribe of Judah offered his gift. He brought his gift, one silver charger of 130 shekels in weight, one silver bowl, of 70 shekels according to the holy shekel, both full of fine flour kneaded with oil for a sacrifice. One golden censer of 10 shekels full of incense. One calf from the herd, one ram, one year-old male lamb for a whole burnt offering, and one goat kid for a sin offering. For a sacrifice of peace offering, two heifers, five rams, five male goats, five year-old female lambs. This was the gift of Nahshon the son of Amminadab.

On the second day Nethanel the son of Zuar, the prince of the tribe of Issachar, brought his offering. He brought his gift, one silver charger, weighing 130 shekels, one silver bowl of 70 shekels according to the holy shekel, both full of fine flour kneaded with oil for a sacrifice. One censer of 10 golden shekels, full of incense. One calf from the herd, one ram, one year-old male lamb for a whole burnt offering, and one goat kid for a sin offering. For a sacrifice, a peace offering, two heifers, five rams, five male goats, five year-old female lambs. This was the gift of Nethanel the son of Zuar.

On the third day the prince of the sons of Zebulun, Eliab the son of Helon. He brought his gift, one silver charger, weighing 130 shekels, one silver bowl of 70 shekels according to the holy shekel, both full of fine flour kneaded with oil for a sacrifice. One golden censer of 10 shekels, full of incense. One calf from the herd, one ram, one year-old male lamb for a whole burnt offering, and one goat kid for a sin offering. For a sacrifice of peace offering, two heifers, five rams, five male goats, five year-old female lambs. This was the gift of Eliab the son of Helon.

On the fourth day Elizur the son of Shedeur, the prince of the children of Reuben. He brought his gift, one silver charger, weighing 130 shekels, one silver bowl of 70 shekels according to the holy shekel, both full of fine flour kneaded with oil for a sacrifice. One golden censer of 10 shekels full of incense. One calf from the herd, one ram, one year-old male lamb for a whole burnt offering, and one goat kid for a sin offering. For a sacrifice of peace offering, two heifers, five rams, five male goats, five year-old female lambs. This was the gift of Elizur the son of Shedeur.

On the fifth day the prince of the children of Simeon, Shelumiel the son of Zurishaddai. He brought his gift, one silver charger, weighing 130 shekels, one silver bowl of 70 shekels according to the holy shekel, both full of fine flour kneaded with oil for a sacrifice. One golden censer of 10 shekels, full of incense. One calf from the herd, one ram, one year-old male lamb for a whole burnt offering, and one goat kid for a sin offering. For a sacrifice of peace offering, two heifers, five rams, five male goats, five year-old female lambs. This was the gift of Shelumiel the son of Zurishaddai.

On the sixth day the prince of the sons of Gad, Eliasaph the son of Deuel. He brought his gift, one silver charger, weighing 130 shekels, one silver bowl of 70 shekels according to the holy shekel, both full of fine flour kneaded with oil for a sacrifice. One golden censer of 10 shekels, full of incense. One calf from the herd, one ram, one year-old male lamb for a whole burnt offering, and one goat kid for a sin offering. For a sacrifice of peace offering, two heifers, five rams, five male goats, five year-old female lambs. This was the gift of Eliasaph the son of Deuel.

On the seventh day the prince of the sons of Ephraim, Elishama the son of Ammihud. He brought his gift, one silver charger, weighing 130 shekels, one silver bowl of 70 shekels according to the holy shekel, both full of fine flour kneaded with oil for a sacrifice. One golden censer of 10 shekels, full of incense. One calf from the herd, one ram, one year-old male lamb for a whole burnt offering, and one goat kid for a sin offering. For a sacrifice of peace offering, two heifers, five rams, five male goats, five year-old female lambs. This was the gift of Elishama the son of Ammihud.

On the eighth day the prince of the sons of Manasseh, Gamaliel the son of Pedahzur. He brought his gift, one silver charger, weighing 130 shekels, one silver bowl of 70 shekels according to the holy shekel, both full of fine flour mingled with oil for a sacrifice. One golden censer of 10 shekels, full of incense. One calf from the herd, one ram, one year-old male lamb for a whole burnt offering, and one goat kid for a sin offering. For a sacrifice of peace offering two heifers, five rams, five male goats, five year-old female lambs. This was the gift of Gamaliel the son of Pedahzur.

On the ninth day the prince of the sons of Benjamin, Abidan the son of Gideoni. He brought his gift, one silver charger, weighing 130 shekels, one silver bowl of 70 shekels according to the holy shekel, both full of fine flour mingled with oil for a sacrifice. One golden censer of 10 shekels, full of incense. One calf from the herd, one ram, one year-old male lamb for a whole burnt offering, and one goat kid for a sin offering. For a sacrifice of peace offering, two heifers, five rams, five male goats, five year-old female lambs. This was the gift of Abidan the son of Gideoni.

On the tenth day the prince of the sons of Dan, Ahiezer the son of Ammishaddai. He brought his gift, one silver charger, weighing 130 shekels, one silver bowl of 70 shekels according to the holy shekel, both full of fine flour kneaded with oil for a sacrifice. One golden censer of 10 shekels, full of incense. One calf from the herd, one ram, one year-old male lamb for a whole burnt offering, and one goat kid for a sin offering. For a sacrifice of peace offering, two heifers, five rams, five male goats, five year-old female lambs. This was the gift of Ahiezer the son of Ammishaddai.

On the eleventh day the prince of the sons of Asher, Phageel the son of Ochran. He brought his gift, one silver charger, weighing 130 shekels, one silver bowl of 70 shekels according to the holy shekel, both full of fine flour mingled with oil for a sacrifice. One golden censer of 10 shekels, full of incense. One calf from the herd, one ram, one year-old male lamb for a whole burnt offering, and one goat kid for a sin offering. For a sacrifice of peace offering, two heifers, five rams, five male goats, five year-old female lambs. This was the gift of Phageel the son of Ochran.

CHAPTER 7

On the twelfth day the prince of the sons of Naphtali, Ahira the son of Enan. He brought his gift, one silver charger, weighing 130 shekels, one silver bowl of 70 shekels according to the holy shekel; both full of fine flour mingled with oil for a sacrifice. One golden censer of 10 shekels, full of incense. One calf from the herd, one ram, one year-old male lamb for a whole burnt offering, and one goat kid for a sin offering. For a sacrifice of peace offering, two heifers, five rams, five male goats, five year-old female lambs. This was the gift of Ahira the son of Enan.

This was the dedication of the altar on the day in which Moses anointed it, by the princes of the sons of Israel, twelve silver chargers, twelve silver bowls, twelve golden censers, each one charger of 130 shekels, and each bowl of 70 shekels, all the silver of the vessels was 2,400 shekels, the shekels according to the holy shekel, as 12 golden censers full of incense, all the gold of the shekels being 120 shekels. All the livestock for whole burnt offerings, twelve calves, twelve rams, twelve year-old male lambs, and their sacrifice, and their drink offerings: and twelve male goat-kids for sin offering. All the livestock for a sacrifice of peace offering, twenty-four heifers, sixty rams, sixty male goats of a year-old, sixty year-old female lambs without imperfection."

This was the dedication of the altar. After that Moses filled his hands, and after he anointed him. When Moses went into the tabernacle of witness to speak to him, then he heard the voice of the Lord speaking to him from off the mercy-seat, which is on the ark of the testimony, between the two cherubs,[1] and he spoke to him.

CHAPTER 7 NOTES

1 Septuagint manuscript 963: ǩeroubein (ⲭⲉⲣⲟⲨⲃⲉⲓⲛ)

• Codex Vaticanus: ǩeroubeim (ⲭⲉⲣⲟⲨⲃⲉⲓⲙ)

• Codex Venetus: ǩeroubin (ⲭⲉⲣⲟⲨⲃⲓⲛ)

• Septuagint manuscript 125: ǩeroubim o estin epi tēs kibōtou tou martyriou (χ̅ρουⲩⲙ οϛⲓⲛ ϭπι ϯ ⳗⲓⲩⲱⲧⲟ ⲧⲟ μαρτυβⲓου). Translation: cherubs that exist on the box of testimony (or martyrdom, evidence)

• Septuagint manuscript 376: ǩairoubim (χαⲅϱουⲩⲙ)

• Leningrad Codex: kərūbîm (כְּרֻבִים). Translation: cherubs (or griffins)

• Peshitta: krwbyn (ܟܪ̈ܘܒܝܢ). Translation: cherubs (or griffins)

• Targum Onkelos: kərûbayyā' (כְּרוּבַיָּא). Translation: cherubs (or griffins)

• Targum Pseudo-Jonathan: kərûbayā' (כְּרוּבַיָא). Translation: cherubs (or griffins)

• Sahidic manuscript 2006: ǩairoubin (ⲭⲁⲓⲣⲟⲨⲃⲓⲛ)

The word "cherub" (ܟܪ̈ܘܒ / כרוב / 𐤊𐤓𐤁 / 𓅨) was the West Semitic term for the mythical creature generally called a 'griffin' today. The oldest form is recorded in the Akkadian word karibu (𒅗𒊑𒁍), meaning "one who blesses." Based on the archaeological record of Canaan, it appears that during the late Bronze Age, the "cherub" was depicted as a sphinx. During the Iron Age, the Assyrian karubu (𒅗𒊒𒁍) iconography was adopted by the Israelites. The term "cherub" appears to have been used as a

73

substitute for śārāp (שָׂרָף) after King Hezekiah or King Manasseh's reforms to the Torah in the early 8th century BCE. Isaiah called Nəḥūštān (נְחֻשְׁתָּן) a seraph when he visited the temple in the late 9th century BCE, before it was destroyed at the beginning of the 8th century BCE. Nəḥūštān was the name or title of the Bronze Serpent statue that Moses made. This suggests that the original "cherubs" on the Ark of the Testimony were seraphs or wadjets. Typically, wadjets were depicted in pairs in older Egyptian literature. During the Middle Bronze Age, paintings and carvings of Egyptian sacred barks, which the Ark of the Testimony was modeled on, were almost always depicted with wadjets. They became less common in the Late Bronze Age, when Amen became the dominant god, and sphinx statues became more common as "guardian gods."

CHAPTER 8

The Lord said to Moses, "Tell Aaron, "Whenever you will set the lamps in order, the seven lamps will give light opposite the candlestick." Aaron did so, on one side opposite the candlestick he lighted its lamps, as the Lord told Moses. This is the arrangement of the candlestick. It is solid gold, its stem and its lilies are all solid, according to the pattern which the Lord showed Moses, so he made the candlestick.

The Lord said to Moses, "Take the Levites out from among the children of Israel and purify them. You will perform their purification like so, you will sprinkle them with water of purification, and a razor will shave their whole body, and they will wash their garments and will be clean. They will take one calf from the herd, and its sacrifice, fine flour mingled with oil, and you will take a year-old calf from the herd for a sin offering. You will bring the Levites before the tabernacle of witness, and you will assemble all the community of the sons of Israel. Bring the Levites before the Lord, and the sons of Israel will lay their hands on the Levites. Aaron will separate the Levites as a gift before the Lord from the children of Israel, and they will be prepared to perform the works of the Lord. The Levites will lay their hands on the heads of the calves, and you will offer one for a sin offering, and the other for a whole burnt offering to the Lord, to make atonement for them. You will set the Levites before the Lord, and before Aaron, and before his sons, and you will give them as a gift before the Lord. Separate the Levites from among the sons of Israel, and they will be mine. Afterward, the Levites will go in to perform the works of the tabernacle of witness, and you will purify them, and present them before the Lord. For these are given to me as a present from among the children of Israel. I have taken them to myself instead of all the firstborn of the sons of Israel that open every womb. For every firstborn among the children of Israel is mine, whether of man or beast, in the day in which I struck every firstborn in the land of Egypt, I sanctified them to myself. I took the Levites in the place of every firstborn among the children of Israel. I gave the Levites as a gift to Aaron and his sons from among the children of Israel, to do the service of the children of Israel in the tabernacle of witness, and to make atonement for the children of Israel, so there will be none among the sons of Israel to draw near to the holy things."

Moses and Aaron, and all the community of the children of Israel, did to the Levites as the Lord commanded Moses concerning the Levites, so the sons of Israel did to them. So the Levites purified themselves and washed their garments, and Aaron presented them as a gift before the Lord, and Aaron made atonement for them to purify them. Afterward, the Levites went in to administer their service in the tabernacle of witness before Aaron, and before his sons. As the Lord appointed Moses concerning the Levites, so they did to them.

The Lord said to Moses, "This is the ordinance for the Levites. From twenty-five years old and upward, they will go in to do the work in the tabernacle of witness. From fifty years old the Levites will cease from the ministry, and will not work any longer. His brother will serve in the tabernacle of witness to keep orders, but he will not do works. So you will do to the Levites in their orders."

CHAPTER 9

The Lord said to Moses in the Wilderness of Sinai, in the second year after they left the land of Egypt, in the first month, "Speak, and let the children of Israel keep the Passover in its season. On the fourteenth day of the first month, in the evening, you will keep it in its season. You will keep it according to its law, and according to its ordinance."

Moses ordered the children of Israel to sacrifice the Passover, on the fourteenth day of the first month in the Wilderness of Sinai, as the Lord appointed Moses, so the children of Israel did. There came men who were unclean because of a dead body, and they were not able to keep the Passover on that day, and they came before Moses and Aaron on that day. These men said to him, "We are unclean because of the dead body of a man. Will we, therefore, fail to offer the gift to the Lord in its season among the children of Israel?"

Moses said to them, "Stand there, and I will hear what order the Lord will give concerning you."

The Lord said to Moses, "Tell the children of Israel, 'Whatever man will be unclean because of a dead body, or on a journey far off, among you, or among your descendants, he will then keep the Passover to the Lord, in the second month, on the fourteenth day. In the evening they will offer it, with unleavened bread and bitter plants will they eat it. They will not leave it until the morning, and they will not break a bone of it. They will sacrifice it according to the ordinance of the Passover."

"Whatever man will be clean, and is not far off on a journey, and will fail to keep the Passover, that mind will be cut off from his people, because he has not offered the gift to the Lord in its season. That man will carry his iniquity. If there should come to you a stranger in your land and should keep the Passover to the Lord, he will keep it according to the law of the Passover and according to its ordinance. There will be one law for you, both for the stranger and for the native of the land."

"In the day in which the tabernacle was pitched the cloud covered the tabernacle, the house of the testimony, and in the evening there was on the tabernacle the appearance of fire until the morning. So it was continually, the cloud covered it by day and the appearance of fire by night. When the cloud went up from the tabernacle, then after that the children of Israel departed, and in whatever place the cloud rested, there the children of Israel camped. The children of Israel will camp by the command of the Lord, and by the command of the Lord, they will leave. All the days in which the cloud overshadows the tabernacle, the children of Israel will camp. Whenever the cloud will be drawn over the tabernacle for many days, then the children of Israel will follow the command of God[1] and they will not move."

"It will be, whenever the cloud overshadows the tabernacle several days, they will camp by the word of the Lord, and will move by the command of the Lord. It will happen, whenever the cloud remains from the evening until the morning, and in the morning the cloud will go up, then they will move by day or by night. When the cloud continues more than a month overshadowing the tabernacle, the children of Israel will camp, and will not depart. For they will depart by the command of the Lord."

They followed the order of the Lord by the command of the Lord by the hand of Moses.

CHAPTER 9 NOTES

1 Codex Vaticanus: T̄U (℮Ῠ). Translation: God
* Leningrad Codex: Yəhwâ (יְהוָ֣ה)
* Peshitta: mryâ (ܡܪܝܐ). Translation: master (or lord)
* Targum Onkelos: Yəyā (??). Translation: Yahweh
* Targum Pseudo-Jonathan: Yəyā (??). Translation: Yahweh

CHAPTER 10

The Lord said to Moses, "Make for yourself two silver trumpets. You will make them of beaten work, and they will be for you to call the assembly, and of moving the camps. You will sound with them, and all the community will be gathered to the door of the tabernacle of witness. If they will sound with one, all the rulers including the princes of Israel will come to you. You will sound an alarm, the camps pitched eastward will begin to move. You will sound a second alarm, and the camps pitched southward will move. If you sound a third alarm, and the camps pitched westward will move forward. If you sound a fourth alarm, and they that camp towards the north will move forward, they will sound an alarm at their departure."

"Whenever you will gather the assembly, you will sound, but not an alarm. The priests, the sons of Aaron will sound with the trumpets, and it will be a perpetual ordinance for you throughout your generations. If you will go out to war in your land against your enemies who oppose you, then you will sound with the trumpets, as a remembrance before the Lord, and you will be saved from your enemies. In the days of your gladness, and your feasts, and your new moons, you will sound with the trumpets at your whole burnt offerings and the sacrifices of your peace offerings. There will be a memorial for you before the gods, I'm the lord of your gods."[1]

CHAPTER 10

(And said Lord to Moses, "I am content to dwell in this mountain which is restored, and you shall be removed from it, and you shall enter into the mountain of the Amorites, and into their subject's mountains, and their subjects in Lebanon and to the coast of the sea of the Canaanites, and from Anti-lebanon to the great river Euphrates. I will concede in front of you the land where you enter, which will be distributed by lottery, the land which I handed to your forefathers Abraham, Isaac, and Jacob, and their descendants.")[2]

It happened in the second year, in the second month, on the twentieth day of the month, the cloud went up from the tabernacle of witness. The children of Israel set forward with their baggage in the Wilderness of Sinai, and the cloud rested in the Wilderness of Paran. The first rank departed by the word of the Lord by the hand of Moses. They first set in motion the order of the camp of the children of Judah with their army, and over their army was Nahshon, son of Amminadab. Over the army of the tribe of the sons of Issachar, was Nethanel the son of Zuar. Over the army of the tribe of the sons of Zebulun, was Eliab the son of Helon. They will take down the tabernacle, and the sons of Gershon will set forward, and the sons of Merari, who carry the tabernacle. The order of the camp of Reuben set forward with their army, and over their army was Elizur the son of Shedeur. Over the army of the tribe of the sons of Simeon, was Shelumiel the son of Zurishaddai. Over the army of the tribe of the children of Gad, was Eliasaph the son of Deuel.

CHAPTER 10

The sons of Kohath set out carrying the holy things, and the others will set up the tabernacle when they arrive. The order of the camp of Ephraim set out with their forces, and over their forces was Elishama the son of Ammihud. Over the forces of the tribes of the sons of Manasseh, was Gamaliel the son of Pedahzur. Over the forces of the tribe of the children of Benjamin, was Abidan the son of Gideoni. The order of the camp of the sons of Dan will set forward the last of all the camps, with their forces: and over their forces was Ahiezer the son of Ammishaddai. Over the forces of the tribe of the sons of Asher, was Phageel the son of Ochran. Over the forces of the tribe of the sons of Naphtali, was Ahira the son of Enan. These are the armies of the children of Israel, and they set forward with their forces. Moses said to Jobab the son of Ragouel the Midianite, the son-in-law of Moses,[3] "We are going forward to the place which the Lord said, 'I will give you this.' Come with us, and we will treat you well, for Lord has spoken good concerning Israel."

He said to him, "I will not go, but I will return to my land and my families"

He said, "Don't leave us, because you have been with us in the wilderness, and you will be an elder among us. It will happen if you will go with us, it will even happen that in whatever things Lord will do us good, we will also do you good."

They departed from the mount of the Lord a three days' journey, and the ark of the covenant of the Lord went before them a three days' journey to provide rest for them. The

CHAPTER 10

cloud overshadowed them by day when they departed from the camp. It came to pass when the ark set forward, that Moses said, "Rise, Lord, and let your enemies be scattered. Let all that hate you flee." When resting he said, "Turn again, Lord, the thousands and tens of thousands of Israel."

CHAPTER 10 NOTES

1 Codex Vaticanus: $\overline{\text{TU}}$ egō $\overline{\text{KS}}$ o $\overline{\text{TS}}$ ymōn (ⲐⲨ ⲉⲅⲱ ⲔⲤ ⲟ ⲐⲤ ⲨⲘⲰⲚ). Translation: Lord I'm lord the god of you

• Leningrad Codex: Yəhōwâ. 'Ănî Yəhōwâ 'ĕlōhêkem (אֲנִי . יְהוָה יְהוָה אֱלֹהֵיכֶם). Translation: Yehowa. I'm Yehowa your god

• Peshitta: mryå ånå ånå mryå ålhkwn (ܡܪܝܐ ܐܢܐ ܐܢܐ ܡܪܝܐ ܐܠܗܟܘܢ). Translation: master I am master your god

• Targum Onkelos: mêmərā' daYyā. 'Ănā' Yəyā 'ĕlāhākôn (מֵימְרָא דַיְיָ . אֲנָא יְיָ אֱלָהֲכוֹן). Translation: command of the Yahweh. I'm Yahweh your god

• Targum Pseudo-Jonathan: 'ĕlāhākôn bəram Saṭānā' mit'arbēb ləqal yabbəbûtəkôn. 'Ănā' hû' Yəyā 'ĕlāhākôn (אֱלָהֲכוֹן בְּרַם סָטָנָא מִתְעַרְבֵב לְקָל יַבְּבוּתְכוֹן. אֲנָא הוּא יְיָ אֱלָהֲכוֹן). Translation: your god however Satan (or adversary, devil) amazed trembling. I'm he: Yahweh your god

• Sahidic manuscript 2006: pjoeis petnnoute (ⲠϪⲞⲈⲓⲤ ⲠⲈⲦⲚⲚⲞⲨⲦⲈ). Translation: the master the hand of god

• Sahidic manuscript 2044: petnnoute anok pe pjoeis petnnoute (ⲠⲈⲦⲚⲚⲞⲨⲦⲈ ⲀⲚⲞⲔ ⲠⲈ ⲠϪⲞⲈⲓⲤ ⲠⲈⲦⲚⲚⲞⲨⲦⲈ). Translation: the hand of god I'm sky the master the hand of god

The phrase Lord the god (Κύριος ὁ θεὸς) only appears a few times in Numbers, although does feature prominently in *Cosmic Genesis*

86

and *Exodus.* It is missing entirely from *Leviticus,* strongly suggesting that *Numbers* is older than *Leviticus,* or compiled of sections that are older than *Leviticus.*

The Aramaic sections of Masoretic *Daniel* that were not translated into Hebrew maintain the term 'ădōnāy hā'ĕlōhîm (אֲדֹנָי הָאֱלֹהִים), meaning the "lord of the gods" where the Septuagint has "Lord the god" (Κύριος ὁ θεὸς). As most books of the Septuagint were translated from Egypto-Aramaic texts, the Egypto-Aramaic text almost certainly used the term "lord of the gods" where the Septuagint has "Lord the god."

2 Septuagint manuscript 78: kai elalēsen kspros Mōsēn legōn ikanoustō umin katoikein en tō oreitouto epistrafētai kai aparatai umeis kai eisporeuestai eis oros amorraiōn kai pros pantas tous perioikous autou tous en tēpaidiadi eis oros kai paidion kai pros liban kaiparalian talassēs gēn kananaiōn kai antilibanon eōs tou megalou potamou eufratoueisseltate paradedōka enōpion umōn tēn gēn eiseltontai klironomēsatai tēngēn ēn ōmosa tois patrasin umōn tō Abraam kai Isaak kai Iakōb dounai tō spermati autou met autous (ℓαϳ ᵷλλℏσαϳ ℓασϱϲ Μοσℳ λόγοοℵ ικϕυ ουοϑοο υμιℵ ℓατⴲℓℓϕℵ αν τοο οϱϕτꙍτο ϭπιϛεϱᵷℏταϳ ℓαϳ Δπαϱℏταϳ υμϫϲ ℓαϳ ϕασοϱϭυϭοϑαϳ ϕϲ οϱϱϲ ΔμοϱⱣραϳοοℵ ℓαϳ πϱϱϲ πϕℵτℏϲ τꙍϲ πϯιⴲℏαꙍ αυτꙍ τꙍϲ αν τℏπαϳΔιΔλι ϕϲ οϱϱϲ ℓαϳ παϳλϕℵ ℓαϳ πϱϱϲ λιℓϕℵ ℓαϳπαϱλλιϕℵ ⴲλλασσℏϲ γℓℳ χϕℵϕℵαϳοοℵ ℓαϳ ϕℵℏλιℓϕⴲ ϭοοϲ τꙍ μόγαⱣυ ποτλμου ϭυϧεϱα τꙍ ϕσσϯⴲλτϭ παϱλΔϭλοοκα ανοοπιⴲ υμϫℵ Ϯϳ γℓℳ ϕσϷⴲⴲταϳ ℓλιⱣⴲομℏⱭαταϳ Ϯϳγℓℳ ℓℳ ωμοⱭα τⴲϲ πλτϱϱσιℵ υμϫℵ τꙍ ᴧιεϱΔμ ℓαϳ ιⱭλδι ℓαϳ ιΔιοοιι λοωαϳ τꙍ ασϱμϱϕℏ Δυτꙍ μϭτ Δυτꙍϲ). Translation: and spoke Lord to Moses, saying, "I am content to dwell in this mountain which is returned, and it shall be removed from you, and you shall enter into the mountain of the Amorites, and into their children's mountains (or subject's mountains), and children (or subjects, slaves) to Lebanon and the coast of the sea of the Canaanites, and Anti-Lebanon to the great river Euphrates. Where you enter, I will concede in front of you the land, which will be distributed by lottery, the land which I shouldered (or carried) to the forefathers Abraham, Isaac, and Jacob, and their descendants."

Septuagint manuscript 767: kai elalēsen kspros Mōsēn legōn ikanoustō umin katoikein en tō orei touto epistrafētai kaiaparatai umeis kai eisporeuestai eis oros amorraiōn kai pros pantas tous perioikousautou tous en tē paidiadi eis oros kai paidion kai pros liban kai paralian talassēsgēn kananaiōn kai antilibanon eōs tou megalou potamou eufratou eisseltatai paradedōka enōpionumōn tēn gēn eiseltontai klironomēsatai tēn gēn ēn ōmosa tois patrasin umōn tō Abraam kai Isaak kai Iakōb dounai tō spermati autou met autous (ωαͳ βαλλ̄σω Ϟασρος Μοσω λόγοον ικ̄ͳ ουᾶ οο υμ̄ν καͳ⊕λͳͳ αν του ορͳͳ τωτο ͷπͳϛρα φλ̄ͳαͳ ωαͳ απαρᾱͳαͳ υμͳс ωαͳ ͳασορͳͳυͳσᾶ αͳ ͳс ορϛс αμορͳͳαͳοον ωαͳ προс πͳͳͳτͳс τωс προⷮ⊕ͳсⷮ αυτω τωс αν ͳͳ παͳͳιͳͳι ͳс ορϛс ωαͳ παͳͳ̄ͳον ωαͳ προс λιͳͳ̄ ωαͳ παρͳͳλιͳͳ̄ Θαλͳͳσσͳͳ͡сͳͳͳ χ͂ͳ ͳ͂ͳ̄ͳ αͳοον ωαͳ ͳ͂ͳͳͳ̄λͳͳͳ̄⊕ ͷοос τω μͳͳͳ̄ͳͳͳ/ͳυ ποτͳͳͳμου ͳ͂υͳͳρα τω ͳͳσͳͳ̄Θͳ̄ͳαͳ παρͳͳͳ̄ͳ̄Θοοκα αν∞πͳ⊕υμͳͳ̄ν ͳͳ͡ͳͳͳ̄υͳ ͳͳσͳͳͳ̄Θͳ̄ͳαͳ ͳͳ̄λͳͳ⊕ομͳͳ̄Cͳͳͳ̄ͳαͳ ͳͳ͡ͳͳͳͳ̄υͳ ͳͳ ∞μͳͳCα τ⊕с πͳͳͳͳ̄ͳͳͳͳ̄ σͳͳ̄ν υμͳͳ̄ν τωσ Αͳͳͳͳ̄ͳͳͳͳ̄μ ωαͳ ιCͳ̄ͳλͳͳ ωαͳ ιͳͳͳͳ̄οοͳͳ ͳͳοωαͳ τωσ σͳͳ̄ϸͳͳͳ̄ͳͳ̄ αυτω μͳ̄τ αυτωс). Translation: and spoke Lord to Moses, saying, "I am content to dwell in this mountain which is returned, and it shall be removed from you, and you shall enter into the mountain of the Amorites, and into their children's mountains (or subject's mountains), and children (or subjects, slaves) to Lebanon and the coast of the sea of the Canaanites, and Anti-Lebanon to the great river Euphrates. Where you enter, I will concede in front of you the land, which will be distributed by lottery, the land which I shouldered (or carried) to the forefathers Abraham, Isaac, and Jacob, and their descendants."

This verse is only found in two known Septuagint manuscripts, however, is consistent with the Hasidic texts of the 2nd century

CHAPTER 10

BCE, and may represent an alternate early Aramaic translation of Numbers.

3 Codex Vaticanus: Obab uiō Ragouēl tō Madianitē tō gambrō Mōysē (ΟΒΑΒΥΙѠΡΑΓΟΥΗΛΤѠΜΑΔΙΑΝΕΙΤΗΤѠΓΑΜΒΡѠΜѠΥϹΗ). Translation: Obab son of Rhagouel the Midianite the groom (or son in law) of Moses

• Codex Alexandrinus: Ōbab uiō Ragouēl tō Madianiti tō gambrō Mōysē (ѠΒΑΒ ΥΙѠ ΡΑΓΟΥΗΛ ΤѠ ΜΑΔΙΑΝΙΤΙ ΤѠ ΓΑΜΒΡѠ ΜѠΥϹΗ). Translation: Obab son of Rhagouel the Midianite the groom (or son in law) of Moses

• Codex Ambrosiano A 147: Iōbab uiō Ragouēl tō Madianitē tō pentherō Mōysē (ιѠΒΑΒΥΙѠ ΡΑΓΟΥΗΛ ΤѠ ΜΑΔΙΑΝΙΤΗ ΤѠ ΠΕΝΘΕΡѠ ΜѠΥϹΗ). Translation: Iobab son of Rhagouel the Midianite the father-in-law of Moses

• Septuagint manuscript 509: Olibath huiō Rhagouēl tō Madianitē tō gambrō Mōysē (Ο λιιλθ γοο Ρλγουλλ τοο Μλλιⲇⲡιτλ τοογαμμεγ Μοουσλ). Translation: Olibath son of Rhagouel the Midianite the groom (or son in law) of Moses

• Septuagint manuscript 131: Ōmab huiō Rhagouēl tō Madianitē tō gambrō Mōysē (Ѡμαι γοο Ρλγουλλ τοο Μλλιⲇⲡιτλ τοογαμμεγ Μοουσλ). Translation: Omabson of Rhagouel the Midianite the groom (or son in law) of Moses

• Septuagint manuscript 319: Hōbab huiō Rhagouēl tō Maadanitē tō gambrō Mōysē (Ѡιⲁⲓ γοο Ρλγουλλ τοο Μλλⲇⲁⲛιτλ τοογαμμεγ Μοουσλ). Translation: Hobab son of Rhagouel the Midianite the groom (or son in law) of Moses

• Septuagint manuscript 16: Hōbab huiō Rhagouēl tō Madianē tō gambrō autou (Ѡιⲁⲓ γοο Ρλγουλλ τοο Μλλιⲇⲡλ τοο γαμμεγ λυτοο). Translation: Hobab son of Rhagouel the Madine the groom of him

89

• Septuagint manuscript 30: Hōbab huiō Rhagouēl tō Maniaditē tō gambrō Mōysē (ⲱⲩⲁⲩ ⲩⲟⲟ Ⲣⲁⲅⲟⲩⲏλ ⲧⲟⲟ Ⲙⲇⲡⲓⲁⲁⲓⲧⲏ ⲧⲟⲟⲅⲁⲙⲩⲣⲱ Ⲙⲟⲟⲩⲟⲏ). Translation: Hobab son of Rhagouel the Maniadite the groom (or son in law) of Moses

• Septuagint manuscript 58: Hōbab huiō Rhagouēl tō Madianiti tō gambrō Mōysē (ⲱⲩⲁⲩ ⲩⲟⲟ Ⲣⲁⲅⲟⲩⲏλ ⲧⲟⲟ Ⲙⲁⲁⲓⲇⲡⲓⲧⲇ ⲧⲟⲟⲅⲁⲙⲩⲣⲱ Ⲙⲟⲟⲩⲟⲏ). Translation: Hobab son of Rhagouel the Midianite the groom (or son in law) of Moses

• Septuagint manuscript 118: Hōbab huiō Rhagouēl tō Madiniatē tō gambrō Mōysē (ⲱⲩⲁⲩ ⲩⲟⲟ Ⲣⲁⲅⲟⲩⲏλ ⲧⲟⲟ Ⲙⲁⲁⲓⲛⲓⲁⲧⲏ ⲧⲟⲟⲅⲁⲙⲩⲣⲱ Ⲙⲟⲟⲩⲟⲏ). Translation: Hobab son of Rhagouel the Midianite the groom (or son in law) of Moses

• Septuagint manuscript 19: Hōbab huiō Rhagouēl tō Madiniati tō gambrō Mōysē (ⲱⲩⲁⲩ ⲩⲟⲟ Ⲣⲁⲅⲟⲩⲏ λ ⲧⲟⲟ Ⲙⲁⲁⲓⲛⲓⲁⲧⲓ ⲧⲟⲟⲅⲁⲙⲩⲣⲱ Ⲙⲟⲟⲩⲟⲏ). Translation: Hobab son of Rhagouel the Midianite the groom (or son in law) of Moses

• Septuagint manuscript 246: Iōabad huiō Rhagouēl tō Madianitē Mōysē (ⲓⲟⲟⲁⲩⲁⲁ ⲩⲟⲟ Ⲣⲁⲅⲟⲩⲏ λ ⲧⲟⲟ Ⲙⲁⲁⲓⲇⲡⲓⲧⲏ Ⲙⲟⲟⲩⲟⲏ). Translation: Ioabadson of Rhagouel the Midianite the groom (or son in law) of Moses

• Septuagint manuscript 130: Abab huiō Rhagouēl tō Madianitē tō gambrō Mōysē (Ⲁⲩⲁⲩ ⲩⲟⲟ Ⲣⲁⲅⲟⲩⲏλ ⲧⲟⲟ Ⲙⲁⲁⲓⲇⲡⲓⲧⲏ ⲧⲟⲟ ⲅⲁⲙⲩⲣⲱ Ⲙⲟⲟⲩⲟⲏ). Translation: Abab son of Rhagouel the Midianite the groom (or son in law) of Moses

• Septuagint manuscript 458: Iōabab uiōn Rhagouēl tō Madianēti tō gambrō Mōysē (ⲓⲟⲟⲁⲩⲁⲩ ⲩⲟⲟⲛ Ⲣⲁⲅⲟⲩⲏλ ⲧⲟⲟ Ⲙⲁⲁⲓⲇⲡⲏⲧⲓ ⲧⲟⲟ ⲅⲁⲙⲩⲣⲱ Ⲙⲟⲟⲩⲟⲏ). Translation: Ioabab son of Rhagouel the Midianite the groom (or son in law) of Moses

• Septuagint manuscript 72: Hōbab huiō Rhagouēl tō Madianē tō gambrō Mōsē (ⲱⲩⲁⲩ ⲩⲟⲟ Ⲣⲁⲅⲟⲩⲏ λ ⲧⲟⲟ Ⲙⲁⲁⲓⲇⲡⲏ ⲧⲟⲟ ⲅⲁⲙⲩⲣⲱ Ⲙⲟⲟⲟⲏ).

Translation: Hobab son of Rhagouel the Midianite the groom (or son in law) of Moses

• Septuagint manuscript 528: Ōbath huiō Rhagouēl tō Madianitē tō gambrō Mōysē (ⲱⲩⲁⲑ ⲩ∞ Ⲣⲁⲅⲟⲩⲏⲗ ⲧ∞ Ⲙⲁⲁⲓⲫⲓⲧⲏ ⲧ∞ ⲅⲁⲙⲙⲉⲱ Ⲙⲟⲟⲩⲥⲏ). Translation: Obath son of Rhagouel the Midianite the groom (or son in law) of Moses

• Septuagint manuscript 44: Iōab huiō Rhagouēl tō Madianitē tō gambrō Mōysē (ⲓ∞ⲁⲩ ⲩ∞ Ⲣⲁⲅⲟⲩⲏⲗ ⲧ∞ Ⲙⲁⲁⲓⲫⲓⲧⲏ ⲧ∞ ⲅⲁⲙⲙⲉⲱ Ⲙⲟⲟⲩⲥⲏ). Translation: Ioabson of Rhagouel the Midianite the groom (or son in law) of Moses

• Leningrad Codex: Hōbāb ben-Rə'û'ēl hammidyānî hōtēn Mōšeh (חֹבָב בֶּן־רְעוּאֵל הַמִּדְיָנִי֙ חֹתֵ֥ן מֹשֶׁ֖ה). Translation: Hobab son of Reuel the Midianite groom (or son-in-law) of Moses

• Peshitta: Ḥwbb: br Rôwåyl Mdynyå ḥmwhy dMwšå (ܟܒ: ܚܒܒ ܕܡܘܫܐ, ܚܡܘܗܝ ܡܕܝܢܝܐ ܕܪܘܐܝܠ). Translation: Hubb son of Rouayl Midianite father-in-law of Moses

• Targum Onkelos: Hōbāb bar Rə'û'ēl midyānā'â ḥămûhî dəMšeh (חֹבָב בַּר רְעוּאֵל מִדְיָנָאָה חֲמוּהִי דְמֹשֶׁה). Translation: Hobab son of Reuel Midianite father-in-law of Moses

• Targum Pseudo-Jonathan: Hôbāb bar Rə'û'ēl midyānā'â ḥămôy dəMšeh (חוֹבָב בַּר רְעוּאֵל מִדְיָנָאָה חֲמוֹי דְמֹשֶׁה). Translation: Hobab son of Reuel Midianite father-in-law of Moses

• Sahidic manuscript 2006: Neliab tšēre nhRagouēl pMadianitēs pšom eMōusēs (Ⲛⲉⲗⲓⲁⲃ ⲡϣⲏⲣⲉ ⲛⲢⲁⲅⲟⲩⲏⲗ ⲡⲘⲁⲇⲓⲁⲛⲓⲧⲏⲥ ⲡϣⲟⲙ ⲉⲘⲱⲩⲥⲏⲥ). Translation: the Neliab the son Ragouel the Midianite the son of Moses

Jobab was also mentioned in *Judges* Chapter 1, however, the texts don't always agree on who he was. In *Judges*, the Codex Alexandrinus refers to him as Jobab the blacksmith the father-in-law of Moses, while the Codex Vaticanus refers to Jethro the blacksmith son-in-law of Moses, and the Masoretic texts omit the name, simply referring to the blacksmith son-in-law of Moses. It is unclear why there are so many variants of the name and relationship in *Judges*, however, *Numbers* is generally consistent between the Septuagint and Masoretic texts in regards to the relationship, with most text reading "son-in-law" (γαμβρῷ / חֹתֵן) of Moses, and only a few Septuagint manuscripts referring to him as the "father-in-law" (πενθερω), or omitting the nature of the relationship. Conversely, both the Peshitta and Targum Onkelos agree that he was the father-in-law of Moses.

CHAPTER 11

The people murmured sinfully before the Lord, and the Lord heard them and was very angry, and fire erupted among them from the Lord and devoured a part of the camp. The people cried to Moses, and Moses prayed to the Lord, and the fire was quenched. The name of that place was called Burning,[1] as a fire was started among them by the Lord.

The mixed multitude among them lusted a lust, and they and the children of Israel sat down and wept and said, "Who will give us flesh to eat? We remember the fish, which we ate in Egypt freely, and the cucumbers, and the watermelons, and the leeks, and the garlic, and the onions. But now our mind is dried up. Our eyes see nothing but the manna. The manna is like coriander seed, and it looks like hoarfrost."

The people went through the field, and gathered, and ground it in the mill, or pounded it in a mortar, and baked it in a pan, and made cakes of it. The sweetness of it was like the taste of wafer made with oil. When the dew came on the camp by night, the manna came down on it. Moses heard them weeping in their families, everyone in his door, and the Lord was very angry. It was evil in the sight of Moses.

Moses said to the Lord, "Why have you afflicted your servant, and why have I not found grace in your sight, that you should lay the weight of these people on me? Have I conceived all these people, or have I born them? That you say to me, 'Take them into your bosom, as a nurse would take her suckling, into the land which you swore to their fathers?' From where have I flesh to give to all these people? For they cry to me, saying, 'Give us flesh, that we may eat. I will not be able to carry these people alone, for this thing is too heavy for me. If you do this to me, kill me completely if I have found favor with you, that I may not see my affliction."

The Lord replied to Moses, "Gather me 70 men from the elders of Israel, whom you yourself know that they are the elders of the people, and their scribes, and you will bring them to the tabernacle of witness, and they will stand there with you. I will go down and speak there with you, and I will take of the spirit that is in you and will put it on them, and they will carry together with you the impetus of the people, and you will not carry them alone. To the people you will say, Purify yourselves for the morning, and you will eat flesh, for you wept before the Lord, saying, 'Who will give us flesh to eat? As it was better for us in Egypt,' and the Lord will allow you to eat flesh, and you will eat flesh. You will not eat one day, nor two, nor five days, nor 10 days, nor twenty days; you will eat for a full month until the flesh comes out of your nostrils, and it will be cholera to you, because you disobeyed the Lord, who is among you, and wept before him, saying, 'Why did we come out of Egypt?"

Moses asked, "The people among whom I am, are an army of 600,000, and you said, 'I will give them flesh to eat, and they will eat a whole month. Will sheep and oxen be butchered for them, and will it be enough for them? Or will all the fish of the sea be gathered together for them, and will it be enough for them?"

The Lord answered Moses, "Will the hand of the Lord not be enough? Now you will know whether my word will take place or not."

Moses went out and spoke the words of the Lord to the people. He gathered 70 men of the elders of the people, and he set them around the tabernacle. The Lord came down in a cloud, and spoke to him, and took of the spirit that was on him, and put it on the 70 men that were elders, and when the spirit rested on them, they prophesied and then ceased. There were two men left in the camp, one named Elidad, and the other named Medad, and the spirit rested on them, and these were of the number of them that were enrolled, but they did not come to the tabernacle, and they prophesied in the camp.

A young man ran and told Moses, and spoke, saying, Elidad and Medad prophesy in the camp. Joshua the son of Nun, who attended on Moses, the chosen one, said, "My lord Moses, forbid them."

Moses asked him, "Are you jealous on my account? If only all the Lord's people were prophets, whenever the Lord will put his spirit on them."

Moses departed the camp along with the elders of Israel. A wind came out from the Lord, and brought quails in from the sea, and it brought them down on the camp a day's journey on this side, and a day's journey on that side, around the camp, as it were two cubits deep off the ground. The people rose up all day, and all night, and all the next day, and gathered quails. He who gathered little gathered 10 measures, and they refreshed themselves around the camp. The flesh was already between their teeth before it died, and the Lord became angry with the people, and the Lord struck the people with a very great plague. The name of that place was called the Graves of Desire,[2] for there they buried the people that lusted. The people departed from the Graves of Desire to Hazeroth, and the people arrived in Hazeroth.

CHAPTER 11 NOTES

1 Codex Vaticanus: empyrismos (ЄМПҮРІⳤМОⳤ). Translation: concentration

- Septuagint manuscript 799: Emprismos (Εμπρισμος)
- Septuagint manuscript 376: Emprysmos (Εμπρυσμος)
- Leningrad Codex: tab'ērâ (תַּבְעֵרָה). Translation: conflagration, burning, fire
- Peshitta: yqdnå (ܝܩܕܢܐ). Translation: burnt offerings
- Targum Onkelos: dəleqtā' (דְּלֶקְתָּא). Translation: burnings (or inflammations)
- Targum Pseudo-Jonathan: dəlêqəta' (דְּלִיקְתָּא). Translation: burnings (or inflammations)
- Sahidic manuscript 2006: pkōht ettmho (ⲡⲕⲱϩⲧ ⲉⲧⲧⲙϩⲟ). Translation: the firey blaze
- Sahidic manuscript 2043: pkōkh (ⲡⲣⲱⲕϩ). Translation: the burning

2 Codex Vaticanus: mnēmata tēs epitymias (ΜΝΗΜΑΤΑ ΤΗC ΕΠΙΘΥΜΙΑC). Translation: graves of desire

• Septuagint manuscript 509: mnēma tēs epitymias (μνｌͅμα ⲅⲉⲛ ⲟ̄πιθυμΑc). Translation: memorials of desire

• Septuagint manuscript 73: bounon tēs epitymiōn (ⲁⲟⲩⲱ⳨ ⲅⲉⲛ ⲟ̄πιθυμⲓⲟⲛ). Translation: hills (or altars) of desires (or wishes). This version of the verse was also quoted in the Clementine literature, dated to between the 1st and 3rd centuries CE.

• Septuagint manuscript 313: mnēmatos tēs epitymias (μνｌͅμαⲅⲟⲥ ⲅⲉⲛ ⲟ̄πιθυμΑc). Translation: memorials of desire.

• Leningrad Codex: qibrôt hatta'ăwâ (קִבְרוֹת הַתַּאֲוָה). Translation: Graves of Lust

• Dead Sea Scroll 4QNumb: qb- (קב-). Only the first two letters survive, however, they do match the letters in the Leningrad Codex.

• Peshitta: qbrå drgtå (ܩܒܪܐ ܕܪܓܬܐ). Translation: tombs (or sepulchers) of permanence

• Targum Onkelos: qibrê dimša'ălê (קִבְרֵי דִמְשַׁאֲלֵי). Translation: tombs (or sepulchers) of the lenders (or borrowers, demanders)

• Targum Pseudo-Jonathan: qibrê dimšayylê bîšərā' (קִבְרֵי דִמְשַׁיְּילֵי בִּישְׂרָא). Translation: tombs (or sepulchers) of the lenders (or borrowers, demanders) of human-flesh (or human-skin)

• Sahidic manuscript 2006: nemhaau ntepitumia (ⲚⲈⲘϨⲀⲀⲨ ⲚⲦⲈⲠⲒⲐⲨⲘⲒⲀ). Translation: the caverns (or tombs) of the desires

• Sahidic manuscript 2169: nemhaou ntepitumeia (ⲚⲈⲘϨⲀⲞⲨ ⲚⲦⲈⲠⲒⲐⲨⲘⲈⲒⲀ)

CHAPTER 12

Mariam and Aaron spoke against Moses, because of the Ethiopian woman that Moses took, as he had taken an Ethiopian woman. They said, "Has the Lord only spoken to Moses? Has he not also spoken to us?"

And the Lord heard it. The man Moses was very meek beyond all the men that were on the land. The Lord immediately called Moses and Aaron and Mariam, "Come up the three of you to the tabernacle of witness."

The three came up to the tabernacle of witness, and the Lord descended in a column of cloud and stood at the door of the tabernacle of witness. Aaron and Mariam were called, and both came forward. He said to them, "Hear my words. If there should be among you a prophet to the Lord, I will be made known to him in a vision, and in sleep will I speak to him. My servant Moses is not so. He is faithful in all my house. I will speak to him face to face openly, and not in dark speeches. He has seen the glory of the Lord. Why were you not afraid to speak against my servant Moses?"

The great anger of the Lord was on them, and he departed, and the cloud departed from the tabernacle. Mariam became leprous as snow, and Aaron looked at Mariam and saw she was leprous. Aaron said to Moses, "I beg you, my lord, do not lay sin on us, for we were ignorant in which we sinned. Let her not be as it were like death, as an abortion coming out of his mother's womb when the disease devours half of the flesh."

Moses cried to the Lord, "El,[1] I beg you, heal her."

The Lord said to Moses, "If her father had only spit in her face, will she not be ashamed seven days? Let her be set apart seven days outside the camp, and afterward, she may come in."

Mariam was separated outside the camp for seven days, and the people did not move forward until Mariam was cleansed.

CHAPTER 12 NOTES

1 Codex Vaticanus: T̄S̄ (ⲑⲥ). Translation: god

• Septuagint manuscript 319: tee (θεε). Translation: god

• Septuagint manuscript 121: teos mou (θεοc μου). Translation: my god

• Leningrad Codex: 'ēl (אֵל). Translation: El (or god)

• Peshitta: ålhå (ܐܠܗܐ). Translation: god

• Targum Onkelos: 'ĕlāhā' (אֱלָהָא). Translation: god

• Targum Jerusalem: 'ĕlāhā' (אֱלָהָא). Translation: god

• Targum Pseudo-Jonathan: 'ĕlāhā' (אֱלָהָא). Translation: god

• Sahidic manuscript 2006: noute (ⲛⲟⲩⲧⲉ). Translation: god

This verse shows the Greeks did translate the term El as "God." As El is a proper name, it is restored from the Leningrad Codex in this translation.

CHAPTER 13

Afterward, the people set out from Hazeroth, and camped in the Wilderness of Paran.[1] The Lord said to Moses, "Send for your men and let them spy the land of the Canaanites, which I give to the sons of Israel as a possession, one man for a tribe, you will send them away according to their families, every one of them a prince."

Moses sent them out of the Wilderness of Paran by the word of the Lord, all these were the princes of the sons of Israel. These are their names:

From the tribe of Reuben, Samuel the son of Zakkur.

From the tribe of Simeon, Shaphat the son of Hori.

From the tribe of Judah, Caleb the son of Jephunneh.

From the tribe of Issachar, Igal the son of Joseph.

From the tribe of Ephraim, Hoshea the son of Nun.

From the tribe of Benjamin, Palti the son of Raphu.

From the tribe of Zebulun, Geuel the son of Sodi.

From the tribe of Joseph of the sons of Manasseh, Gaddi the son of Susi.

From the tribe of Dan, Ammiel the son of Gemalli.

From the tribe of Asher, Sethur the son of Michael.

From the tribe of Naphtali, Nahbi the son of Sabi.

From the tribe of Gad, Geuel the son of Maki.

These are the names of the men that Moses sent to spy out the land. Moses called Hoshea the son of Nun, Joshua. Moses sent them to spy out the land of Canaan, and said to them, "Go up by this wilderness, and you will go up to the mountain, and you will see the land, what it is, and the people that live in it, whether it is strong or weak, or whether they are few or many. What the land is on which they live, whether it is good or bad, and what the cities are in which these live, whether they live in fortified cities or unfortified. What the land is, whether rich or neglected, whether there are trees in it or not, and you will persevere and take of the fruits of the land."

It was springtime, before the time of the grape. They went up and surveyed the land from the Wilderness of Sin[2] to Rehob, as men go into Ephaath.[3] They went up by the wilderness and departed as far as Hebron, and there were Ahiman, Sheshai, Talmai; the descendants of Anak.[4] Hebron was built seven years before Avaris[5] in Egypt. They came to the valley of the cluster and surveyed it, and they cut down there a bough and one cluster of grapes on it and carried it on staffs, and they took of the pomegranates and the figs. They called that place, The valley of the cluster, because of the cluster which the children of Israel cut down from there.

They returned from there, having surveyed the land, after forty days. They proceeded and came to Moses and Aaron and all the community of the children of Israel, to the Wilderness of Paran Kadesh. They brought word to them and to all the community, and they showed the fruit of the land. They reported to him, "We came into the land into which you sent us, a land flowing with milk and honey, and this is the fruit of it. Only the nation that dwells on it is bold, and they have very great and fortified towns, and we saw there Anakites.[6] Amalekites[7] live in the southern region of the land, and the Cypriots,[8] Mitannians,[9] Jebusites, and the Amorites live in the hill country. The Canaanites live by the sea, and by the Jordan River."

Caleb stopped the people from speaking to Moses, and said to him, "No, but we will go up by all means, and will inherit it, for we will surely prevail against them."

But the men that went up together with him said, "We do not go up, for we will not by any means be able to go up against the nation, for it is much stronger than we."

They brought a horror of that land which they surveyed on the children of Israel, saying, "The land which we passed by to survey it, is a land that eats up its inhabitants, and all the people whom we saw in it are men of extraordinary stature. There we saw the Gigantes (sons of Anak, from the Nepilim),[10] and we were like locusts before them. This is how we compared to them."

CHAPTER 13 NOTES

1 Codex Vaticanus: Faran (ⲫⲀⲢⲀⲚ)

- Septuagint manuscript 630: Fara (Φαρὰ)
- Leningrad Codex: Pā'rān (פָּארָן)
- Peshitta: Prn (ڢܪܢ)
- Targum Onkelos: Pā'rān (פָּארָן)
- Targum Jerusalem: Pā'rān (פָּארָן)
- Targum Pseudo-Jonathan: Pā'rān (פָּארָן)
- Sahidic manuscript 2169: Farran (ⲫⲀⲢⲢⲀⲚ)

The Wilderness of Paran was mentioned in *Cosmic Genesis*, *Numbers*, *Deuteronomy*, *3rd Kingdoms* (Masoretic *Kings*), and Masoretic *Habakkuk*, however, the location of Paran is debated. The book of *Numbers* states that Paran was Kadesh, and the book of *Deuteronomy* locates it in the Arabah Desert of southern modern Jordan and Israel. In the 2nd century CE, the Christian geographer Claudius Ptolemy located it in the southern Sinai Peninsula, at the region now called the Wadi Feiran, while Islamic scholars have interpreted it as the Hijaz region of western Saudi Arabia, around Mecca.

2 Codex Vaticanus: Sein (ⲤⲈⲒⲚ)

- Codex Venetus: Sina (Σινὰ)
- Septuagint manuscript 30: Sēna (Σηνὰ)
- Septuagint manuscript 56: Sēn (Σην)
- Septuagint manuscript 528: Sin (Σιν)
- Septuagint manuscript 59: Siēr (Σιηβ)
- Leningrad Codex: Sin (סִן)
- Dead Sea Scroll 4QNum[b]: Ṣyn (צין)

CHAPTER 13

- Peshitta: Syn (ܣܝܢ)
- Targum Onkelos: Sîn (צִין)
- Targum Pseudo-Jonathan: Sîn (צִין)
- Sahidic manuscript 2006: Sin (ⲤⲒⲚ)
- Sahidic manuscript 2045: Sein (ⲤⲈⲒⲚ)

See the note in chapter 1 for more information on the Wilderness of Sin.

3 Codex Vaticanus: Efaaṯ (ⲉⲫⲁⲁⲑ)

- Codex Colberto-Sarravianus: Eglaaam (ⲉⲅⲗⲁⲁⲁⲙ)
- Codex Alexandrinus: Aimaṯ (ⲁⲓⲙⲁⲑ)
- Septuagint manuscript 28: Aiṯam (ⲁⲓⲑⲁⲙ)
- Septuagint manuscript 318: Ēmaṯ (Ⲉμαθ)
- Septuagint manuscript 319: Samaṯ (Ⲥλμαθ)
- Septuagint manuscript 129: Emae (Ⲉμαϛ)
- Septuagint manuscript 75: Emmaōṯ (Ⲉμμαωθ)
- Septuagint manuscript 246: Nifaṯ (Ⲛιϧλθ)
- Septuagint manuscript 799: Enfaṯ (Ⲉⲛϧλθ)
- Septuagint manuscript 56: Nefaṯ (Ⲛϭϧλθ)
- Leningrad Codex: ḥămāt (חֲמָת). Translation: fortress (or Hama)
- Peshitta: ḥmt (ܚܡܬ). Translation: fortress (or Hama)
- Targum Onkelos: ḥămāt (חֲמָת). Translation: fortress (or Hama)
- Targum Pseudo-Jonathan: 'Antûkəyā'ya (אַנְטוּכְיָא). Translation: Antioch
- Sahidic manuscript 2006: Emaaṯ (Ⲉⲙⲁⲁⲑ)
- Sahidic manuscript 2045: Efaaṯ (Ⲉⲫⲁⲁⲑ)

The Greek and Hebrew translations differ here, with most Greek translations referring to a place generally called Ephaath, although there are many variants of the name in Greek. The Hebrew translation refers to either to a fortress, or the city of Hama in northern Syria. The Syrian city of Hama was known to the ancient Arameans and Canaanites as Ḥmt (חמת / חלף / +𐤂𐤉), derived from the word "fortress," and has existed since before 5000 BCE. Under the Seleucid Dynasty, the city was renamed Epifaneia (Επιφανεια), which the Translators at the Library of Alexandria would have known how to spell, as it was the Greek word meaning 'manifestation.' Some Greek and Coptic manuscripts due use Greek transliterations of ḥmt (חמת). including the 5th century Codex Alexandrinus, however, the Alexandrinus is known to have included names transliterated from the Hebrew translations then in circulation.

The Greek term Efaaṯ (Εφααθ) is less clear, however, similar to the name Efraṯa / 'Eprātâ (Εφραθα / אֶפְרָתָה) in *Cosmic Genesis / Bereshít*, which was identified as the old name of Bethlehem. The term in *Cosmic Genesis / Bereshít* appears to be corrupted Canaanite transliteration of the Egyptian name r-pr-t (𓏏 𓉐 𓏏 𓉔), which translates as "temple of bread," one meaning of the Canaanite name bêt leḥem (𐤌𐤄𐤋 +𐤕𐤉𐤁). If Efaaṯ (Εφααθ) is a transliteration of the same name from an old Aramaic translation of Numbers, it would then be a reference to Bethlehem, not Hama. As the Greek and Hebrew texts appear to be referring to different places, the Greek name is used in this translation.

The name Antioch, found in the Targum Jonathan, referred to the city of Antakya in southernmost modern Turkey, which was founded by Seleucus I Nicator, one of Alexander the Great's generals in approximately 300 BCE. It is unclear why anyone would have thought that Antioch was the city in the verse, however, it was built it was near Mount Zephon. Prior to the Greek city, a Canaanite town was located on the site, named Meroe, where a major shrine to the virgin goddess Anat was located. This suggests the substitution was theological, not political, as Anat was the wife of Yahweh in the early-Persian era.

4 Codex Vaticanus: Enak̆ (ⲈⲚⲀⲭ)
- Codex Alexandrinus: Enak (ⲈⲚⲀⲕ)
- Septuagint manuscript 15: Ainak (ⲀⲓⲚⲀⲕ)
- Septuagint manuscript 75: Nak (ⲚⲀⲕ)
- Septuagint manuscript 126: Anak (ⲀⲚⲀⲕ)
- Septuagint manuscript 767: Ainak̆ (ⲀⲓⲚⲀⲭ)
- Leningrad Codex: 'Ănāq (עֲנָק). Translation: giant, huge, large, big, neck, necklace
- Peshitta: ånq (ܐܢܩ)
- Targum Onkelos: gibbārayyā' (גִּבָּרַיָּא). Translation: mighty ones
- Targum Pseudo-Jonathan: gibbārā' (גִּבָּרָא). Translation: heroes (or strong men, giants)
- Vetus Latina manuscripts: Senac (ЅⲈⲚⲀⲤ)
- Sahidic manuscript 2006: Enak̆ (ⲈⲚⲀⲭ)
- Armenian manuscripts: Enak (Ենակ)

The Anakites were a tribe of people also referred to in the books of *Deuteronomy, Joshua*, and *Judges.* According to the Book of Judges, they lived in Hebron. Egyptian execration texts from the Middle Kingdom Era, record a group of Canaanites in the region called the Ånq (𓊃𓂝𓈎) who are generally considered to be the same people. This term was also adopted by the Mycenaean Greeks as wakana (𐀷𐀙𐀏), meaning "lord." In the Iron Age, this evolved into the Dorian Greek wanax (ϝαναξ), meaning "king," and later into the Koine Greek anax (αναξ), meaning "lord." The Greek digamma (ϝ) was used in the early Iron Age for words adopted from Semitic languages to represent the W (ו / 𐤅) vowel, but later dropped from Greek in favor of the ō (ω) or o (o), which were natural vowels in

Greek. The Semitic word was also adopted into Cypriot as wanakse (ᚲᛏ𐤗) and Old Phrygian as vanaktei (φανακτει), both meaning "lord."

Anax (Αναξ) was also the name of the legendary king of Anaktoria (Ανακτορια), a Bronze Age kingdom in southeast Anatolia. While the archaeological evidence of the civilization exists, the only surviving records are via Greek interpretations of Minoan stories of the culture. Wanax was likely the title of the leader, and not his name, and Anakt oria (Ανακτ ορια) simply translates as "Anax's boundaries."

The land of Anaktoria was later conquered by the legendary Minoan warrior Miletus, who renamed the city of Anaktoria to Miletus (Μίλητος). This may simply be a Greek legend about the Minoanization of the region in the Middle Bronze Age, as there was also a plant in the region called Miletus. In the late Bronze Age, the region was known as Mirati (𝑉Ⴑ𐌍) in Greek, and Millawanda (𒈪𒆗𒇲𒉿𒀭𒁕) in Neshite. The archaeological evidence supports the culture going through a rapid Minoanization starting around 1900 BCE, so the legend of a Minoan conquering the region may be accurate. The older "Wanaxian" culture appears in the archaeological record only a century earlier, around 2000 BCE, and appears to have been an Amorite colony.

The original meaning of Enak̆ (Εναχ) / 'Ănāq (עֲנָק) was likely the Amorite ānak (𒉌𒀖𒁹), meaning "tin," or ānakum (𒀖𒌷𒁹𒈬), meaning "metalworkers." The Amorite civilization's economic strength was built on mining during their war against the Neo-Sumerian Empire. Israelite texts often use the term 'ănāk (אֲנָק) and qênî (קֵינִי) interchangeably, suggesting that qyny (𐤒𐤉𐤍𐤉) was the early Iron Age translation of ānakum (𒀖𒌷𒁹𒈬), while ānak (𒉌𒀖𒁹) was transliterated directly as ånq (𐤏𐤍𐤒).

CHAPTER 13

Based on the following implied reference to Hebron being established seven years before Avaris, this would place the establishment of Hebron around the beginning of the 2nd millennium BCE. The name Ḥebrôn (חֶבְרוֹן) is based on the Amorite word meaning "friendship," or "alliance." This suggests the town was founded in the border region of the Egyptian Empire and the Amorites, after the Amorites and Elamites defeated the Neo-Sumerians circa 2004 BCE. Hebron was in the northern region of the "copper belt" in southern Canaan and Sinai during the era, which spanned the region from Moab to the Sinai.

5 Codex Vaticanus: Tanin (ΤΑΝΙΝ). Translation: Tanis
- Septuagint manuscript 318: Taēan (ΤΑμαν)
- Septuagint manuscript 319: Tanin (Ταινιν)
- Septuagint manuscript 509: Tani (Ταινι)
- Septuagint manuscript 64: Tanis (Ταινιc)
- Septuagint manuscript 55: Taēin (Ταλιν)
- Septuagint manuscript 128: Taneōs (Ταινοοc)
- Septuagint manuscript 313: Tanēn (Ταινω)
- Septuagint manuscript 381: Tēs (Τλc)
- Septuagint manuscript 458: Tanyn (Ταινω)
- Leningrad Codex: Ṣō'an (צֹעַן). Translation: Tanis
- Peshitta: Ṣōn (ܨܥܢ). Translation: Tanis
- Targum Onkelos: Tānas (טָנֵס)
- Targum Jerusalem: Tā'nês (טָאנֵיס)
- Sahidic manuscript 2006: Jaane (ϪΑΑΝΕ)
- Bohairic manuscripts: Jani (Ϫανι)

Tanis and Ṣō'an were the Greek and Hebrew names for an ancient city in northeast Egypt. This sentence is either an odd scribal note about Tanis that was added later, or a name that was updated in the early Iron Age. Hebron is much older than Tanis, and Tanis was not significant in any way until the 19th dynasty (circa 1290 to 1190 BCE) when it became the capital of the 14th nome (province). During the 21st and 22nd Dynasties, circa 1070 to 720 BCE Tanis became the capital of Egypt, which is likely when this line was added. The 22nd dynasty Pharaoh Shoshenq I invaded Judah during the reign of King Rehoboam, circa 935 BCE, while the later 22nd dynasty Pharaoh Osorkon II was an ally of Samaria during their war against Assyria circa 725 BCE.

The 22nd dynasty disintegrated into multiple competing dynasties after the Assyrians defeated the allied Samaritan-Egyptian forces, and Tanis was no longer a capital city, meaning this line could have been added at any point in ancient Israelite-Samaritan history up until circa 725 BCE. Conversely, Hebron existed by 1800 BCE, and according to the Book of Joshua, Joshua conquered Hebron circa 1540 BCE in the Septuagint's chronology.

The city of Tanis was built on part of the ruins of Pi-Ramesses, near the Iron Age city of Ramesses. Pi-Ramesses had been founded by Ramesses II in the 1200s BCE, at the docks of old Avaris, the former Hyksos capital. Avaris had been founded by 12th dynasty king Amenemhat I in the 2000s BCE, suggesting the original name in the verse was Avaris. This would indicate the original text of this chapter likely dates to much after the city of Avaris was destroyed in approximately 1572 BCE, based on the carbon dating of King Ahmose I's mummy.

6 Codex Vaticanus: Enak̆ (ⲉⲚⲁⲭ)

• Codex Colberto-Sarravianus: Enek (ⲉⲚⲉⲕ)

• Codex Alexandrinus: Ainak (ⲀⲓⲚⲁⲕ)

• Septuagint manuscript 767: Einak (ⲈⲓⲚⲁⲕ)

• Septuagint manuscript 16: Enaak (ⲈⲚⲁⲁⲕ)

- Leningrad Codex: 'Ănāq (עֲנָק). Translation: giant, huge, large, big, neck, necklace
- Peshitta: gnbrå (ܓܢܒܪܐ). Translation: heroes (or strong men, giants). Translation: heroes (or strong men, giants)
- Targum Onkelos: gibbārayyā' (גִּבָּרַיָּא). Translation: heroes (or strong men, giants). Translation: heroes (or strong men, giants)
- Targum Pseudo-Jonathan: gibbārā' (גִּבָּרָא). Translation: heroes (or strong men, giants). Translation: heroes (or strong men, giants)
- Sahidic manuscript 2006: Enak̆ (Ɛnax)

See the previous note on the "Anak" for more information. This reference to Anak is in a list with Amalek, indicating that they were viewed as separate groups, even though they appear to both be general references to groups living under the rule of the Hyksos dynasty. Åmw (𓄿𓄿𓅓𓏤) was the Egyptian name of the Amorites, whose kings were known as hqâ-ǩåst (𓃀𓄿𓄿𓈎𓏏) during the Egyptian Middle Kingdom. Hqâ-ǩåst was an Egyptian title meaning "foreign kings," which gave rise to the Egyptological term Hyksos. While this isn't clear evidence that the Amorites were the original Hyksos rulers, it certainly suggests they were. However, the Hyksos dynasty appears to have originally been republican, electing a new "king" every 3 years. They eventually became Egyptianized and developed a royal family that ended when the Theban dynasty recaptured the Nile Delta and Canaan.

7 Codex Alexandrinus: Amalēk (ΑΜΑΛΗΚ)
- Septuagint manuscript 108: Amalik (Αμαλικ)
- Leningrad Codex: 'Ămālēq (עֲמָלֵק)
- Targum Onkelos: 'Ămālēq (עֲמָלֵק)
- Targum Pseudo-Jonathan: 'Ămālēq (עֲמָלֵק)
- Vetus Latina manuscripts: Amalech (Amalech)

• Sahidic manuscript 2006: Amalēk (ⲀⲘⲀⲖⲎⲔ)

In the Israelite books, the Amalek are periodically present in Canaan and the Sinai peninsula from the time of Abraham until the time of King David; however, there is no archeological evidence of a tribe called "Amalek." The name is a transliteration of the Egyptian term åmw-rqî (𓄿𓄿𓆑𓏤 𓂋𓈖), which can be translated as "hostile Asiatics," "opposing Amorites," or "defiant fires." The presence of the term supports this section of text having once been translated into Egyptian. The same word was pronounced as åmw-lqî in the Fayyumic dialect. The Fayyumic dialect was spoken in the Faiyum Oasis, as well as the region of the Nile where the canal that carried water into the Faiyum Oasis connected to the Nile. In this region was the Egyptian city of Nn-nswt (𓎛𓎛 𓊃𓏏𓈉), from which the dialect was likely derived. The name is commonly anglicized as Henen-Nesut, and was one of the capitals of Egypt during the First Intermediate Period, specifically during the 9th and 10th dynasties.

The dialect is believed to have become dominant in the Faiyum Oasis during the 12th dynasty, when the Faiyum basin was flooded with Nile flood water diverted via a canal, turning the oasis into a lake the size of Lake Superior in North America. During this era, the Faiyum was colonized by Egyptians and refugees from the rebellion in Amorite-controlled Syria and Canaan. This suggests the inversion of the L and R sounds in this name was absorbed into written Canaanite during this era.

An Egyptian named Ahmose pen-Nekhbet reported fighting at Avaris and Sharuhen in the autobiography carved into his tomb. He also noted that the Egyptians fought the šåsw (𓈙𓄿𓋴𓅱), meaning "nomads," in the Sinai peninsula during these campaigns. These nomads do not appear to have been the Israelites, who, according to the Israelite texts, would have been deep in the wilderness east of Edom by that point. However, the Book of Numbers also places the "Amalek" north of the Negev, indicating these were the Amorite remnants of the Hyksos regime. In the time of Abraham, the Amorites began a rebellion against King Shulgi's Neo-Sumerian Empire, and therefore the term is translated literally.

8 Codex Vaticanus: Ǩettaios (ⲭⲉⲧⲧⲁⲓⲟⲥ)

- Septuagint manuscript 120: Ǩegaios (ⲭⲟⲅⲁⲓⲟⲥ)
- Septuagint manuscript 458: Aǩettaios (ⲁⲭⲟⲧⲁⲓⲟⲥ)
- Septuagint manuscript 618: Ǩetaios (ⲭⲟⲧⲁⲓⲟⲥ)
- Leningrad Codex: Hittî (חִתִּי). Translation: Cypriots
- Peshitta: Hytyå (ܚܝܬܐ). Translation: living (or animals, beasts, pure, vitals)
- Targum Onkelos: Hittā'â (חִתָּאָה)
- Targum Pseudo-Jonathan: Hittā'ê (חִתָּאֵי)
- Sahidic manuscript 2006: Ǩeddaios (ⲭⲉⲗⲗⲁⲓⲟⲥ)

This term has created a great deal of confusion since the misidentification of the ruins of the Neshites as being "Hittite" in the 1800s. The modern archaeological name "Hittite," is not derived from an ancient name for the culture applied by themselves, or anyone else, but rather adopted from the biblical reference to a then-unknown civilization somewhere in the region. There was an ancient culture in the region called the Hattians, however, they were conquered by the Nesites before 1700 BCE, and subsequently disappeared from the historic records.

The name was applied to a culture today referred to as "Hittites," before the "Hittite" language had been translated, and is incorrect. Since 1906, excavations at Boğazköy, the ancient "Hittite" capital Hattusa have uncovered more than 10,000 "Hittite" texts, including the royal achieve. The actual name of the "Hittite" language and people was Nešili (𒉌𒅆𒇷), which is now rendered in some academic literate as Nesite or Neshite. As early as the mid-1800s some scholars disputed the identification of the Nesites as the Biblical Hittites, including the Orientalist Max Müller, who was one of many claiming the Biblical Hittites were ancient Greeks or some other Mediterranean people. Later in the Septuagint's translation of the Maccabees, the similar term Ḱettiim (Χεττιιμ) as a reference to all Greek-speaking lands.

In the 1st century CE, the Jewish historian Josephus reported that Keṭima (Κεθιμα) was the name of "Cyrus" in Aramaic, and the Ḱettim (Χεττιμ) were the descendants of Noah's grandson Ḱeṭimus (Χεθιμυσ), who had settled on Cyprus. Josephus reported that the name was preserved in the Greek name of the town Kition (Κίτιον). Most historians view it as more likely that the Aramaic name was derived from the city-state of Kition, which was known as Kåtjåy (𒄥 𒁹𒋼𒈝) in Egyptian records from the New Kingdom Era in the late Bronze Age, and Kt (𐤊𐤕) or Kty (𐤊𐤕𐤉) in Phoenician records from the early Iron Age. While this may be the origin of the term, by the era of the Neo-Assyrian era, the term must have also referred to other Greek islands, as both the prophets Isaiah and Ezekiel used the term "Islands of Kittim." As the term referred to the entire island of Cyprus in Aramaic, the translation of "Cypriots" is used.

9 Codex Vaticanus: Euaios (ЄΥΑΙΟϹ)

- Septuagint manuscript 30: Ebaios (Єυαγοϲ)
- Vetus Latina: Eucheus (Єucheuѕ)
- Bohairic manuscripts: Euaios (ЄΤΑΙΟϹ)
- Sahidic manuscript 2006: Euhaios (ЄΥϨΑΙΟϹ)

The word is missing from this list of nations in the Leningrad Codex, Peshitta, and Targums. In other verses, it is hā'Awwîm (הָעַוִּים) in the Leningrad Codex. The term is believed to have been derived from a name of the Hurrians, however, is derived

114

separately from the other term Ḥōrî (חֹרִי). Ḥōrî is accepted as referring to the Hurrians, whom the Egyptians called Ǩårw (𓈏𓏤𓅱𓏭), and the Babylonians called Ǩuurri (𒄷𒌨𒊑). The Hurrians were one of the oldest cultures in the Middle East, however, became largely a slave culture within the Akkadian and Old Babylonian empires. Under the Mitanni empire, they rose to a position of wealth, and formed the noble caste. The Greek transliteration of this term was variations of Ǩorr̩aious (Χορραιους), which, like the Hebrew term, was used interchangeably in the texts with Euaion (Ευαιον) / Ḥiwwî (חִוִּי), although that term generally applied to the rules and priests.

The ultimate origin of the terms Euaion (Ευαιον) / Euaios (Ευαιος) and hā'Awwîm (הָעַוִּים) / Ḥiwwî (חִוִּי), both appear to be the cuneiform word Éan (𒂍𒀭), meaning temple or sacred. In the Amarna Letters, which date to the 1330s BCE, the term Éan (𒂍𒀭) was the name of a people, who appear to be the Mitanni, or the Mitanni-Aryan priesthood within the Mitanni. A similar correlation between the terms is found in the Septuagint's *1ˢᵗ Paralipomenon* and Masoretic *Dibrê-hayyāmîm*, where the Greek translation uses Baiṭani (Βαιθανι), however, the Hebrew uses the term Mitnî (מִתְנִי). This term also refers to a group of people, meaning the underlying Edomite text the Greeks translated would have been 'people of the House of Ån' (𐤏𐤍‎+𐤕𐤁), a direct Canaanite translation of É An (𒂍𒀭).

While Mitni was the transliteration used in the Edomite text that formed the basis of the Hebrew translation of *Dibrê-hayyāmîm*, it was replaced with Ḥiwwî (חִוִּי) in the Judahite texts, which served as the basis of most of the Masoretic texts. This likely originated in a Judahite copy of the text, after the Aramaic translation had been made, where an N (𐤍) was replaced with a W (𐤅). The Aramaic translation would have already been made in the time of King

Manasseh, were the term was transliterated as Hyån (ח־ן^א׳), itself a transliteration of the early Canaanite Hyån (𐤄𐤉𐤀𐤍).

The term Ebaiôn (Εβαιων) / Ebaios (Εβαιος), which is found as a substitute for Euaion (Ευαιον) / Euaios (Ευαιος) in some copies of the Septuagint for term, must have originated in an intentional alteration to the text, as there are no similar letters for B (ב ,ך ,פ) and Y (י ,^ ,ז) in the Semitic alphabets the text was previously in. This probable origin was an Ebionite translation in the 1st century CE. The Ebionites were an early Judeo-Christian sect based in Judea before the First Jewish-Roman war. Many fled east to Mesopotamia with the Mandeans and other smaller Judahite religious groups, while others fled south into Arabia. The Arabian Ebionites are generally viewed as shaping the Islamic view of the prophet Jesus (عِيسَى).

10 Codex Vaticanus: gigantas (ΓΙΓΑΝΤΑΣ). Translation: Gigantes

• Codex Colberto-Sarravianus: gigantas uious enak ek tōn gigantōn (ΓΙΓΑΝΤΑΣ ΥΙΟΥΣ ΕΝΑΚ ΕΚ ΤΩΝ ΓΙΓΑΝΤΩΝ). Translation: Gigantes sons of Enak of the Gigantes

• Septuagint manuscript 128: gigantas uious gigantōn (ΓΙΓΑΝΤΑΣ ΥΙΟΥΣ ΓΙΓΑΝΤΩΝ). Translation: Gigantes son of Gigantes

• Septuagint manuscript 18: gigantas uious Ainak ek tōn gigantōn (γιγαντας ψους Αιναλ ελ τῶ γιγαντῶ). Translation: Gigantes son of Ainac of the Gigantes

• Leningrad Codex: nəpîlîm bənê 'ănāq min-hannəpilîm (נְפִילִים בְּנֵי עֲנָק מִן־הַנְּפִלִים). Translation: nepilim sons of Anaq from the nepilim

• Peshitta: gnbrå: bny gnbrå: dmn gnbrå (ܓܢܒܪ̈ܐ: ܒܢܝ ܓܢܒܪ̈ܐ: ܕܡܢ ܓܢܒܪ̈ܐ). Translation: heroes (or strong men, giants) sons of heroes (or strong men, giants). blood of heroes (or strong men, giants)

- Targum Onkelos: gibbārayyā' bənê 'ănāq min gibbārayyā' (גִּבָּרַיָּא
בְּנֵי עֲנָק מִן גִּבָּרַיָּא). Translation: heroes (or strong men, giants) sons of
Anaq of heroes (or strong men, giants)

- Targum Jerusalem: gabrayā' bənê 'ănāq mignîsat gûbərayā'
(גִּבְרַיָּא בְּנֵי עֲנָק מִגְנִיסַת גּוּבְרַיָּא). Translation: heroes (or strong men,
giants) sons of Anaq of the family (or decedents) of Guberaya (or
Orion)

- Vetus Latina manuscripts: gigantum (ϹΙϹΑΝΤϢϺ). Translation:
giants

- Sahidic manuscript 2006: gigas (ⲅⲓⲅⲁⲥ). Translation: giants

The Aramaic translators appear to have simplified the text, as the
Greeks would have transliterated the names. The term Gigantes
(γιγαντας) was used as a translation in the Septuagint for the both of
the words that were transliterated as Anaq and Nepilim in the
Leningrad Codex, suggesting the Aramaic translation generally
used the same term for both. While most Christian translations of
both the Septuagint and the Leningrad Codex translate this word as
"giant," neither the Greek nor Hebrew terms mean "giant."

The 'Ănāq (עֲנָק) mentioned in the Leningrad Codex, were also
recorded in the Middle Kingdom era Execration Texts, as the Ảnq
(𓃛𓂝𓈖), a people that lived in the region around Mount Hermon.

The Hebrew term nəpilîm (נְפִלִים) is accepted as meaning "fallen,"
and, the term is likely related to the Aramaic name for the Orion
constellation Npylyå (𐡍𐡐𐡉𐡋𐡉𐡀). The term nəpilîm (נְפִלִים) likely
originated as a description of the Orionid meteor shower that
happens each year, between October 2 and November 7, as the
Earth passes through the debris left by Halley's Comet. Peaks of 70
meteors a minute have been recorded, and these meteors fall from
the region of the sky where Orion's upstretched arm is located.

The region of the sky where the constellations Orion and Lepus
are located was known as the asterism Sâh (𓊃𓄿𓎛𓇳) in the religion

of the Egyptian Old Kingdom, which represented Såḫ, the father of the gods. The Sumerian version of Såḫ was Ān (𒀭), who was also the father of the gods. The name Greek name Ōriōn (Ωριων) is derived from the Amorite name Uru-Ān (𒌷𒀭𒈾), meaning "Light of An," as the early Greeks learned of the asterism from the Canaanites that had settled in Cyprus.

As the Greeks neither translated nor transliterated the term Nepilim, it is unlikely it was in the Aramaic text they translated, suggesting whatever term they found in the text was either conceptually or phonetically similar to the Greek Gigas (Γίγας). A more detailed version of this story appears in the Books of Enoch, where the term was translated into Ge'ez as 'äyärän (ዐየረየን) meaning "watchers" or "guardians." A similar term, egirō (ἐγείρω) meaning "awaken," appears to have been used in the Greek translation of Secrets of Enoch, which was later transliterated into Old Slavonic as Grigori (ⰃⰓⰉⰃⰑⰓⰉ). This indicates the original term was likely something that meant "watcher" and sounded like Gigas, and given the connections to Mount Hermon, the Orion constellation, and thereby the god An, and his children the ^{an}Ānuna (𒀭𒀀𒉣𒈾), the original term in the Cuneiform text was almost certainly Igigi (𒅆𒄀𒄀).

The Igigi were described as being a group of lesser gods that rebelled against the rule of the ^{an}Ānuna, which translates as "sons of the ^{deity}Ān/sky," and their name was the homophone of the Akkadian word igigi (𒅆𒄀) meaning to "observe and measure."

As the original Edomite text probably included the terms found in the Leningrad Codex, the longer text is imported and placed in parentheses.

CHAPTER 14

All the community lifted their voice and cried, and the people wept all that night. All the children of Israel murmured against Moses and Aaron, and all the community said to them, "We should have died in the land of Egypt! Or in this wilderness, we should have died! Why does the Lord bring us into this land to die in war? Our wives and our children will be victims. Now then it is better to return to Egypt."

They said one to another, "Let us choose a ruler, and return to Egypt."

Moses and Aaron fell on their face before all the community of the children of Israel. But Joshua the son of Nun, and Caleb the son of Jephunneh, of those who had spied out the land, tore their garments, and spoke to all the community of the children of Israel, saying, "The land which we surveyed is actually extremely good. If the Lord chooses us, he will bring us into this land, and give it to us. A land that flows with milk and honey! Only don't abandon the Lord, and don't fear the people of the land, for they are meat for us! For the season of prosperity has departed from them, but the Lord is among us. Don't fear them!"

All the community shouted, "Stone them with stones," and the glory of the Lord appeared in the cloud on the tabernacle of witness to all the children of Israel.

The Lord asked Moses, "How long will these people provoke me? How long will they don't believe me for all the signs which I have worked among them? I will strike them dow dead and destroy them, and I will make of you and your father's house a great nation, and much greater than this."

Moses replied to the Lord, "Then Egypt will hear, that you have brought up these people from them by your might. Moreover, all the residents in this land have heard that you are the Lord of these people, who, the Lord, have been seen by them face to face, and your cloud rests among them, and you go before them by day in a pillar of a cloud, and by night in a pillar of fire. If you will destroy this nation as one man, then all the nations that have heard your name will speak, saying, 'Because the Lord could not bring these people into the land which he swore to them, he has destroyed them in the wilderness.' Now, the Lord, let your strength be exalted, as you said. The Lord is restraint and merciful, and true, removing transgressions and iniquities and sins, and he will by no means clear the guilty, visiting the sins of the fathers on the children to the third and fourth generation. Forgive these people their sin according to your great mercy, as you were favorable to them from Egypt until now."

The Lord said to Moses, "I am gracious to them according to your word. But as I live and my name is living, so the glory of the Lord will fill all the land. For all the men who see my glory, and the signs which I worked in Egypt, and in the wilderness, and have tempted me this tenth time, and have not listened to my voice, surely they will not see the land, which I swore to their fathers, but their children which are with me here, as many as don't know good or evil, every inexperienced youth, to them will I give the land. But none who have provoked me will see it. My servant Caleb, because there was another spirit in him, and he followed me, I will bring him into the land into which he entered, and his seed will inherit it. But Amalekites and the Canaanites live in the valley. Tomorrow, turn and depart for the wilderness by the way of the Sea of Edom."[1]

The Lord said to Moses and Aaron, "How long will I endure this wicked community? I have heard their murmurings against me, even the murmuring of the children of Israel, which they have murmured concerning you. Say to them, 'As I live, says the Lord, surely as you spoke into my ears, so will I do to you. Your carcasses will fall in this wilderness, and all those of you that were surveyed, and those of you that were counted from twenty years old and up, all that murmured against me, you will not enter into the land for which I stretched out my hand to establish you on, except only Caleb the son of Jephunneh, and Joshua the son of Nun. Your little ones, who you said would become prey, them will I bring into the land, and they will inherit the land, from which you turned away. Your carcasses will fall in this wilderness. Your sons will be fed in the wilderness for forty years, and they will carry your fornication until your carcasses are consumed in the wilderness. According to the number of the days during which you spied the land, forty days, a day for a year, you will carry your sins forty years, and you will know my fierce anger. I, the Lord have said,

'Surely will I do this to this evil community that has risen together against me. In this wilderness, they will be completely consumed, and there they will die.'"

The men that Moses sent to spy out the land, and who came and murmured against it to the assembly to bring out evil words concerning the land, the men that spoke evil reports against the land, died of the plague before the Lord. Joshua the son of Nun and Caleb the son of Jephunneh still lived out of those men who went to spy out the land. Moses spoke these words to all the children of Israel, and the people mourned greatly. They rose early in the morning and went up to the top of the mountain, saying, "Look, these men that are here will go up to the place of which the Lord has spoken because we have sinned."

Moses asked, "Why do you transgress the word of the Lord? You will not prosper. Don't go up, for the Lord is not with you, and will you fall before the face of your enemies. For Amalek and the Canaanites are there before you, and you will fall by the sword, because you have disobeyed the Lord and turned aside, and the Lord will not be among you."

Having forced their way through, they went up to the top of the mountain, but the ark of the covenant of the Lord and Moses stirred would not leave the camp. The Amalekites and Canaanites that lived in that mountains came down, and routed them, and destroyed them to Herman, and they returned to the camp.

CHAPTER 14 NOTES

1 Codex Vaticanus: ṭalassan Eruṭran (ⲐⲀⲗⲗⲀⳓⳓⲀⲚ ⲉⲣⲨⲐⲣⲀⲚ). Translation: Erythrean Sea

• Septuagint manuscript 128: ṭalassēs Eruṭras (θἀλλσοℎℂ Εℛⲩθℯℊ c). Translation: Erythrean Sea

• Septuagint manuscript 799: ṭalassē Eruṭra (θλλσοℎ Εℛⲩθℯℊ). Translation: Erythrean Sea

• Leningrad Codex: yam-sûp (יַם־סֽוּף). General Translation: sea of papyrus (or reeds)

• Peshitta: ymå dswp (ܝܡܐ ܕܣܘܦ). Translation: sea of papyrus (or reeds)

• Targum Onkelos: yammā' dəsûp (יַמָּא דְסוּף). Translation: sea of papyrus (or reeds)

• Targum Pseudo-Jonathan: yammā' dəsûp (יַמָּא דְסוּף). Translation: sea of papyrus (or reeds)

• Sahidic manuscript 2044: Eruṭra ṭalassa (ⲈⲣⲨⲐⲣⲀ ⲐⲀⲗⲗⲀⳓⳓⲀ). Translation: Eruthra Sea

The Greek term is not geographically specific, however, by this point the Israelites should have been at the Gulf of Aqaba. The Greek name appears to be a translation of the Persian term Erostras, which referred to the entire Persian Gulf, Red Sea, and the Indian Ocean. The Greeks were likely interpreting this as the Gulf of Aqaba, however, this was known to the ancient Egyptians as the "Sea of Edom" (𓄿𓈖𓏤𓂋𓏤𓇋𓇌) which is what the Israelites would have called it if that was where they were. The Egyptian name is accepted as being adopted from the Canaanite name of the Gulf of Aqaba, which was ym Ådm (𐎊𐎎𐎀𐎄𐎎) in Ugaritic, ym Ådm (𐤉𐤌𐤀𐤃𐤌) in Phoenician, and ymå hÅydm (𐡀𐡃𐡌𐡄𐡉𐡌) in Aramaic, all of which translate as "Sea of Edom." As "Edom" and "red" were both spelled as ådm (𐤀𐤃𐤌) in Canaanite (Judahite,

CHAPTER 14

Samartian, Edomite), and åydm (𐤄𐤃𐤀) and Aramaic, the Aramaic
texts that the Greeks translated probably used the name Sea of
Edom/red, suggesting the Aramaic translator believed that the Sea
of Papyrus was the Sea of Edom. Based on the writings of Jeremiah,
the Sea of Papyrus was accepted as having been the Sea of Edom by
the 600s BCE, which was the earliest that the ancient collection of
texts composing Numbers could have been complied and added to
the Torah, based on their language. As the sea in the verse must
have originally been the Sea of Edom, the name is restored in this
translation.

CHAPTER 15

The Lord said to Moses, "Tell the children of Israel, 'When you have come into the land of your habitation, which I give to you, and you will offer whole burnt offerings to the Lord, a whole burnt offering or a sacrifice to magnify a vow, or a free-will offering, or to offer in your feasts a sacrifice of sweet savor to the Lord, whether from the herd or the flock, then he that offers his gift to the Lord will bring a sacrifice of fine flour, a tenth part of a bushel mingled with oil, even with a quarter of a hin.[1] For a drink offering you will offer a quarter of a hin on the whole burnt offering or the sacrifice. For every lamb, you will offer so much, as a sacrifice, a smell of sweet savor to the Lord. For a ram, when you offer it as a whole burnt offering or as a sacrifice, you will prepare as a sacrifice two-tenths of fine flour mingled with oil, the third part of a hin.'"

"'You will offer for a smell of sweet savor to the Lord wine for a drink offering, a third of a hin. If you sacrifice a whole burnt offering or a sacrifice, to perform a vow or a peace offering to the Lord, then the worshiper will offer the calf as a sacrifice, three tenths of fine flour mixed with a half of oil. Wine for a drink offering the half of a hin, a sacrifice for a smell of sweet savor to the Lord. This you will do to one calf or one ram, or one lamb of the sheep or goat kid. According to the number of whatever you will offer, so will you do to each one, according to their number. Every native of the country will do this to offer such things as sacrifices for a smell of sweet savor to the Lord. If there should be a stranger among you in your land or one who should be born to you among your generations, and he will offer a sacrifice, a smell of sweet savor to the Lord as you do, so the whole community will offer to the Lord. There will be one law for you and the strangers living among you, a perpetual law for your generations. As you are, so will the stranger be before the Lord. There will be one law and one ordinance for you, and for the stranger that abides among you.'"

The Lord said to Moses, "Tell the sons of Israel, 'When you are entering into the land, into which I bring you, then it will happen when you will eat of the bread of the land, you will separate a wave-offering, a special offering to the Lord, the first fruits of your dough. You will offer your bread a heave-offering: as a heave-offering from the threshing floor, so will you separate it, even the first fruits of your dough, and you will give the Lord a heave-offering throughout your generations. But whenever you will transgress, and not perform all these commands, which the Lord spoke to Moses, as the Lord ordered you by the hand of Moses, from the day which the Lord ordered you and forward throughout your generations, then it will happen, if a trespass is committed unwillingly, unknown to the community, then will all the community offer a calf from the herd without imperfection for a whole burnt offering of sweet savor to the Lord, and its sacrifice and its drink offering according to the ordinance, and one goat kid for a sin offering."

"The priest will make atonement for all the community of the children of Israel, and the trespass will be forgiven them, because it is involuntary, and they have brought their gift, a burnt offering to the Lord for their trespass before the Lord, even for their involuntary sins. It will be forgiven as respects all the community of the children of Israel, and the stranger that is living among you, because it is involuntary to all the people.'"

"'If one mind sins unwillingly, he will bring one male goat of a year-old for a sin offering. The priest will make atonement for the mind that committed the trespass unwillingly, and that sinned unwillingly before the Lord, to make atonement for him. There will be the same law for the native among the children of Israel, and for the stranger that abides among them, whoever will commit a trespass unwillingly. Whichever mind either of the natives or the strangers will do anything with a presumptuous hand, he will provoke God, and that mind will be cut off from his people, for he has set at nothing the word of the Lord and broken his commands, that mind will be completely destroyed, his sin is on him.'"

The children of Israel were in the wilderness, and they found a man gathering sticks on the sabbath day. They who found him gathering sticks on the sabbath day brought him to Moses and Aaron, and all the community of the children of Israel. They placed him in custody, for they did not determine what they should do to him.

The Lord said to Moses, "Let the man be by all means put to death, let all the community stone him with stones."

CHAPTER 15

All the community brought him out of the camp, and all the community stoned him with stones outside the camp, as the Lord commanded Moses.

The Lord said to Moses, "Speak to the children of Israel, and tell them, and let them make for themselves fringes on the borders of their garments throughout their generations. You will put on the fringes of the borders a lace of blue. It will be on your fringes, and you will look at them, and you will remember all the commands of the Lord, and do them, and you will not turn back after your imaginations, and after the sight of your eyes in the things after which you go whoring, that you may remember and perform all my commands, and you will be holy to your god. I am the lord of the gods who brought you out of the land of Egypt, to be your god. I am the lord of your gods!"[2]

CHAPTER 15 NOTES

1 Codex Vaticanus: in (ܝܢ)

• Leningrad Codex: hîn (הִין)

• Peshitta: hmynå (ܗܡܝܢܐ). Translation: hmyna (or belt, girdle)

• Targum Onkelos: hînā' (הִינָא)

• Targum Pseudo-Jonathan: hînā' (הִינָא)

• Sahidic manuscript 2006: ši (ϣι). Translation: measurement (or weight)

The hin was an ancient Israelite and Judean unit of measurement. Estimated around 3.7 liters, or 3.9 quarts.

2 Codex Vaticanus: egō K̄S̄ o T̄S̄ umōn o exagagōn umas ek gēs Aiguptou einai umōn ths, egō K̄S̄ o T̄S̄ umōn (ⲈⲄⲰⲔⲤⲞⲐⲤⲨⲘⲰⲚⲞ ⲈⲌⲀⲄⲀⲄⲰⲚ ⲨⲘⲀⲤ ⲈⲔ ⲅⲎⲤ ⲀⲓⲅⲨⲡⲧⲞⲨ ⲈⲓⲚⲀⲓ ⲨⲘⲰⲚ ⲐⲤ ⲈⲄⲰ K̄C̄ Ⲟ ⲐⲤ ⲨⲘⲰⲚ). Translation: I am Lord the god of you who exported you from the land Egypt to be your god. I am Lord the god of you.

• Septuagint manuscript 318: egō kurios o ṯeos umōn o exagagōn umas ex Aiguptou einai umōn ṯeos, egō kurios o ṯeos umōn (ϵγω ⲕⲩⲣⲓⲟⲥ ⲟ ⲑ̄ⲥ̄ⲟⲥ ⲩⲙⲱⲛ ⲟ ⲉⲝⲁⲅⲁⲅⲟⲟⲛ ⲩⲙⲁⲥ ⲉⲝ ⲁⲓⲅⲩⲡⲧⲱ ⲇⲛⲁⲓ ⲩⲙⲱⲛ ⲑ̄ⲥ̄ⲟⲥ, ϵγω ⲕⲩⲣⲓⲟⲥ ⲟ ⲑ̄ⲥ̄ⲟⲥ ⲩⲙⲱⲛ). Translation: I am Lord the god of you who exported you from Egypt to be your god. I am Lord the god of you

• Septuagint manuscript 130: egō kurios o ṯeos umōn o exagōn umas ek gēs Aiguptou einai umōn ṯeos, egō kurios o ṯeos umōn (ϵγω ⲕⲩⲣⲓⲟⲥ ⲟ ⲑ̄ⲥ̄ⲟⲥ ⲩⲙⲱⲛ ⲟ ⲉⲝⲁⲅⲟⲟⲛ ⲩⲙⲁⲥ ⲉⲕ ⲅⲏⲥ ⲁⲓⲅⲩⲡⲧⲱ ⲇⲛⲁⲓ ⲩⲙⲱⲛ ⲑ̄ⲥ̄ⲟⲥ, ϵγω ⲕⲩⲣⲓⲟⲥ ⲟ ⲑ̄ⲥ̄ⲟⲥ ⲩⲙⲱⲛ). Translation: I am Lord the god of you who exported you from the land Egypt to be your god. I am Lord the god of you

• Septuagint manuscript 72: egō kurios o ṯeos umōn o exagagōn umas ek gēs Aiguptou einai umin ṯeos, egō kurios o ṯeos umōn (ϵγω ⲕⲩⲣⲓⲟⲥ ⲟ ⲑ̄ⲥ̄ⲟⲥ ⲩⲙⲱⲛ ⲟ ⲉⲝⲁⲅⲁⲅⲟⲟⲛ ⲩⲙⲁⲥ ⲉⲕ ⲅⲏⲥ ⲁⲓⲅⲩⲡⲧⲱ ⲇⲛⲁⲓ ⲩⲙⲓⲛ ⲑ̄ⲥ̄ⲟⲥ, ϵγωⲕⲩⲣⲓⲟⲥ ⲟ ⲑ̄ⲥ̄ⲟⲥ ⲩⲙⲱⲛ). Translation: I am Lord the god of you who exported you from the land of Egypt to be your god. I am Lord the god of y'll

• Septuagint manuscript 528: egō kurios o ṯeos umōn o exagagōn umas ek tēs Aiguptou einai umōn ṯeos, egō kurios o ṯeos umōn (ϵγω ⲕⲩⲣⲓⲟⲥ ⲟ ⲑ̄ⲥ̄ⲟⲥ ⲩⲙⲱⲛ ⲟ ⲉⲝⲁⲅⲁⲅⲟⲟⲛ ⲩⲙⲁⲥ ⲉⲕ ⲑ̄ ⲁⲓⲅⲩⲡⲧⲱ ⲇⲛⲁⲓ ⲩⲙⲱⲛ ⲑ̄ⲥ̄ⲟⲥ, ϵγω ⲕⲩⲣⲓⲟⲥ ⲟ ⲑ̄ⲥ̄ⲟⲥ ⲩⲙⲱⲛ). Translation: I am Lord the god of you who exported you from the Egypt to be your god. I am Lord the god of you

• Leningrad Codex: 'ănî Yəhwâ 'ĕlōhêkem 'ăšer hôsē'tî 'etkem mē'ereṣ miṣrayim lihyôt lākem lē'lōhîm 'ănî Yəhwâ 'ĕlōhêkem (אֲנִי יְהוָה אֱלֹהֵיכֶם אֲשֶׁר הוֹצֵאתִי אֶתְכֶם מֵאֶרֶץ מִצְרַיִם לִהְיוֹת לָכֶם לֵאלֹהִים אֲנִי

יְהוָה אֱלֹהֵיכֶם). Translation: I am Yahweh your god who removed you from the land of Egypt to be for you the elohim. I am Yahweh elohim of yours.

• Peshitta: ånå ånå mryå ålhkwn: dåpqtkwn mn åröå dmsryn: dåhwå lkwn ålhå: ånå ånå mryå ålhkwn (ܐܢܐ ܐܢܐ ܡܪܝܐ ܐܠܗܟܘܢ: ܕܐܦܩܬܟܘܢ ܡܢ ܐܪܥܐ ܕܡܨܪܝܢ: ܕܐܗܘܐ ܠܟܘܢ ܐܠܗܐ: ܐܢܐ ܐܢܐ ܡܪܝܐ ܐܠܗܟܘܢ). Translation: I am Master (or lord) your god who removed you from the land of Egypt to be for you god. I am Master (or lord) your god.

• Targum Onkelos: 'ånā' Yəyā 'ĕlāhākôn dî 'appēqît yātəkôn mē'ar'ā' dəMisrayim ləmēhăwê ləkôn lē'ĕlāhā' 'ånā' Yəyā 'ĕlāhākôn (אֲנָא יְיָ אֱלָהְכוֹן דִּי אַפֵּקִית יָתְכוֹן מֵאַרְעָא דְמִצְרַיִם לְמֶהֱוֵי לְכוֹן לֶאֱלָהָא אֲנָא יְיָ אֱלָהְכוֹן). Translation: I'm Yahweh your god who exported you from the land of Egypt to be for you a god. I'm Yahweh your god.

• Targum Pseudo-Jonathan: 'ånā' hû' Yəyā 'ĕlāhākôn dî pərāqît wə'appēqît yatkôn pərîqîn mē'ar'ā' dəMisrayim mətôl ləmehĕwê ləkôn le'ĕlāhā' 'ånā' hû' Yəyā 'ĕlāhākôn (אֲנָא הוּא יְיָ אֱלָהְכוֹן דִּי פְרָקִית וְאַפֵּקִית יַתְכוֹן פְּרִיקִין מֵאַרְעָא דְמִצְרַיִם מְטוֹל לְמֶהֱוֵי לְכוֹן לֶאֱלָהָא אֲנָא הוּא יְיָ אֱלָהְכוֹן). Translation: I'm he: Yahweh your god, who separated and exported you spreading out from the land of Egypt, for the reason that is to be a god. I'm he: Yahweh your god.

• Sahidic manuscript 2006: pentafntēutn ebol hm pkah nkēme etrašōpe nētn nnoute anok pe pjoeis petnnoute (ⲡⲉⲛⲧⲁϥ̄ⲛⲧⲏⲩⲧⲛ ⲉⲃⲟⲗ ϩⲙ ⲡⲕⲁϩ ⲛ̄ⲕⲏⲙⲉ ⲉⲧⲣⲁϣⲱⲡⲉ ⲛⲏⲧⲛ ⲛⲛⲟⲩⲧⲉ ⲁⲛⲟⲕ ⲡⲉ ⲡⲭⲟⲉⲓⲥ ⲡⲉⲧⲛⲛⲟⲩⲧⲉ). Translation: he who brought you out from within the land of the black (or Egypt) to exist to you the god I'm sky the Lord of the god

The word in the Leningrad Codex is commonly translated as "God," but is a plural form of the Aramaic ålhå (ܐܠܗܐ), meaning "gods," or a plural form of the Hebrew 'ēlâ (אֱלָה) meaning "goddesses." The term ålhym (ܐܠܗܝܡ), and ålhym (ܐܠܗܝܡ), are also direct transcriptions of the Neo-Assyrian word elium (𒂊𒇷𒌝), which by the Iron Age meant "god," indicating that text had previously been written in cuneiform, and was translated into Aramaic or Phoenician during the iron age. During the bronze age, the word was pronounced as Alium (𒀀𒇷𒌝), and referred to a specific god, deityĀn (𒀭𒀭) the highest god, and father of the other gods. His Akkadian name was derived from the word elûm (𒂊𒇻𒌝), meaning 'higher,' as the term was intended to convey the meaning of "highest." During the Sumerian era, he was believed to live in the polar region of the sky, where the modern constellation of Draco is located, making him the highest in the sky, around which all the gods (stars) circled. By the Akkadian era, Ellil was believed to be the highest god, living in the polar region, however, the name 'Highest' continued to be used for An. By the Babylonian era be was believed to be the god governing the ecliptic, specifically the asterism later known as Orion, which was ultimately named after him in Greek from the Akkadian úru An (𒌷𒀭), meaning "Light of An."

The term 'ēl 'elyôn (אֵל עֶלְיוֹן), meaning "highest god," was translated into Hebrew in Bereshít Chapter 14, where the Greeks translated it as ṯeō tō usistō (θεω τω υψιστω), also meaning "highest god." El Elyon is known to have been a major god of the Canaanites, called ål wålyn (𐡀𐡋 𐡅𐡏𐡋𐡉𐡍), meaning "God and Highest" in an Aramaic language Sefire Treaty from circa 750 BCE. The Greek translations of Sanchuniathon's bronze age writing that has survived to the present, referred to the primordial creator god of the Canaanites as Elioun (Ελιουν), which appears to be the same god. According to Sanchuniathon, Elioun was the highest (ὕψιστος) god, who made the sky and the land, and they made the rest of the gods.

During the Old Babylonian and Old Assyrian eras, the gods Marduk and Ashur, the national gods of Babylon and Assyria, replaced the Akkadian An as the primary god of the Mesopotamian pantheons, and by the iron age, the word elium had came to mean "god," explaining why the Aramaic term ålhym (ﬦﬧﬦﬡ) would have been interpreted as "god," by the Greeks.

CHAPTER 16

Korah the son of Jezer the son of Kohath the son of Levi, and Dathan and Abiram, the sons of Eliab, and On the son of Peleth the son of Reuben, rose up and spoke before Moses, and 250 men of the sons of Israel, chiefs of the assembly, chosen councilors, and men of renown. They rose up against Moses and Aaron, and said, "Let it be enough for you that all the community are holy, and the Lord is among them. Why do you set up yourselves against the community of the Lord?"

When Moses heard it, he fell on his face. He said to Korah and all his assembly, "God has visited and known those that are his, and who are holy, and has brought them to himself. Whom he has chosen for himself, he has brought to himself. Do this, take for yourselves censers, Korah and all his company, and put fire in them, and put incense on them before the Lord tomorrow, and it will happen that the man whom the Lord has chosen, he will be holy. Let it be enough for you, you sons of Levi."

Moses said to Korah, "Listen to me, you sons of Levi. Is it a little thing for you, that God of Israel has separated you from the community of Israel, and brought you near to himself to minister in the services of the tabernacle of the Lord, and to stand before the tabernacle to minister for them? He has brought you near and all your brothers the sons of Levi with you, and do you seek to be priests also? So it is with you and all your community which is gathered together against God, and who is Aaron, that you murmur against him?"

Moses called Dathan and Abiram, the sons of Eliab, and they replied, "We will not go up. Is it a minor thing that you have brought us out of a land flowing with milk and honey, to kill us in the wilderness, and that you alone rule over us? You are a prince, but have you brought us into a land flowing with milk and honey, and have you given us an inheritance of land and vineyards? Would you have cut out the eyes of those men? We will not go up."

Moses was exceedingly indignant, and said to the Lord, "Pay no attention to their sacrifice. I have not taken away the desire of any one of them, neither have I hurt any one of them."

Moses said to Korah, "Sanctify your company and be ready before the Lord, you and Aaron and them, tomorrow. Take each man his censer, and you will put incense on them and will bring each one his censer before the Lord, 250 censers, and you and Aaron will bring each his censer."

Each man took his censer, and they put fire in them and laid incense on them, and Moses and Aaron stood by the doors of the tabernacle of witness. Korah raised against them all his company by the door of the tabernacle of witness, and the glory of the Lord appeared to all the community.

the Lord said to Moses and Aaron, "Separate yourselves from the middle of this community, and I will consume them at once."

CHAPTER 16

They fell on their faces and asked, "El, god[1] of spirits and all flesh, if one man has sinned, will the anger of the Lord be on the whole community?"

The Lord said to Moses, "Tell the community, 'Depart from the company of Korah and around him.'"

Moses rose up and went to Dathan and Abiram, and all the elders of Israel went with him. He said to the community, "Separate yourselves from the tents of these stubborn men, and touch nothing that belongs to them, in case you are consumed with them in all their sin."

They stood apart from the tent of Korah and around it. Dathan and Abiram went out and stood by the doors to their tents, and their wives and their children and their store.

Moses said, "Now will you know that the Lord has sent me to perform all these works, that I have not done them of myself. If these men will die according to the death of all men, if also their visitation will be according to the visitation of all men, then the Lord has not sent me. But if the Lord will show by a vision, and Adamah[2] will open her mouth and swallow them up, and their houses, and their tents, and all that belongs to them, and they will go down alive into Hades, then you will know that these men have provoked the Lord."

When he finished saying these words, the ground ripped apart beneath them. The ground[3] opened and swallowed them up, and their houses, and all the men that were with Korah, and their livestock. They went down and all that they had, alive into Hades, and the ground covered them, and they perished from among the community. All Israel around them fled from the sound of them, saying, "In case the ground swallows us up also."

Fire went out from the Lord and devoured the 250 men that offered incense.

The Lord said to Moses, and to Eleazar the son of Aaron the priest, "Pick up the bronze censers from among the men that have been burnt, and scatter the strange fire, for they have sanctified the censers of these sinners against their minds, and make them beaten plates a covering for the altar, because they were brought before the Lord and consecrated, and they became a sign to the children of Israel. Eleazar the son of Aaron the priest took the bronze censers, which the men who had been burnt brought near, and they put them as a covering on the altar, a memorial to the children of Israel that no stranger might draw near, who is not of the seed of Aaron, to offer incense before the Lord, so he will not be as Korah and as they that conspired with him, as the Lord spoke to him by the hand of Moses.

The children of Israel murmured the next day against Moses and Aaron, saying, "You have killed the people of the Lord. It came to pass when the community united against Moses and Aaron, that they ran impetuously to the tabernacle of witness, and the cloud covered it, and the glory of the Lord appeared. Moses and Aaron went in, in front of the tabernacle of witness.

CHAPTER 16

The Lord said to Moses and Aaron, "Depart out of the middle of this community, and I will consume them at once, and they fell on their faces.

Moses said to Aaron, "Take a censer, and put on it fire from the altar, and put incense on it, and carry it away quickly into the camp, and make atonement for them, for anger has gone out from the presence of the Lord, and it has begun to destroy the people."

Aaron took as Moses told him, and ran among the community, for already the plague had begun among the people, and he put on the incense and made an atonement for the people. He stood between the dead and the living, and the plague ceased. They who died in the plague were 14,700, besides those that died on account of Korah. Aaron returned to Moses to the door of the tabernacle of witness, and the plague ceased.

CHAPTER 16 NOTES

1 Codex Vaticanus: T̄S T̄S (ΘСΘС). Translation: god god

• Codex Colberto-Sarravianus: tee tee (ΘΕΕ ΘΕΕ). Translation: god god

• Septuagint manuscript 707: Teos o teos (Θ6ос о θ6ос). Translation: God the god

• Septuagint manuscript 75: Teos (Θ6ос). Translation: God

• Leningrad Codex: 'ēl 'ĕlōhê (אֵל אֱלֹהֵי). Translation: El (or god, strong) god

CHAPTER 16

- Peshitta: åyl ålhå (ܐܠܗܐ ܐܝܠ). Translation: El (or god, strong) god
- Targum Onkelos: 'ēl 'ĕlāhā' (אֵל אֱלָהָא). Translation: El (or god in Hebrew) god
- Targum Jerusalem: 'ĕlāhā' (אֱלָהָא). Translation: god
- Targum Pseudo-Jonathan: 'ēl 'ĕlāhā' (אֵל אֱלָהָא). Translation: El (or god in Hebrew) god
- Vetus Latina: deus deus fortis domine (ᴅєus ᴅєus ꜰᴏʀᴛɪꜱ ᴅᴏᴍɪɴє). Translation: god god powerful (or strong) lord
- Sahidic manuscript 2006: pnoute pnoute (ⲡⲛⲟⲩⲧⲉ ⲡⲛⲟⲩⲧⲉ). Translation: the god the god

In this verse, the word Ṭeos (Θεὸς) is being used as a proper name, and so 'Ēl (אֵל) is restored from the Leningrad Codex. El, which means 'God,' was also the name of the ancient Canaanite creator-god. El is also the name of the god that Jacob worshiped in Genesis, as he built the Temple of El near Shiloh, which continued to be the main temple in Samaria until Yahweh supplanted El shortly before the Assyrians conquered Samaria.

2 Codex Vaticanus: Gē (ⲅⲏ). Translation: Ge (or Earth)
- Codex Venetus: Gē ē (ⲅⲏⲏ). Translation: Ge (or Earth) she
- Leningrad Codex: 'Ădāmâ (אֲדָמָה). Translation: Adama
- Peshitta: årôå (ܐܪܥܐ). Translation: land
- Targum Onkelos: 'ar'ā' (אַרְעָא). Translation: land
- Targum Pseudo-Jonathan: 'ar'ā' (אַרְעָא). Translation: land
- Sahidic manuscript 2006: kah (ⲕⲁϩ). Translation: land (or soil)

Adamma was the Elbaite name of an earth goddess, generally associated with the underworld, not the surface. In the 3rd millennium BCE Elbaite texts, she was the wife the god Rašaap (𒀭𒊮𒀊), later known as Ršp (𒀭𒊮𒀊 / ⲣⲉⲥⲉⲫ / רשף) by the

Amorites and Canaanites, more commonly known as Resheph (רֶשֶׁף)
today, from the version of his name in the Masoretic Text. During
the Hyksos Dynasty, Rašaap was also viewed as being the Egyptian
god Atum (𓇋𓏏𓐝) by a cult based in Íwnw (Heliopolis), although this
association ended with the fall of the Hyksos dynasty. During the
early New Kingdom era, his worship was suppressed in Egypt and
Canaan, where he was replaced by Shed / Shaddai (𓈙𓂧𓏤𓀭 / 𐤔𐤃𐤅).

With the exception of Ishara, the Amorites did not view
goddesses as important, however, the Hurrian culture which had
been dominated by the Amorites continued to view Adamma as the
wife of Rašaap after the fall of the Hyksos Dynasty. The fact that the
name Adamma was mentioned supports the text of Numbers
originating during the bronze age, as Adamma was not worshiped
in Canaan during the iron age, having been supplanted by the
Canaanite earth-goddess Eretz.

The Earth (Eretz / Adamma) is depicted as the same type of
primordial deity in the Septuagint as she was in the Greek myths
and called on to witness blessings and curses, implying
consciousness. As the goddess' name was Adamma, not Earth or Ge,
that name is restored from the Leningrad Codex.

3 Codex Vaticanus: ēnoiķtē ē Gē (ΗΝΟΙΧΘΗ Η ΓΗ). Translation:
opened the Earth (or Ge, land)

• Leningrad Codex: tiptaḥ hā'Āres 'et-pîhā (תִּפְתַּח הָאָרֶץ אֶת־פִּיהָ).
Translation: opened the Earth (or Eretz, dirt) it's (or his, her) mouth

• Peshitta: ptḥ åråå pwmh (ܘܦܬܚܬ ܐܪܥܐ ܦܘܡܗ). Translation:
opened land's mouth

• Targum Onkelos: iptaḥ hā'Āres 'et pîhā (תִּפְתַּח הָאָרֶץ אֶת פִּיהָ).
Translation: opened land it's (or his, her) mouth

• Targum Pseudo-Jonathan: pətāhat 'ar'ā' yat pûmāh (פְּתָחַת אַרְעָא
יַת פּוּמָהּ). Translation: opened land it's (or his, her) mouth

CHAPTER 16

• Sahidic manuscript 2006: afōmk mmoou (ⲁϥⲱⲙⲕ ⲙⲙⲟⲟⲩ). Translation: opened the waters

The Earth (Eretz / Adamma) is depicted as the same type of primordial deity in the Septuagint as she was in the Greek myths and called on to witness blessings and curses, implying consciousness. As the goddess' name was Eretz, not Earth or Ge, that name is restored from the Leningrad Codex. The text varies between Eretz, the common Canaanite word for "Mother Earth" and Adamma, the Canaanite and Hurrian name for "Goddess of the underworld," both names are restored from the Leningrad Codex in their respective places. The Greeks translated both as Gē (Γη), the name of the primordial Greek "Mother Earth," later renamed Gaia in the Roman Era.

CHAPTER 17

The Lord said to Moses, "Speak to the children of Israel, and take wands from them, according to the houses of their families, a wand from all their princes, according to the houses of their families, twelve wands, and write the name of each on his wand. Write the name of Aaron on the wand of Levi, as it is one wand for each. They will give them according to the tribe of the house of their families. You will put them in the tabernacle of witness, before the testimony, where I will be made known to you. The wand will blossom for the man whom I choose, and I will remove the murmuring of the children of Israel, which they murmur against you."

Moses spoke to the children of Israel, and all their chiefs gave him a wand each, for one chief a wand, according to the house of their families, twelve wands, and the wand of Aaron was among the wands. Moses set up the wands before the Lord in the tabernacle of witness. It came to pass in the morning, that Moses and Aaron went into the tabernacle of witness, and saw the wand of Aaron for the house of Levi had blossomed, and put out a bud, and bloomed blossoms and produced almonds.

Moses brought out all the wands from before the Lord to all the sons of Israel, and they looked, and each one took his wand. The Lord said to Moses, "Set up the wand of Aaron before the testimonies to be kept as a sign for the children of the disobedient, and let their murmuring cease from me, and they will not die."

Moses and Aaron did as the Lord commanded Moses.

The children of Israel said to Moses, "Look, we are cut off, we are destroyed, we are consumed. Everyone that touches the tabernacle of the Lord, dies. Will we all die?"

CHAPTER 18

The Lord said to Aaron, "You and your sons and your father's house will carry the sins of the holy things, and you and your sons will carry the iniquity of your priesthood. Take with yourself your brothers the tribe of Levi, the family of your father, and let them be joined to you, and let them minister to you, and you and your sons with you will minister before the tabernacle of witness. They will keep your orders and the orders of the tabernacle. Only they will not approach the holy vessels and the altar, so both they and you will not die."

"They will be joined to you and will keep the orders of the tabernacle of witness, in all the services of the tabernacle, and a stranger will not approach you. You will keep the orders of the holy things, and the orders of the altar, and so there will not be anger in the children of Israel. I have taken your brothers the Levites out of the middle of the children of Israel, a present given to the Lord, to minister in the services of the tabernacle of witness. You and your sons after you will keep up your priestly administration, according to the whole manner of the altar, and that which is within the veil, and you will minister in the services as the office of your priesthood, and the stranger that comes near will die."

The Lord said to Aaron, "Look! I have given you the order of the first fruits of all things consecrated to me by the children of Israel. I have given them to you as an honor, and to your sons after you for a perpetual ordinance. Let this be to you from all the holy things that are consecrated to me, even the burnt offerings, from all their gifts, and all their sacrifices, and every trespass-offering of theirs, and from all their sin offerings, whatever things they give to me of all their holy things, they will be yours and your sons.' In the holiest place will you eat them, every male will eat them, you and your sons, they will be holy to you."

"This will be for you of the first fruits of their gifts, of all the wave offerings of the children of Israel, to you have I given them and to your sons and your daughters with you, a perpetual ordinance. Every clean person in your house will eat them. Every first-offering of oil, and every first-offering of wine, their first fruits of grain, whatever they may give to the Lord, to you have I given them."

"All the first fruits that are in their land, whatever they will offer to the Lord, will be yours. Every clean person in your house will eat them. Every devoted thing among the children of Israel will be yours. Everything that opens the womb of all flesh, whatever they bring to the Lord, whether man or beast, will be yours. Only the firstborn of men will be surely redeemed, and you will redeem the firstborn of unclean livestock. The redemption of them will be from a month old, their valuation of five shekels, it is twenty gerahs according to the holy shekel. But you will not redeem the firstborn of calves and the firstborn of sheep and the firstborn of goats."

"They are holy, and you will pour their blood on the altar, and you will offer the fat as a burnt offering for a smell of sweet savor to the Lord. The flesh will be yours, as also the breast of the wave-offering and as the right shoulder, it will be yours. Every special offering of the holy things, whatever the children of Israel will especially offer to the Lord, I have given to you and your sons and your daughters with you, a perpetual ordinance. It is a covenant of perpetual salt forever before the Lord, for you and your seed after you."

The Lord said to Aaron, "You have no inheritance in their land, neither will you have any portion among them, for I am your portion and your inheritance among the children of Israel. And, Look, I have given to the sons of Levi every tithe in Israel for an inheritance for their services, whenever they perform ministry in the tabernacle of witness. The children of Israel will no longer draw near to the tabernacle of witness to incur fatal guilt. The Levite himself will perform the service of the tabernacle of witness, and they will carry their iniquities, it is a perpetual statute throughout their generations, and among the children of Israel, they will not receive an inheritance. Because I have given as a distinct portion to the Levites for an inheritance the tithes of the children of Israel, whatever they will offer to the Lord, therefore I said to them, 'Among the children of Israel they have no inheritance.'"

The Lord said to Moses, "You will also speak to the Levites, and will say to them, 'If you take the tithe from the children of Israel, which I have given you from them for an inheritance, then will you separate from it a heave-offering to the Lord, a tenth of the tenth. Your heave offerings will be reckoned to you as grain from the floor, and an offering from the winepress. So you will also separate them from all the offerings of the Lord out of all your tithes, whatever you will receive from the children of Israel, and you will give of them an offering to the Lord to Aaron the priest. Of all your gifts you will offer an offering to the Lord and of every first-fruit the consecrated part from it."

"You will say to them, When you will offer the first fruits from it, then will it be reckoned to the Levites as produce from the threshing floor, and as produce from the winepress. You will eat it in any place, you and your families, for this is your reward for your services in the tabernacle of witness. You will not carry sin because of it, because you have offered an offering of first fruits from it, and you will not profane the holy things of the children of Israel, that you don't die."

CHAPTER 19

The Lord said to Moses and Aaron, "This is the constitution of the law, as the Lord has commanded, 'Speak to the sons of Israel and let them take for you a red heifer outside spots, that has no spot on her, and on which no yoke has been put. You will give her to Eleazar the priest, and they will bring her out of the camp into a clean place and kill her before his face. Eleazar will take of her blood, and sprinkle her blood seven times in front of the tabernacle of witness. They will burn her to ashes before him, and her skin and her flesh and her blood, with her dung, will be burnt. The priest will take cedarwood and hyssop and scarlet wool, and they will throw them onto the burning heifer."

"The priest will wash his garments, and bathe his body in water, and afterward, he can go into the camp, and the priest will be unclean until evening. He that burns her will wash his garments, and bathe his body, and will be unclean until evening. A clean man will gather up the ashes of the heifer, and lay them up in a clean place outside the camp, and they will be for the community of the children of Israel to keep. It is the water of sprinkling, a purification.'"

"'He that collects the ashes of the heifer will wash his garments and will be unclean until evening, and it will be a perpetual statute for the children of Israel and the strangers joined to them. He that touches the dead body of any man, will be unclean for seven days. He will be purified on the third day and the seventh day and will be clean, but if he is not be purged on the third day and the seventh day, he will not be clean. Everyone that touches the carcass of the body of a man, if he should have died, and the other not have been purified, has defiled the tabernacle of the Lord. That mind will be cut off from Israel because the water of sprinkling has not been sprinkled on him. He is unclean, and his uncleanness is yet on him.'"

"'This is the law. If a man dies in a house, everyone that goes into the house, and all things in the house, will be unclean for seven days. Every open vessel that had no lid covering it will be unclean. Everyone who touches a man slain by violence, or a corpse, or human bone, or sepulcher, will be unclean for seven days. They will take for the unclean of the burnt ashes of purification, and they will pour on them running water into a vessel. A clean man will take hyssop, and dip it into the water, and sprinkle it on the house, and the furniture, and all the minds that are therein, and on him that touched the human bone, or the slain man, or the corpse, or the tomb. The clean man will sprinkle the water on the unclean on the third day and on the seventh day, and on the seventh day he will purify himself and the other will wash his garments, and bathe himself in water, and will be unclean until evening.'"

"'Whichever man is defiled and will not purify himself, that mind will be cut off from among the community because he has defiled the holy things of the Lord because the water of sprinkling has not been sprinkled on him. He is unclean. It will be for you a perpetual statute, and he that sprinkles the water of sprinkling will wash his garments. He that touches the water of sprinkling will be unclean until evening. Whatever the unclean man will touch will be unclean, and the mind that touches it will be unclean until evening.'"

CHAPTER 20

The entire community of the children of Israel came into the Wilderness of Sin, in the first month, and the people lived in Kadesh. Mariam died there and was buried there. There was no water for the community, and they gathered themselves together against Moses and Aaron. The people criticized Moses, saying, "We should have died in the destruction of our brothers before the Lord! Why have you brought the community of the Lord into this wilderness, to kill us and our livestock? Why is this? You have brought us out of Egypt, that we should come into this evil place where there is no sowing or figs, or vines, or pomegranates. There isn't even water to drink!"

Moses and Aaron went from before the assembly to the door of the tabernacle of witness, and they fell on their faces, and the glory of the Lord appeared to them. The Lord said to Moses, "Take your wand, and call the assembly, you and Aaron your brother, and speak to the rock before them, and it will give out its waters. You will bring water out of the rock for them, and give drink to the community and their livestock."

Moses took his wand which was before the Lord, as the Lord commanded. Moses and Aaron assembled the community before the rock, and said, "Hear me, you disobedient ones! Must we bring water out of this rock for you?" Moses lifted his hand and struck the rock with his wand twice, and a great deal of water came out, and the community drank, and their livestock.

The Lord said to Moses and Aaron, "Because you have not believed me to sanctify, me before the children of Israel, therefore you will not bring this community into the land which I have given them." This is the Water of Strife because the children of Israel spoke insolently before the Lord, and he was sanctified in them.

Moses sent messengers from Kadesh to the king of Edom, saying, "So says your brother Israel, 'You know all the trouble that has found us. How our fathers went down into Egypt, and we stayed in Egypt for many days, and the Egyptians afflicted us and our fathers. We cried to the Lord, and the Lord heard our voice, and sent a messenger and brought us out of Egypt. Now we are in the city of Kadesh, at the extremity of your frontiers. We will pass through your land, we will not go through the fields, nor through the vineyards, nor will we drink water out of your cistern. We will go by the king's highway. We will not turn aside to the right hand or the left until we have passed your borders."

Edom replied to him, "You will not pass through me, and if otherwise, I will go out to meet you in war."

The children of Israel said to him, "We will pass by the mountain, and if I and my livestock drink of your water, I will pay you, but it is no matter of importance, we will go by the mountain.

CHAPTER 20

He replied, "You will not pass through me," and Edom went out to meet him with a great army, and a mighty hand. So Edom refused to allow Israel to pass through his borders, and Israel turned away from him. They departed from Kadesh, and the children of Israel, even the whole community, came to Mount Hor.[1]

The Lord said Moses and Aaron in Mount Hor, on the borders of the land of Edom, "Let Aaron be added to his people, for you will certainly not go into the land which I have given the children of Israel because you provoked me at the Water of Strife. Take Aaron, and Eleazar his son, and bring them up to Mount Hor before all the community, and take Aaron's apparel from off him and put it on Eleazar his son. Let Aaron die there and be added to his people."

Moses did as the Lord commanded him, and took him up to Mount Hor, before all the community. He took Aaron's garments off him and put them on Eleazar his son, and Aaron died on the top of the mountain, and Moses and Eleazar came down from the mountain. All the community saw that Aaron was dead, and they wept for Aaron thirty days, including all the house of Israel.

CHAPTER 20 NOTES

1 Codex Vaticanus: Ōr to oros (ⲱⲣⲧⲟⲟⲣⲟⲥ). Translation: Or the mountain

CHAPTER 20

- Septuagint manuscript 416: Sōr to oros (Σωῤ το ορϲ). Translation: Sor the mountain.

- Septuagint manuscript 126: oros Ōr (ορϲ ωῤ). Translation: Mount Or.

- Leningrad Codex: hōr hāhār (הֹר הָהָר). Translation: Hor the mountain

- Peshitta: hwr twrå (ܛܘܪܐ ܚܘܪ). Translation: Hwr hill (or mountain)

- Targum Onkelos: hōr ṭûrā' (הֹר טוּרָא). Translation: Hor hill (or mountain)

- Targum Pseudo-Jonathan: tawwrôs 'ûmānôs (טַוְורוֹס אוּמָנוֹס). Translation: Nur mountains (from the Greek Taurus Amanus – Ταῦρος Ἀμανός)

- Sahidic manuscript 2006: ōr ptoou (ⲱⲣ ⲡⲧⲟⲟⲩ). Translation: Or the highland (or desert)

The book of Numbers includes two distinct mountains called Hor, one south of Edom, and the other to the far north, somewhere. The locations of both of these Mount Hors have been debated since the Second Temple Era, as they define the northern and southern borders of the lands the Israelites were to live in.

The southern Mount Hor was located on the "edge of the land of Edom" according to Numbers and was where Aaron died. In the 1st century CE, Josephus identified this Mount Hor, as the mountain today called Jebel Nebi Harun, a mountain near Petra, which he claimed was Kadesh Barne. This location was adopted by Islamic historians, and today has a "tomb" of the Prophet Harun (Aaron) on it.

While Mount Hor may be Jebel Nebi Harun, it is also notable that Mount Horeb (Χωρηβ / חֹרֵב) is not mentioned in Numbers, even though it played such a significant role in Exodus, and, therefore, Horeb may be another name of the southern Hor. Throughout most references to Mount Horeb and Mount Sinai they appear to be references to the same mountain, both in the Torah, and later in other works, such as *3rd Kingdoms* (Masoretic *Kings*). To further complicate the geography, a third name was applied to it in the *Book of Judges*, which is considered by scholars to be the oldest surviving texts that have not been heavily redacted by later priesthoods. In Song of Deborah, found in *Judges*, the mountain where God came down to the Israelites is called Mount Seir, and the details of the story she repeats are the same as those of the Horeb / Sinai event. Fortunately, this does narrow the list of possible mountains to the southern Abarim mountains in modern Jordan, south of the Dead Sea.

The 1st century Judean Historian Josephus, who was given the ancient scrolls from the Second Temple when Rome destroyed it, identified Kadesh Barnea as Petra, which he claimed was known as Rekem in ancient times. The location of Kadesh Barnea is central to identifying the location of Sinai, as the Israelites went to Kadesh Barnea after leaving Mount Sinai, and both were outside of Edomite territory, which by the 700s BCE included the southern Abarim mountains. Nevertheless, Josephus reported that Petra was part of Midian during the Exodus, meaning the Edomites were still only in the northern Abarim mountains, east of the Dead Sea. Josephus' claims about ancient Petra being named Rekem has been confirmed by archaeology, as has the fact that the region was not Edomite until after 800 BCE, meaning it could have been Midianite before that, and also could have been Kasdeh Barnea.

The Egyptian el-Amarna Letters, written between 1360 and 1332 BCE do mention the Shasu of Sôr, which is translated as the "nomads of Seir," implying someone was living in the Seir region of the southern Abarim mountains. If Mount Seir was near Petra (Kadesh Barnea) in the 1300s BCE, the mountain would have been Jebel al-Madhbah, which translates as "The Mountain of the Altar."

CHAPTER 20

The Mountain of the Altar has been associated with Moses since at least the pre-Christian era and includes a Valley of Moses and a Spring of Moses. The mountain's summit is covered in rock-cut ceremonial structures and is reached by a rock-cut staircase. There are two giant obelisks, carved out of the rocky surface, near a large rectangular promenade hollowed out so the edges for benches. The site also included large cisterns for collecting rainwater. It is unclear when this complex was carved out of the rock, as the site was later quarried for blue slate, which archaeologists believed once covered the site. This blue slate was likely what was later identified as sapphire in the Septuagint.

The northern Mount Hor is more difficult to identify, however, many attempts have been made. During the Second Temple Era, the most common northern Mount Hor was Mount Nur (also called Amanus, Amanah, Manus, Umanis), near the modern Turkish-Syrian border. The Targum Jonathan uses the Greek name of the Nur Mountains: Taurus Amanus (Ταῦρος Ἀμανός) transliterated into Aramaic.

The text of Numbers supports the identification of the northern Hor being at Nur, as the mountain is described as being near Hama, the major city of the Syrian northwest, which has been inhabited constantly for more than 7000 years. Additionally, in other Hebrew scriptures, such as Isaiah, the northern border is called Zephon (צפון), which is known to have been the Canaanite name of a mountain in the Nur Mountains. The original version of Numbers likely used the name Zephon, which was then redacted to Hor in Josiah's 'authorized' version of the Torah, as he went to great lengths to purge the old gods from his country, and Mount Zephon was the holy mountain of the Canaanite god of thunder Ba'al Hadad.

In order to simplify the reading of this translation, the southern Hor in translated as Mount Hor, while the northern Hor is called Mount Nur.

CHAPTER 21

Arad the Canaanite king who lived by the wilderness heard that Israel came by the way of Atharin, and he made war against Israel and carried off many captives from among them. Israel vowed a vow to the Lord, and said, "If you will deliver these people into my power, I will devote it and its cities to you."

The Lord listened to the voice of Israel and delivered the Canaanites into his power, and Israel devoted him and his cities, and they called the name of that place Anathema. Having departed from Mount Hor by the way leading to the Sea of Edom, they circled the land of Edom, and the people lost courage along the way. The people spoke against God and Moses, saying, "Why is this? Have you brought us out of Egypt to kill us in the wilderness? There is no bread or water, and our minds hate Lahem the worthless."[1]

The Lord sent among the people deadly serpents, and they bit the people, and many people among the children of Israel died. The people came to Moses and said, "We have sinned, for we have spoken against the Lord, and against you. Pray to the Lord, and let him take away the serpent from us."

Moses prayed to the Lord for the people, and the Lord said to Moses, "Make a serpent, and put it on a signal-staff, and it will come to be that whenever a serpent bites a man, everyone bit that looks at it will live." Moses made a serpent

CHAPTER 21

of brass and put it on a signal-staff, and it happened that whenever a serpent bit a man, and he looked on the bronze serpent, he lived.

The children of Israel departed and camped in Oboth. Having departed from Oboth, they traveled past the ruins of the Habirus,[2] on the farther side in the wilderness beyond Moab to the east. There they departed and camped in the valley of Zared. They departed there and camped on the other side of Arnon in the wilderness, the country which extends from the frontiers of the Amorites, for Arnon is the borders of Moab, between Moab and the Amorites. Therefore it is said in a book, 'A war of the Lord has set on fire Zoob, and the brooks of Arnon.' He has appointed brooks to cause Ar to live there, and it lies near the border of Moab. There they came to the well, this is the well of which the Lord said to Moses, "Gather the people, and I will give them water to drink."

Then Israel sang this song at the well, 'Begin to sing of the well for it.' The princes dug it, the kings of the nations in their kingdom, in their lordship sank it in the rock, and they went from the well to Mattanah, and from Mattanah to Nahaliel, and from Nahaliel to Bamoth, and from Bamoth to Janen, which is in the plain of Moab as seen from the top of the quarried rock that looks towards the wilderness.

Moses sent ambassadors to Sihon king of the Amorites, with peaceful words, saying, "We will pass through your land, we will go by the road. We will not turn aside to the field or the vineyard. We will not drink water out of your well. We will go by the king's highway until we have passed your boundaries."

Sihon did not allow Israel to pass through his borders, and Sihon gathered all his people and went out to set the battle formation against Israel into the wilderness, and he came to Jahaz and set the battle in array against Israel. Israel attacked him and slaughtered by the sword, and they became possessors of his land, from Arnon to Jabbok, as far as the children of Amman, for Jaazer is the borders of the children of Amman. Israel took all their cities, and Israel lived in all the cities of the Amorites, in Heshbon, and all cities belonging to it. Heshbon is the city of Sihon king of the Amorites, and he before fought against the king of Moab, and they took all his land, from Ar to Arnon.

Therefore they say, those who deal in dark speeches, "Come to Heshbon, that the city of Sihon may be built and prepared. For a fire has gone out from Heshbon, a flame from the city of Sihon, and has consumed as far as Moab, and devoured the pillars of Arnon. Woe to you, Moab. You are lost, you people of Chamos! Their sons are sold for preservation, and their daughters are captives to Sihon king of the Amorites. Their seed will perish from Heshbon to Dibon, and their women have yet further started a fire against Moab. Israel lived in all the cities of the Amorites. Moses sent to spy out Jaazer, and they took it, and its villages, and threw out the Amorites that lived there. Having returned, they went up the road that leads to Bashan, and Og the king of Bashan went out to meet them, and all his people to war to Edrei.

CHAPTER 21

The Lord said to Moses, "Don't fear him, for I have delivered him and all his people, and all his land, into your hands, and you will do to him as you did to Sihon king of the Amorites, who lived in Heshbon."

He killed him and his sons, and all his people, until he left none of his to be taken alive, and they inherited his land.

CHAPTER 21 NOTES

1 Codex Vaticanus: artō tō diakenō (ΑΡΤѠ ΤѠ ΔΙΑΚΕΝѠ). Translation: bread the emptiness

• Septuagint manuscript 630: artō tō diakeimenō (αρτοο τοο Διλλιϥμϕοο). Translation: bread is to be served

• Septuagint manuscript 129: artō tō dikenō (αρτοο τοο Διлιϲνοο)

• Septuagint manuscript 646: arḱonti toutō tō diakenō (αρχ℗⫯ι τοͻτοο τοο Διλλιϲνοο). Translation: ruler here is ruined

• Septuagint manuscript 767: artō tō diakenō kai koufō (αρτοο τοο Διλλιϲνοο ꙡɑⱪ κϱυϕοο). Translation: bread is ruined and lightweight

• Leningrad Codex: lehem haqqəlōqēl (לְחֶם הַקְּלֹקֵל). Translation: bread the ruined

• Peshitta: lhmå zȯwrå (ܠܚܡܐ ܙܘܪܐ). Translation: bread the ruined

• Targum Onkelos: mannā' hādēn dəmêkəlêh qālîl (מַנָּא הָדֵין דְּמֵיכְלֵיהּ קָלִיל). Translation: manna troublesome (or legal) containers are lightweight

• Targum Pseudo-Jonathan: manā' hādēn dimzônêh qālîl (מָנָא הָדֵין דִּמְזוֹנֵיהּ קָלִיל). Translation: manna troublesome (or legal) food is lightweight

160

- Sahidic manuscript 292L: asmestepoeik etšooue (ⲁⲥⲙⲉⲥⲧⲉⲡⲟⲉⲓⲕ ⲉⲧⲱⲟⲟⲩⲉ). Translation: to hate flour when it's dry

- Sahidic manuscript 2006: asmestepoeik etšoueit (ⲁⲥⲙⲉⲥⲧⲉⲡⲟⲉⲓⲕ ⲉⲧⲱⲟⲩⲉⲓⲧ). Translation: to hate flour that is empty

- Sahidic manuscript 2196: asmoste hm poeik etšoueit (ⲁⲥⲙⲟⲥⲧⲉ ϩⲙ ⲡⲟⲉⲓⲕ ⲉⲧⲱⲟⲩⲉⲓⲧ). Translation: to hate all flour that is empty

As the Hebrew text claims the bread was gone, the original phrase appears to have been about hating the god Lehem, the Canaanite god of bread.

2 Codex Vaticanus: Ǩalglei (ⲭⲁⲁⲅⲗⲉⲓ)
- Codex Ambrosiano A 147: Aǩellai (ⲁⲭⲉⲗⲗⲁⲓ)
- Codex Venetus: Iaēl (ⲓⲁⳑⳑⲗ)
- Septuagint manuscript 509: Aǩalgaei (ⲁⲭⲁⲗⳋⲁ∤)
- Septuagint manuscript 392: Ǩelgei (ⲭⱥⳋⳋ∤)
- Septuagint manuscript 319: Gai (ⲅⲁⳋ)
- Septuagint manuscript 343: Aǩalǩagi (ⲁⲭⲁⲗⲭⲁⳋⳋ)
- Septuagint manuscript 426: Aiē (ⲁⳑⳑ)
- Septuagint manuscript 118: Aǩileim gaiei (ⲁⲭⳋⲗ∤ⲙ ⳋⲁⳋ∤)
- Septuagint manuscript 56: Aǩalgai (ⲁⲭⲁⲗⳋⲁⳋ)
- Septuagint manuscript 82: Aǩeltaic (ⲁⲭⱥⳋⲧⲁⳋⳑ)
- Septuagint manuscript 417: Ǩalǩai (ⲭⲁⲗⲭⲁⳋ)
- Septuagint manuscript 19: Aǩileim ǩaieim (ⲁⲭⳋⲗ∤ⲙ ⲭⲁⳋ∤ⲙ)
- Septuagint manuscript 458: Aǩelseein en geēl (ⲁⲭⱥⲥⳋⲇ∤ⲛ ⲁⳝ ⳋⳋⳑⲗ)
- Septuagint manuscript 767: Aǩelseein en gaiein (ⲁⲭⱥⲥⳋⲇ∤ⲛ ⲁⳝ ⳋⲁⳋ∤ⲛ)
- Septuagint manuscript 528: Aǩalǩai (ⲁⲭⲁⲗⲭⲁⳋ)
- Septuagint manuscript 799: Aǩelge (ⲁⲭⱥⳋⳋⳏ)
- Septuagint manuscript 53: Faǩelgai (ⲫⲁⲭⱥⳋⳋⲁⳋ)

- Leningrad Codex: bə'iyyê hā'Ăbārîm (בְּעִיֵּי הָעֲבָרִים). Translation: ruins of the Hebrews (or Eberites)

- Peshitta: bŏynå dŎbryå (ܚܣܝܐ ܕܥܒܪܝܐ). Translation: ruins of the Hebrews (or Eberites)

- Targum Onkelos: 'Ăbārā'ê (עֲבְרָאֵי)

- Targum Pseudo-Jonathan: məgiztā' (מְגִזְתָא). Translation: fortress

- Vetus Latina: Achiin (Achiin)

- Sahidic manuscript 2006: Aǩirgaein hi pekro hn terēmos (ⲁⲭⲓⲣⲅⲁⲉⲓⲛ ϩⲓ ⲡⲉⲕⲣⲟ ϩⲛ ⲧⲉⲣⲏⲙⲟⲥ). Translation: Akhirgaein at the edge of the desert (or wilderness, ruins)

- Sahidic manuscript 2169: Aǩalgaei ebol hm pekro hn terēmos (ⲁⲭⲁⲗⲅⲁⲉⲓ ⲉⲃⲟⲗ ϩⲙ ⲡⲉⲕⲣⲟ ϩⲛ ⲧⲉⲣⲏⲙⲟⲥ). Translation: Akhalgaei out at the edge of the desert (or wilderness, ruins)

Multiple Greek versions of this name exist, some of which mirror the Hebrew and Aramaic terms, however, most do not. As the Masoretic version claims the Israelites camped at the 'ruins of the Hebrews,' it means the Hebrews were not considered to be Israelites at the time, which is not something the Hebrew translator would have likely added to the text. This suggests that the Hebrew translation was at least partially made from a Canaanite (Judahite or Samaritan) copy of *Numbers* which included this line. The Targum Onkelos contains a variant, in treating the term as a proper place: 'Ăbārā'ê, implying that it was not universally viewed as the "ruins of the Hebrews" by Aramaic speaking people in the early-Christian era.

This likely began as a reference to the ruins of Íabru (𒌷𒅁𒊏), a city destroyed by King Amar-Sin of Ur centuries earlier, during the life of Abraham. The location is not known, however, the city was associated with four cities in the Dead Sea region, and the name suggests it was somewhere in the desert between the Iraqi marshlands and the Dead Sea. In the aftermath of the destruction of

CHAPTER 21

Íabru, Habirus began raiding all regions bordering the Syrian desert. If Moses did lead the Israelites to the ruins of Íabru, it suggests they went a long way into the desert to escape the Egyptians, and possibly to what they viewed as their ancestral homeland, as they appear to be a Habiru people.

CHAPTER 22

The children of Israel departed and camped to the west of Moab by Jordan near Jericho. When Balak son of Zippor saw all that Israel did to the Amorites, then the Moabites were extremely afraid of the people because they were many, and Moab was worried before the face of the children of Israel. Moab said to the elders of Midian, "Now will this assembly eats up all that is around us, as a calf would eat up the green plants of the field."

Balak son of Zippor was king of Moab at that time. He sent ambassadors to Balaam the son of Beor, in Ur, [1] which is in the river land, to the sons of his people,to call him, saying, "Look, people have come out of Egypt, and have covered the surface of the land, and have camped close to me. Now come and help me curse these people, for they are stronger than we are. If we can kill some of them, I will drive them out of the land, as I know that whoever you bless, they are blessed, and whoever you curse, they are cursed."

The elders of Moab went, and the elders of Midian with their divining instruments in their hands. They went to Balaam and told him the words of Balak.

He replied to them, "Wait here tonight, and I will tell you what the Lord tells me," and the princes of Moab stayed with Balaam.

CHAPTER 22

God came to Balaam, and asked him, "Who are these men with you?"

Balaam answered God, Balak son of Zippor, king of Moab, sent them to me, saying, "Look, people have come out of Egypt, and have covered the face of the land, and have camped near to me. Now come and curse them for me, so I will be able to hit them and cast them out of the land."

God said to Balaam, "You will not go with them or curse the people, for they are blessed."

Balaam rose in the morning, and told the princes of Balak, "Leave quickly to your lord, God does not permit me to go with you."

The princes of Moab rose, and returned to Balak, and told him, "Balaam will not come with us."

Balak sent more princes, more honorable princes than the first. They came to Balaam, and they said to him, "Balak the son of Zippor says, 'I beg you, don't delay coming to me. For I will greatly honor you and will do for you whatever you will say. Come then, curse these people for me."

Balaam answered the princes of Balak, "If Balak would give me his house full of silver and gold, I will not be able to go against the word of the lord of the gods, to make those people little or great in just my mind. Now, you also wait here this night, and I will hear what the Lord will say to me."

CHAPTER 22

God came to Balaam by night, and said to him, "If these men have come to call you, rise and follow them, however, the word which I will speak to you, it will you do."

Balaam rose in the morning, and saddled his donkey, and went with the princes of Moab. God was very angry because he went, and the messenger of God rose up to stop him. He had mounted his donkey, and his two servants were with him. When the donkey saw the messenger of God standing in the way, with his sword drawn in his hand, then the donkey turned away and went into the field, and Balaam struck the donkey with his wand to direct her back along the way. The messenger of God stood in the avenues of the vines, fences being on both sides. When the donkey saw the messenger of God, she thrust herself against the wall and crushed Balaam's foot against the wall, and he struck her again. The messenger of God went farther, and came and stood in a narrow place where it was impossible to turn to the right or the left. When the donkey saw the messenger of God, she lay down under Balaam, and Balaam became angry and struck the donkey with his wand. God opened the mouth of the donkey, and she asked Balaam, "What have I done to you, that you have struck me this third time?"

Balaam answered the donkey, "You have mocked me, and if I had had a sword in my hand, I would now have killed you."

The donkey replied to Balaam, "Am I not your donkey on which you have ridden since your youth until today? Did I ever do this to you, completely ignore you?"

CHAPTER 22

And he answered, "No."

God opened the eyes of Balaam, and he saw the messenger of God standing in the way, with his sword drawn in hand, and he kneeled down and worshiped on his face. The messenger of God said to him, "Why have you struck your donkey this third time? And, Look, I came out to stop you, as your path did not seem right to me, and when the donkey saw me she turned away from me this third time. If she had not turned away, I would have killed you, but would have left her alive."

Balaam replied to the messenger of God, "I have sinned, for I did not know that you were standing in the way to meet me, and now if you do not want me to go on, I will return."

The messenger of God said to Balaam, "Go with the men, however the words which I will speak to you, you will carefully repeat."

Balaam went with the princes of Balak. When Balak heard that Balaam had arrived, he went out to meet him, to a city of Moab, which is on the borders of Arnon, which is at the farthest part of the borders. Balak said to Balaam, "Didn't I send to you, and call you? Why haven't you come to me? Won't I be able to honor you?"

Balaam replied to Balak, "Look, I have now come to you. Will I be able to say something? God has put into my mouth words that I will speak."

Balaam went with Balak, and they came to the fortified city.[2] Balak offered sheep and calves and sent to Balaam and to

CHAPTER 22

his princes who were with him. It was morning, and Balak took Balaam, and brought him up to steles of Ba'al,[3] and showed him some of the people.

CHAPTER 22 NOTES

1 Codex Alexandrinus: Baṯoura (ʙᴀⲟⲟⲨⲢᴀ). Translation: of olive oil

- Septuagint manuscript 318: Baitoura (Βαιθουϱα)
- Septuagint manuscript 120: Fatourṛa (Φαθουῥϱα)
- Septuagint manuscript 121: Faṯouras (Φαθουϱας)
- Septuagint manuscript 129: Faṯyra (Φαθυϱα)
- Septuagint manuscript 616: Faboura (Φαμουϱα)
- Septuagint manuscript 75: Faṯoura (Φαθουϱα)
- Septuagint manuscript 29: Paṯoura (ΠΑθουϱα)
- Septuagint manuscript 458: Para (παϱα)
- Septuagint manuscript 550: Faṯara (Φαθαϱα)
- Septuagint manuscript 528: Fṯṯoura (Φθθουϱα)
- Septuagint manuscript 618: Baṯourō (Βαθουϱω)
- Septuagint manuscript 664: Baṯyra (Βαθυϱα)
- Septuagint manuscript 376: Fatoura (Φαⲧⲟϱα)
- Leningrad Codex: Pətôrâ (פְּתֹ֫ורָה). Translation: Petora
- Peshitta: Pšwrâ (ܦܬܘܪܐ)
- Targum Onkelos: Pərāt (פְּרָת). Translation: Euphrates
- Targum Pseudo-Jonathan: 'Ărām də'al Pərāt (אֲרָם דְּעַל פְּרָת). Translation: Aram (or Syria) on the Euphrates
- Sahidic manuscript 2006: Faṯoura (ⲫⲁⲑⲟⲨⲢⲁ)
- Sahidic manuscript 2044: Faroua (ⲫⲁⲣⲟⲨⲁ)

This city is often assumed to be the town of Pitíru (𐎓𐎐𐎚) in Assyria; however, that town was not founded until circa 1100 BCE by King Tiglath-Pileser I. The name of the city Pǝtôrâ (פְּתוֹרָה), appears to be a transliteration of the Babylonian cuneiform word paššuru (𐎁𐎗𐎛𐎜𐎍), which meant "table." The related Aramaic word was pāṯūrā (מְתוּרָא), the Syriac word was pāṯūrā (ܦܳܬܘܪܐ), and the related Arabic word is fāṯūr (فَاثُور), all of which mean "table," or "tray." The older Akkadian spelling was paššuru (𒉿), which was also the spelling of the name of the city of Ur, in southern modern Iraq. If the original text of this section of text was written before the development of the Phoenician alphabet, it would have been written in Akkadian Cuneiform, the script used in Canaan under Egyptian rule during the New Kingdom era, suggesting the transliteration error took place when the Phoenician translation was made in the early Iron Age. Wherever "Petora" was located, it was accepted in the Classical era as being somewhere along the Euphrates, as evidenced by the Targums.

2 Codex Vaticanus: poleis epauleōn (ΠΟΛΕΙC ΕΠΑΥΛΕΩΝ). Translation: city of farming (or pasture, grassland)

• Codex Ambrosiano A 147: polin epauleōn (ΠΟΛΙΝΕΠΑΥΛΕΩΝ). Translation: city of farming (or pasture, grassland)

• Septuagint manuscript 767: polis epauleōs (πολϛ ϭπΔυλϭϭοc).Translation: city of farming (or pasture, grassland)

• Leningrad Codex: qiryat ḥūṣôt (קִרְיַת חֻצוֹת). Translation: city of midnight (or noon)

• Peshitta: qwryt ḥṣrwt (ܩܘܪܝܬ ܚܨܪܘܬ). Translation: the city of scribe's reeds (pens)

• Targum Onkelos: qiryat māḥôzôhî (קִרְיַת מָחוֹזוֹהִי). Translation: city in his territories

CHAPTER 22

- Targum Pseudo-Jonathan: qartā' dəSîhôn hî' Bîrôšā' (קַרְתָּא דְסִיחוֹן הִיא בִּירוֹשָׁא). Translation: city of Sihon it's Birosha (or of cypress)

- Sahidic manuscript 2006: polis nnpsooue (ⲡⲟⲗⲓⲥ ⲛⲛⲣⲥⲟⲟⲩⲉ). Translation: town will not get wheat (or grain)

The term in the Leningrad Codex is not proper Hebrew, and appears to be an older Canaanite dialect transliterated into Hebrew. The term appears to be the Phoenician qārt ḥsrt (𐤕𐤓𐤒 𐤇𐤑𐤓𐤕), which means a "fortified town," in which a transcription error resulted in ḥsrt being copied as ḥswt. The Greek translation appears to have been from the Aramaic "city of ḥsyrh (חצירה)," meaning the "city of pasture," or "city of grass." Both "fortified" and "pasture" were spelled similarly in Aramaic (חצירה and חצר) and Phoenician (𐤇𐤑𐤓𐤕 and 𐤇𐤑𐤓), suggesting that a translation error may have happened when the name was translated into Aramaic from Phoenician, resulting in "pasture" instead of "fortified." As the Greek and Hebrew names are not directly related, the Greek name is transliterated in this translation.

3 Codex Vaticanus: stēlēn tou Baal (ⲥⲧⲏⲗⲏⲛ ⲧⲟⲩ ⲃⲁⲁⲗ). Translation: steles (or columns) of Baal

- Septuagint manuscript 407: stēlēn tou balal (ⲥⲧⲏⲗⲏⲛ ⲧⲟ ⲩⲁⲗⲁⲗ). Translation: steles (or columns) of Balal

- Septuagint manuscript 318: stēlēn tou balaak (ⲥⲧⲏⲗⲏⲛ ⲧⲟ ⲩⲁⲗⲁⲁⲕ). Translation: steles (or columns) of Balaak

- Septuagint manuscript 29: stēlēn tou balaam (ⲥⲧⲏⲗⲏⲛ ⲧⲟ ⲩⲁⲗⲁⲁⲙ). Translation: steles (or columns) of Balaam

- Septuagint manuscript 458: stolēn tou boual (ⲥⲟⲗⲏⲛ ⲧⲟ ⲩⲟⲩⲁⲗ). Translation: robes (or equipment) of Boual

- Septuagint manuscript 46: stēlēn tō balam (ⲥⲧⲏⲗⲏⲛ ⲧⲟ ⲩⲁⲗⲁⲙ). Translation: steles (or columns) of Balam

- Septuagint manuscript 72: stēlēn tō baal (ܤܛ‌ܠܘ ܛܘܘ ܘܐܐܠ). Translation: steles (or columns) of Baal
- Septuagint manuscript 528: stēlēn tō balaal (ܤܛ‌ܠܘ ܛܘ ܘܐܠܐܐܠ). Translation: steles (or columns) of Balaal
- Septuagint manuscript 664: stēlēn tou balak (ܤܛ‌ܠܘ ܛܘ ܘܐܠܐܠ). Translation: steles (or columns) of Balak
- Leningrad Codex: bāmôt Bā'al (בָּמוֹת בָּעַל). Translation: bamahs of the Lord (or Baal)
- Peshitta: bmwt bôlå (ܒܥܠܐ ܕܒܡܘܬ). Translations: bamahs of the Lord (or master, husband)
- Targum Onkelos: rāmat daḥaltêh (רָמַת דַּחַלְתֵּיהּ). Translations: hills of ossuary
- Targum Pseudo-Jonathan: rāmat daḥaltā' diP'ôr (רָמַת דַּחַלְתָּא דִּפְעוֹר). Translations: hills of the ossuary of Peor
- Vetus Latina: titulum suum ollus balac (ᴛɪᴛᴜʟᴜᴍ sᴜᴜᴍ ᴏʟʟᴜs Bᴀʟᴀᴄ). Translation: his tablets (or inscriptions) of Balac
- Sahidic manuscript 2006: stēlē mpbahal (ⲤⲦⲎⲎ ⲘⲠⲂⲀ2ⲀⲀ). Translation: pillar of Ba'al

The ancient Canaanites used to worship the gods on mountaintops or hilltops, where they erected altars as Moses had described in Exodus, along with Asherah (oak) trees. In Phoenician and Hebrew, these were known as Bamahs, which the Greeks translated as steles. The term Greek word βααλ is clearly a transliteration of the Hebrew term ba'al (בַּעַל), which translates as Lord, however, was applied to many lords.

The Balaam ben Beor is known from the Deir Alla Inscription (KAI 312) to have been the prophet of multiple gods, including Elohim (𐤉𐤆𐤀𐤋�), Shaddai (𐤉𐤆𐤀𐤅), Ishtar (𐤀𐤕𐤅𐤏), and Saggar (𐤀𐤂𐤅𐤔). While the inscription dates to the 800s BCE, the inclusion of Saggar placed to origin of the list in the bronze age, as Saggar was a

CHAPTER 22

Mesopotamian god whose worship had disappeared in Canaan and Syria by the early iron age. Earlier in the 3rd millennium BCE, he had been viewed as the husband of Ishara in Elba, however, like many older gods from the region, was not viewed as important to the Amorites. He later resurfaced in the Hurrian religion with Adamma and other older gods under the rule of the Mitanni Empire, however, his worship disappeared in Canaan and Syria after the fall of the Mitanni Empire. This suggests that the prophecy of Balaam was made no later than the 1300s BCE.

The Targums use variations of the term dahaltêh, meaning ossuary, which is also used as a translation for Asherah in other verses. In Canaan, oak trees were planted above the graves of important kings as "living gravestones," and according to the Targum Jerusalem, this was the ossuary of the Lord of Peor.

CHAPTER 23

Balaam said to Balak, "Build seven altars for me here, and prepare more calves for me, and seven rams."

Balak did as Balaam told him, and he offered up a calf and a ram on each altar. Balaam said to Balak, "Stand by your sacrifice, and I will go and see if God will come and meet me, and the words which he will tell me, I will report to you."

Balak stood by his sacrifice. Balaam went to inquire of God, and he went straight forward, and God appeared to Balaam, and Balaam said to him, I have prepared the seven altars, and have offered a calf and a ram on every altar. God put a word into the mouth of Balaam, and said, "You will return to Balak, this is what you will say."

He returned to him, and moreover, he stood over his whole burnt offerings, and all the princes of Moab with him, and the Spirit of God came on him. He told his story, and said, "Balak king of Moab sent for me out of Mesopotamia, out of the mountains of the east, saying, 'Come, curse Jacob for me, and come, call a curse for me on Israel.' How will I pray if not calling down curse of the Lord, or what will I curse if not calling down the curse of god?[1] From the top of the mountains, I will see him, and from the hills, I will watch him. Look, the people will live alone, and will not be considered among the nations. Who has exactly calculated the seed of Jacob, and who will number the families of Israel? Let my mind die with the minds of the righteous, and let my seed be as their seed."

Balak said to Balaam, "What have you done to me? I called you to curse my enemies, and you have greatly blessed them!"

Balaam said to Balak, "Whatever the Lord will put into my mouth, won't I speak it exactly?"

Balak said to him, "Come with me to another place where you will not see them, and you will see only a part of them and will not see them all. Curse them from there." He took him to a high place of the field to the top of the quarried rock, and there he built seven altars, and offered a calf and a ram on each altar."

Balaam said to Balak, "Stand by your sacrifice, and I will go to inquire of God. God met Balaam, and put a word into his mouth, and said, "Return to Balak, and is what you will say."

He returned to him, and stood by his whole burnt sacrifice, and all the princes of Moab were with him, and Balak asked him, "What has the Lord said?"

He continued his parable, and said, "Rise Balak and hear, listen as a witness, you son of Zippor. God is not as man to waver, nor like a human[2] to be threatened. Won't he do what he says? Will he speak and not keep to his word? Look, I have received commandment to bless, and I will bless, and not turn back. There will not be trouble in Jacob, neither will sorrow be seen in Israel, the lord of the gods is with him, the glories of rulers are in him. It was God who brought him out of

Egypt like the glory of his gazelle.[3] For there is no divination against Jacob, nor enchantment in Israel. In time, it will be told to Jacob and Israel what will God perform. The people will rise like a lion's cub who will exalt himself as a lion, he will not lie down until he has eaten the prey, and he will drink the blood of the slain."

Balak said to Balaam, "Neither curse him at all for me nor bless them at all."

Balaam answered and said to Balak, "Didn't I say to you, 'Whatever God will tell me, that will I do?'"

Balak said to Balaam, "Come, and I will move you to another place if it will please God, and curse them for me from there. Balak took Balaam to the top of Peor, which extends to the wilderness.

Balaam said to Balak, "Build here seven altars for me, and prepare seven calves from me, and seven rams."

Balak did as Balaam told him, and offered a calf and a ram on every altar.

CHAPTER 23 NOTES

1 Codex Vaticanus: ti arasōmai on mē kataratai $\overline{KS}$ ē ti katarasōmai on mēkataratai o $\overline{TS}$ (ΤΙ ΑΡΑϹΩΜΑΙ ΟΝ ΜΗ ΚΑΤΑΡΑΤΑΙ $\overline{KC}$ Η ΤΙ ΚΑΤΑΡΑϹΩΜΑΙΟΝΜΗΚΑΤΑΡΑΤΑΙΟ$\overline{ΘC}$). Translation: what will I pray to if not call down curse of lord, or what will I call down curses if not calling down curse of god

• Codex Alexandrinus: ti arasomai on mē aratai o $\overline{KS}$ ē tikatarasomai onmēkatarataio $\overline{TS}$ (ΤΙΑΡΑϹΟΜΑΙΟΝΜΗΑΡΑΤΑΙΟ $\overline{KC}$Η ΤΙΚΑΤΑΡΑϹΟΜΑΙΟΝΜΗΚΑΤΑΡΑΤΑΙΟ $\overline{ΘC}$). Translation: what will I pray to if not praying to the lord, or what will I call down curses if not calling down curse of god

• Codex Venetus: ti arasomai on mē aratai $\overline{KS}$ ē ti epikatarasomai on mē kataratai o $\overline{TS}$ (ΤΙ ΑΡΑϹΟΜΑΙ ΟΝ ΜΗ ΑΡΑΤΑΙ $\overline{KC}$ Η ΤΙ ΕΠΙΚΑΤΑΡΑϹΟΜΑΙ ΟΝ ΜΗ ΚΑΤΑΡΑΤΑΙ Ο $\overline{ΘC}$). Translation: what will I pray to if not praying to lord, or what will I call down curses if not calling down curse of the god

• Septuagint manuscript 55: ti arasamai on mē kataratai o kurios ṯeos ē ti katarasomai on mēkataratai o ṯeos (Ἡ αρλϹαμαι ⊕ μ̀λ καταρλται ο ιυβιος θόος λ Ἡ καταρλσομαι ⊕ μ̀λκαταρλται ο θόος). Translation: what will I pray to if not call down curse of lord god, or what will I call down curses if not calling down curse of god

• Septuagint manuscript 58: ti katarasomai on mē kataratai o kurios ē ti arasomai on mē aratai o ṯeos (Ἡ καταρλσομαι ⊕ μ̀λ καταρλται ο ιυβιος λ Ἡ αρλσομαι ⊕ μ̀λ αρλται ο θόος). Translation: what will I call down curses if not calling down curses of lord, or what will I pray to if not praying to the god

• Septuagint manuscript 73: ti arasomai on mē aratai o $\overline{KS}$ ē ti kataratai KS ē ti arasomai on mē aratai o $\overline{TS}$ (Ἡ αρλσομαι ⊕ μ̀λ αρλται ο ΚΣ λ Ἡ καταρλται ΚΣ λ Ἡ αρλσομαι ⊕ μ̀λ αρλται ο ΘΣ). Translation: what will I pray to if not praying to lord or calling down curses from lord, or what will I pray to if not praying to the god

• Septuagint manuscript 426: ti arasomai on mē aratai o $\overline{KS}$ ē ti katarasomai on mē kataratai o $\overline{TS}$ $\overline{KS}$ (Ἡ αρλσομαι ⊕ μ̀λ αρλται ΚΣ λ Ἡ καταρλσομαι ⊕ μ̀λ καταρλται ο ΘΣ ΚΣ). Translation: what will I pray to if not praying to lord or what will I call down curses to if not calling down curses from the god lord

• Septuagint manuscript 458: ti arasomai on tropon mē kataratai o kurios kai eti katarasomai on mē kataratai o teos (ʈɩ αρλσομαɩ ⊕ τϱϱπ⊕ μλ κατορλται ο ιυβιος ιɩαɩ σ̌ι κατορλσομαɩ ⊕ μλ κατορλται ο θσ̌ος). Translation: what will I pray to if not decreeing down curses of lord, and furthermore will I bring down curses if not cursing by the god

• Septuagint manuscript 767: ti arasōmai on mē arasetai kurios kai eti katarasōmai on mē katarasetai o teos (ʈɩ αρλϚωμαɩ ⊕ μλ αρλσσ̌ται ιυβιος ιɩαɩ σ̌ι κατορλϚωμαɩ ⊕ μλ κατορλσσ̌ται ο θσ̌ος). Translation: what will I pray to if not praying to lord, and what will I bring down curses from if not bringing down curses by the god

• Leningrad Codex: mâ 'eqqōb lō' qabbōh 'Ēl ûmâ 'ez'ōm lō' zā'am Yəhwâ (מֶה אֶקֹּב לֹא קַבֹּה אֵל וּמֶה אֶזְעֹם לֹא זָעַם יְהוָה). Translation: how will I declare something not declared by El and how do I curse not cursed by Yehwah

• Peshitta: mnâ âlwtywhy: dlâ lth âlhå: wmnâ âwbdywhy: dlå âwbdh mryâ (ܡܢܐ ܐܠܘܛܝܘܗܝ: ܕܠܐ ܠܬܗ ܐܠܗܐ: ܘܡܢܐ ܐܘܒܕܝܘܗܝ: ܕܠܐ ܐܘܒܕܗ ܡܪܝܐ). Translations: how do I curse when not cursed by god and how do I curse when not cursed by master

• Targum Onkelos: mā' 'ălôtêh dəlā' latyēh 'ēl ûmā' 'ătārəkêh dəlā' tārəkêh Yəyā (מָא אֲלוֹטֵיה דְלָא לַטְיֵה אֵל וּמָא אֲתָרְכֵיה דְלָא תָרְכֵיה יְיָ). Translations: how do I purify when not purifying by god (or El) and how do I divine anger when not enraging Yahweh

• Targum Jerusalem: mâ 'ănā' layît dəbêt ya'ăqb ûmêmərā' daYyā məbārēk yathôn ûmâ 'ănā' maz'êr dəbêt Yišrā'ēl ûmêmərā' daYyā masgê yathôn (מָה אֲנָא לַיְיט דְבֵית יַעֲקב וּמֵימְרָא דַיְיְ מְבָרֵךְ יַתְהוֹן וּמָה אֲנָא מַזְעֵיר דְבֵית יִשְׂרָאֵל וּמֵימְרָא דַיְיְ מַסְגֵי יַתְהוֹן). Translation: what can I purify the house of Jacob and the command of Yahweh himself, and how can I make small the house of Israel and the command of Yahweh himself?

179

CHAPTER 23

• Sahidic manuscript 2006: naš nhe einašcalhou mpetempepnoute sahou mmof ē je etbe ou tnahoouš mpetempepnoute hoouš erof (ⲚⲀϢ ⲚϨⲈ ⲈⲒⲚⲀϢⲤⲀϨⲞⲨ ⲘⲠⲈⲦⲈⲘⲠⲈⲠⲚⲞⲨⲦⲈ ⲤⲀϨⲞⲨ ⲘⲘⲞϤ Ⲏ ⲬⲈ ⲈⲦⲂⲈ ⲞⲨ ⲦⲚⲀϨⲞⲞⲨϢ ⲘⲠⲈⲦⲈⲘⲠⲈⲠⲚⲞⲨⲦⲈ ϨⲞⲞⲨϢ ⲈⲢⲟϥ). Translation: and who fell and will draw a curse from him and because of a commandment which is not from God to curse regarding him

2 Codex Vaticanus: uios antrōpou (ⲨⲒⲞⲤ ⲀⲚⲐⲢⲰⲠⲞⲨ). Translation: son of human

• Leningrad Codex: ben-'ādām (בֶן־אָדָם). Translation: son of Adam (or human)

• Peshitta: brnšå (ܒܪܢܫܐ). Translation: son of mortal (or human)

• Targum Onkelos: bənê 'ĕnāšā' (בְּנֵי אֲנָשָׁא). Translations: son of mortal (or human)

• Targum Jerusalem: bənê 'ĕnāšā' (בְּנֵי אֲנָשָׁא). Translations: son of mortal (or human)

• Targum Pseudo-Jonathan: bənê bîšărā' (בְּנֵי בִישְׂרָא). Translation: sons of flesh (or meat, milk)

• Sahidic manuscript 2006: šēre nrōme (ϢⲎⲢⲈ ⲚⲢⲰⲘⲈ). Translation: child of human

3 Codex Vaticanus: ōs doxa monokerōtos autō (ⲰⲤ ⲆⲞⲜⲀ ⲘⲞⲚⲞⲔⲈⲢⲰⲦⲞⲤ ⲀⲨⲦⲰ). Translation: just like like glory (or splendor) unicorn (one-horn) his (or hers, its)

• Leningrad Codex: kətô'ăpōt rə'ēm lô (כְּתוֹעֲפֹת רְאֵם לוֹ). Translation: like flying-symbol gazelle (or onyx) his

• Peshitta: bŏwšnh wbrwmh (ܒܥܘܫܢܗ ܘܒܪܘܡܗ). Translation: with (or in, from) power (or strength, mass, firmness) and with (or in, from) glory (or elevation, height)

- Targum Onkelos: tûqəpā' wərûmā' dîlÊh (תּוּקְפָּא וְרוֹמָא דִּילֵיהּ).
Translation: strength (or solidness) and greatness of the Yah

- Targum Jerusalem: tûqəpā' wətûšəbaḥtā' wərôməmûtā' dîdêh
hî' (תּוּקְפָּא וְתוּשְׁבַּחְתָּא וְרוֹמְמוּתָא דִּידֵיהּ הִיא). Translation: strength (or
anger, attacking) and praise (or singing, wisdom) and great-death
(or great Mot) which is his (or hers, its)

- Targum Pseudo-Jonathan: tûqəpā' wərôməmûtā' tûšəbəhā'
ûgəbûrətā' dîdêh hû' (תּוּקְפָּא וְרוֹמְמוּתָא תּוּשְׁבְּחָא וּגְבוּרְתָּא דִּידֵיהּ הוּא).
Translation: strength (or anger, attacking) and and great-death (or
great Mot) great glory (or praise) and superiority which are his (or
hers, its)

- Vetus Latina manuscripts: cujus fortitudo similis est unicornis
(ᴄᴜᴊᴜꜱ ꜰᴏʀᴛɪᴛᴜᴅᴏ ꜱɪᴏɪʟɪꜱ ᴇꜱᴛ ᴜɴɪᴄᴏʀɴɪꜱ). Translation: with strength
like a unicorn (or one-horn)

- Codex Gothicus Legionensis (VL 91): cujus fortitudo similis est
rhinocerotis (ᴄᴜᴊᴜꜱ ꜰᴏʀᴛɪᴛᴜᴅᴏ ꜱɪᴏɪʟɪꜱ ᴇꜱᴛ ʀʜɪɴᴏᴄᴇʀᴏᴛɪꜱ).
Translation: with strength like a rhinoceros.

- Sahidic manuscript 2006: nṬE mpeoou noumonokerōs (ⲚⲐⲈ
ⲘⲠⲈⲞⲞⲨ ⲚⲞⲨⲘⲞⲚⲞⲔⲈⲢⲰⲤ). Translation: the God in glory of your
unicorn

The Greek word monokerōtos (μονοκερωτος) referred to the
Asian rhinoceros, which, unlike the African rhinoceros, only has
one horn. This term was translated directly into the old Latin
translation as unicornis, the origin of the English word unicorn. By
the beginning of the 5th century, Greek influence in Persia and
India had been lost, and the term monokerōtos was rare enough that
Jerome substituted the more common rhinoceros (rhinocerotis) in
his Orthodox Latin translation.

The Greek interpretation of monokerōtos for the animal referred
to as rə'ēm (רְאֵם) in the Masoretic text, appears to be based on the
description of the animal in the book of Job, which appears to have

been translated either earlier than, or at the same time as the Torah, however, all commentators agree that the translation of 'Asian rhinoceros' is almost certainly incorrect in this verse. Most modern translations either use the term unicorn, from the Greek text, or gazelle or oryx from the Hebrew text.

The Hebrew word rə'ēm (רְאֵם) is descended from the Akkadian rimu (𒌑) meaning wild bull, and the Ugaritic rwm (𐎗𐎆𐎎) meaning gazelle or wild buffalo. The related Arabic word rīm (ريم) means oryx. Based on the reference in *Daniel*, Rə'ēm was probably the old Canaanite name of a constellation, either Taurus or Aries, however, this is also probably not what this verse was in reference to.

The gazelle or oryx was also the symbol of the Amorite god Resheph, and his subsequent reinterpretation as Shed during the Egyptian New Kingdom era. As Resheph, later reinterpreted as Shaddai, appears to be the god of Abraham and Moses, this would be a reference to his power leading the Israelites out of Egypt.

Alternatively, the Hebrew word rā'im (רָאֵם) could be interpreted as "high," which influenced the Peshitta and Targums. In Judeo-Aramaic, rûmā' (רוּמָא) translates as "great;" however, this interpretation is clearly not how the Greek translators viewed the term. It appears to have been part of the ongoing attempts to make the text fit the theology of the era. As the translations of rhinoceros and unicorn both appear to be incorrect, the term gazelle is imported from the Leningrad Codex.

CHAPTER 24

When Balaam saw that it pleased God to bless Israel, he did not do according to his custom to cast the omens but turned his face towards the wilderness. Balaam lifted his eyes and saw Israel camped in their tribes, and the spirit of God came over him. He continued, and Balaam son of Beor said, "The man who sees honestly says; he who claims he hears the words of El, who sees Shaddayin,[1] he who sees in sleep with his eyes open says: How good are your habitations, Jacob, and your tents, Israel? Like shady groves, and like gardens by a river, and like tents which God pitched, and like cedars by the waters."

"There will come a man out of his seed, and he will rule over many nations, and be exalted over Agog[2] his king, and his kingdom will be increased. God led him out of Egypt like the glory of the gazelle! He will consume the nations of his enemies, and he will suck the marrow out of their fat bones, and with his darts, he will shoot through the enemy. He laid down, and he rested like a lion, and like a lion cub, who will stir him up? They who bless you are blessed. And they who curse you are cursed."

Balak was angry with Balaam and clasped his hands together. Balak said to Balaam, "I called you to curse my enemy, and Look! You have decidedly blessed him three times! Now flee to your home! I said, 'I will honor you,' but now the Lord has deprived you of glory."

CHAPTER 24

Balaam said to Balak, "Did I not tell the messengers you sent to me, 'If Balak should give me his house full of silver and gold, I will not be able to go against the word of the Lord to make it good or bad by myself? Whatever things God will say, them will I speak. Now, Look, I return to my home. Come, I will advise you of what these people will do to your people in the last days."

He continued his parable and said, "Balaam the son of Beor says; the man who sees truly says; hearing the words of El, knowing knowledge from Elyon, (and seeing Shaddayin; who forecasts) with open eyes.[3] I will point to him, but not now. I bless him, but he does not come close. A star will rise out of Jacob, a man will spring out of Israel, and will crush the princes of Moab, and will ruin all the sons of Seth. Edom will be an inheritance, and Esau his enemy will be an inheritance of Israel, and Israel will be valiant. One will arise out of Jacob, and destroy out of the city he who escapes."

Having seen Amalek, he continued and said, "Amalek is the first of the nations, yet his seed will perish."

Having seen the blacksmiths,[4] he continued and said, "Your living-place is strong, yet though you should put your nest in a rock, and though Beor should have a nest of cunning, the Assyrians will carry you away captive."

He looked at Og, and continued his parable, and said, "Oh, oh, who will live, when God will put these things? A hand will come from Cyprus,[5] and will attack Assyria, and will attack the Habirus,[6] and they will die together."[7]

CHAPTER 24

Balaam rose and departed and returned to his place, and Balak went to his own home.

CHAPTER 24 NOTES

1 Codex Vaticanus: fēsin akouōn logia $\overline{TU}$ ostis orasin $\overline{TU}$ eiden en upnō, apokekalummenoi oi oftalmoi autou (ΦΗⲤΙΝ ΑΚΟΥⲰΝ ΛΟΓΙΑ $\overline{ΘΥ}$ ⲞⲤΤΙⳅ ⲞⲢΑⳅΙΝ $\overline{ΘΥ}$ ⲈΙΔⲈΝ ⲈΝ ΥΤΤΝⲰ ΑΤΤⲞΚⲈΚΑΛΥΜΜⲈΝⲞΙ ⲞΙ ⲞΦⲐΑΛΜⲞΙ ΑΥΤⲞΥ). Translation: says hears (or listens, understands) words (or logic) god who sees god perceives in sleep (or trance) revealed the eyes his

• Codex Alexandrinus: fēsin akouōn logia $\overline{TU}$ iskǔrou ostis orasin $\overline{TU}$ eiden en upnō apokekalummenoi oi oftalmoi autou (ΦΗⲤΙΝ ΑΚΟΥⲰΝ ΛΟΓΙΑ $\overline{ΘΥ}$ ΙⲤΧΥⲢⲞΥ ⲞⲤΤΙⳅ ⲞⲢΑⳅΙΝ $\overline{ΘΥ}$ ⲈΙΔⲈΝ ⲈΝ ΥΤΤΝⲰ ΑΤΤⲞΚⲈΚΑΛΥΜΜⲈΝⲞΙ ⲞΙ ⲞΦⲐΑΛΜⲞΙ ΑΥΤⲞΥ). Translation: says hears (or listens, understands) words (or logic) strong who sees god strong perceives in sleep (or trance) revealed the eyes his

• Codex Ambrosiano A 147: fēsin ostis orasin $\overline{TU}$ eiden en upnō apokekalummenoi oi oftalmoi autou (ΦΗⲤΙΝ ⲞⲤΤΙⳅ ⲞⲢΑⳅΙΝ $\overline{ΘΥ}$ ⲈΙΔⲈΝ ⲈΝ ΥΤΤΝⲰ ΑΤΤⲞΚⲈΚΑΛΥΜΜⲈΝⲞΙ ⲞΙ ⲞΦⲐΑΛΜⲞΙ ΑΥΤⲞΥ). Translation: says words (or logic) god who sees god perceives in sleep (or trance) revealed the eyes his

• Codex Venetus: fēsin o akouōn logia teou ostis orasin teou eiden en upnō, apokekalummenoi oi oftalmoi autou (ϕ⳱σιν ο ἀκουων ϐγιἀ θ⳱ου οϛις οϱασιν θ⳱ου ᶲλαν αν υπνοο, ἀπολιⳙκα λυμμ⳵ϴ ϴ οϕⲐΑλμϴ λυτω). Translation: says the hears (or listens, understands) words (or logic) god who sees god perceives in sleep (or trance) revealed the eyes his

• Septuagint manuscript 616: fēsin akouōn logia iskǔrōs ostis orasin teou eiden en upnō, apokekalummenoi oi oftalmoi autou (ϕ⳱σιν

185

ακουοον /ογιλ ισχυρως ος ις ορα σιν θεου ϳλαν αν υπνοο, απολιϭκα λυμμϕⲱ ⲱ οϣθλλμⲱ λυτο). Translation: says hears (or listens, understands) words (or logic) strong who sees god perceives in sleep (or trance) revealed the eyes his

- Septuagint manuscript 246: fēsin akouōn logia isǩurou fēsin oantrōpos oalētinōs orōn ostis orasin teou eiden en upnō, apokekalummenoi oi oftalmoi autou (ϣⳑⲟⲓⲛ ακουοον /ογιλ ισχυρου ϣⳑⲟⲓⲛ οϕⳡϸⲟⲟⲡⲟⲥ οαλⳑϸⲛⲟⲟⲥ ορων ος ις ορα σιν θεου ϳλαν αν υπνοο, απολιϭκα λυμμϕⲱ ⲱ οϣθλλμⲱ λυτο). Translation: says hears (or listens, understands) words (or logic) of strong speaks as human genuine (or truthful) watcher (or eyes) who sees god perceives in sleep (or trance) revealed the eyes his

- Septuagint manuscript 72: fēsin logia isǩura ostis orasin isǩuraeiden en upnō, apokekalummenoi oi oftalmoi autou (ϣⳑⲟⲓⲛ /ογιλ ισχυρα ος ις ορα σιν ισχυρα ϳλαν αν υπνοο, απολιϭκα λυμμϕⲱ ⲱ οϣθλλμⲱ λυτο). Translation: says hears (or listens, understands) words (or logic) strong who sees god perceives in sleep (or trance) revealed the eyes his

- Septuagint manuscript 59: fēsin kai akouōn logia isǩura ostis orasin teou eiden en upnō, apokekalummenoi oi oftalmoi autou (ϣⳑⲟⲓⲛ ⳑⲁⳇ ακουοον /ογιλ ισχυρα ος ις ορα σιν θεου ϳλαν αν υπνοο, απολιϭκα λυμμϕⲱ ⲱ οϣθλλμⲱ λυτο). Translation: says and hears (or listens, understands) words (or logic) of strength who sees god perceives in sleep (or trance) revealed the eyes his

- Leningrad Codex: nə'ūm šōmēa' 'imrê-'Ēl 'ăšer mahăzēh Šadday yehĕzeh nōpēl ûgəlûy 'ênāyim (נְאֻם שֹׁמֵעַ אִמְרֵי־אֵל אֲשֶׁר מַחֲזֵה שַׁדַּי יֶחֱזֶה נֹפֵל וּגְלוּי עֵינָיִם). Translation: declares hears pronouncement of El (or god) who sees Shaddai (or demonic) forecasts fall and manifest eyes

- Peshitta: åmr dšmȯ måmrå dålhå: whzwå dålhå hzå: kd rmå wptyhn ȯynwhy (ܐܡܪ ܕܫܡܥ ܡܐܡܪܐ ܕܐܠܗܐ: ܘܚܙܘܐ ܕܐܠܗܐ ܚܙܐ: ܟܕ ܪܡܐ ܘܦܬܝܚܝܢ ܥܝܢܘܗܝ

CHAPTER 24

‎בד דתכא ܗܦܠܐܣ ܚܣܗܡ,). Translation: he spoke the discourse of god, and prophesied for god visions, with wide open eyes

• Targum Onkelos: 'ēmar dišma' mēmar min qŏdām 'Ēl wəhēzû min qŏdām Šadday hāzē šəkîb ûmitgəlê lêh (אֲמַר דְּשָׁמַע מֵימַר מִן קֳדָם ‎אֵל וַחֲזוֹ מִן קֳדָם שַׁדַּי חֲזֵי שְׁכִיב וּמִתְגְּלֵי לֵיהּ). Translations: he spoke and heard the command (or word) proceeding from god (or El) and saw proceeding from god (or El) Shaddai (or powerful) and recognizes while laying down and revealed by Yah (or woe)

• Targum Jerusalem: 'êmar gabrā' dišma' mamlēl min qŏdām Yəyā wədî ḥăzā' min qŏdām Šaday ḥăzê wəkad ḥăwâ bā'ê ḥăwâ ništataḥ 'al 'appôy wərāzē nəbû'ātā' mitgalîn lêh wahăwâ mitnabbê 'al napšêh dəhû' nāpîl bəharbā' wəsôp nəbû'ātā' ləmitqayymā' (אֵימַר ‎גַבְרָא דְּשָׁמַע מַמְלֵל מִן קֳדָם יְיָ וְדִי חֲזָא מִן קֳדָם שַׁדַי חֲזֵי וְכַד הֲוָה הֲוָה ‎נִשְׁתַּטַּח עַל אַפּוֹי וְרָזֵי נְבוּאֲתָא מִתְגְּלִין לֵיהּ וַהֲוָה מִתְנַבֵּי עַל נַפְשֵׁיהּ דְּהוּא נָפִיל ‎בְּחַרְבָּא וְסוֹף נְבוּאֲתָא לְמִתְקַיְּימָא). Translation: spoke man the heard speech from before Yahweh, and perceived knowledge from before Shaddai's vision (or aperture), and when he himself saw it, he stretched out on his face, and came to him revelation of Yah, and produced prophecies from the mind (or soul) of he, Orion's (or Napil's) sword (or dry gust). And he penned (or finished, wrote) his prophecy, and it will happen.

• Targum Pseudo-Jonathan: 'êmar dišma' mēmar min qŏdām 'ĕlāhā' hayāy' dəhēziyû min qŏdām 'Ēl Šaday ḥăwâ ḥāmê wəkad bā'ê dəmitgəlê lÊh ḥăwâ mištataḥ 'al 'anpôy wərazyā' sətîmayā' mâ də'itkasê min nəbiyā' mitgəlê lÊh (אֵימַר דְּשָׁמַע מֵימַר מִן קֳדָם אֱלָהָא ‎חַיָּיא דְּחֲזִיּוּ מִן קֳדָם אֵל שַׁדַי הֲוָה חֲמֵי וְכַד בָּעֵי דְּמִתְגְּלֵי לֵיהּ הֲוָה מִשְׁתַּטַּח עַל ‎אַנְפּוֹי וְרָזַיָּא סְתִימַיָא מָה דְּאִתְכַּסֵּי מִן נְבִיָּא מִתְגְּלֵי לֵיהּ). Translation: spoke the heard command (or word) from before god and perceived the heat within from god Shaddai, who produced the vision, and when he saw from Yahweh, he fell on his face, and a powerful (or strong) storm (or winter storm) of revelation departed the prophet praising to Yahweh.

• Sahidic manuscript 2006: entafnay etorasis mpnoute efobal holp ebol (ⲉⲛⲧⲁϥⲛⲁⲩ ⲉⲑⲟⲣⲁⲥⲓⲥ ⲙⲡⲛⲟⲩⲧⲉ ⲉϥⲟⲃⲱ ⲉⲣⲉⲛⲉϥⲃⲁⲗ ϭⲟⲗⲡ ⲉⲃⲟⲗ). Translation: then he saw the vision of the god in his sleep when his eyes were revealed

• Sahidic manuscript 2169: entafnay etorasis mpnoute hn ouōbš holp ebol (ⲉⲛⲧⲁϥⲛⲁⲩ ⲉⲑⲟⲣⲁⲥⲓⲥ ⲙⲡⲛⲟⲩⲧⲉ ϩⲛ ⲟⲩⲱⲃⲱ ⲉⲣⲉⲛⲉϥⲃⲁⲗ ϭⲟⲗⲡ ⲉⲃⲟⲗ). Translation: then he saw the vision of the god in white when his eyes were revealed

The shortened Greek verse was almost certainly already in the Aramaic translations they worded from, as it is part of a pattern of redacting Shaddai from the version of the Torah that ended up in the Septuagint. The name was translated into Greek as "omnipotent" (παντοκρατοροσ) in the Septuagint's *Job*, and transliterated directly into Greek as Saddai (Σαδδαι) in *Ezekiel*, however, is entirely missing from *Cosmic Genesis* while appearing six times in the *Bereshít*, the Hebrew translation.

The term "god Šdy" (אל-שדי) is used repeatedly in Bereshít regarding the god of Abraham, Isaac, and Jacob, however, does not show up in the Septuagint's *Cosmic Genesis*, where "the Lord" or "god" are used instead. The term ål Šdy was only used 48 times in the Masoretic texts, including 31 times in *Job*, 6 times in *Bereshít*, and once in *Names*, when Moses' god identified himself as the god of Jacob, however, the name Ōn (Ὠν) is used *Exodus'* version of the verse. *Cosmic Genesis* and *Names* appear to have been both redacted in regards to the identity of ål Šdy, as there is no reference to ål Šdy in *Cosmic Genesis*, and there is no reference to Ōn in *Names*. In Numbers, it appears the Aramaic translator simply omitted it, as it appears twice in the Leningrad Codex version, both times in the list of gods that Balaam was the prophet of, making it easy to omit.

CHAPTER 24

The Septuagint and Masoretic translations often differ in regards to the name or title Shaddai, suggesting that the Aramaic and Canaanite source texts they worked from differed in regards to this word. The cause of the confusion over the term Shaddai, is likely due to the difference between the meaning of the word in Canaanite versus Aramaic. In Akkadian cuneiform, which was adopted as the written script by many cultures, the term was ^{deity}šēdu (✳⽥), however, it referred to a "protective spirit" or "lesser god." In the later Aramaic language, the word became šydå (ᴎ𐤉^Ʋ), meaning 'demon' in the classical sense, as a type of muse or nymph. Whereas in Canaanite, šdy (ᴢ𐤀ᴡ) took on different meaning, generally interpreted as "powerful" by the Early Classical Era, which is likely where the Greeks ultimately derived the term "omnipotent" (παντοκράτοροσ), which was used later in the Septuagint where the Masoretic Text generally uses the term šdy.

This alternate interpretation of the šdy (ᴢ𐤀ᴡ) in Canaanite is likely due to the Egyptian New Kingdom era rule over Canaan, when Shed (🖙╾⽥, transliteration: šd), was worshiped in the region. Shed, who was often referred to as 'the savior,' was virtually identical to the earlier Canaanite god Resheph who was largely suppressed after the fall of the Hyksos dynasty.

In the Masoretic Book of Job, Eliphaz referred to humanity as the "sons of Resheph" (בני-רשף) instead of the 'sons of Adam,' and then uses Šdy as the name of a god. This god Šdy was explicitly listed alongside the god El in Masoretic Job, whereas in the Septuagint's Job they are not explicitly listed as two separate gods. The Greek translation of Šdy (שדי) in Job is consistent with most of the Septuagint, using a term that translates as "omnipotent" (παντοκράτοροσ), however, the name El (אל) is generally translated as a word meaning "strong" (ἰσχυρὸσ). It is likely because the Masoretic Text lists them side by side, as 'god El and god Šdy,' (אל-אל ואל-שדי), which the Greek translators did not do, instead

189

routinely dropping the second reference to a god when they were listed together.

The terms "god Šdy" (אל-שדי) and "god El" (אל-אל) are repeatedly found in Masoretic Job, and are themselves direct translations of the same terms in Akkadian Cuneiform: deityšēdu (✳⊟) and deityAn (✳✳). Unfortunately, the Akkadian meaning of the word šēdu was "demonic," which is likely the cause of it's redaction. Based on the linguistics of Masoretic Job, the text book existed in a hieratic Canaanite form during the Hyksos Dynasty, and therefore the name Resheph is not out of place, as Resheph was one of the main gods of the Hyksos rulers.

During subsequent the New Kingdom era, Resheph worship was suppressed due to his associated with the earlier Hyksos dynasty. During the early New Kingdom era, holy texts about Resheph would have been updated to Shed (𓏏𓂝𓈙), which would have been transliterated into Canaanite using the Akkadian Cuneiform script in the late New Kingdom era as deityšēdu (✳⊟), before being translated into Canaanite using the Phoenician script in the early iron age as šdy (𐤔𐤃𐤉), resulting in the confusing "demonic" (𐤔𐤉𐤃) god in Aramaic.

This word has not survived among the Dead Sea Scrolls, however, 4QNumb does have a partial copy of this verse which is significantly shorter than the Masoretic version, indicating that the verse was still being rewritten during the Hasmonean Dynasty (140 to 37 BCE). As the Deir Alla Inscription (KAI 312), which was carved in Moabite between 880 and 770 BCE confirms that Balaam was a prophet of several gods, including Šdyn (𐤔𐤃𐤉𐤍), generally anglicized as Shaddayin, the Moabite name of the god is restored in this translation, along with the names of El and Elyon from the Leningrad Codex.

2 Codex Vaticanus: Gōg (ܪܘܓ)

- Septuagint manuscript 319: Ōg (ωγ)
- Septuagint manuscript 127: Agōg (Ἀγωγ)
- Septuagint manuscript 44: Gōb (ܪܘܒ)
- Leningrad Codex: 'Ăgag (אֲגַג)
- Peshitta: Ăgg (ܐܓܓ)
- Targum Onkelos: 'Ăgag (אֲגַג)
- Targum Jerusalem: 'Ăgag (אֲגַג)
- Targum Pseudo-Jonathan: 'Ăgag (אֲגַג)
- Vetus Latina: Gog (Ϛοϛ)
- Sahidic manuscript 2006: Gōg (Ϩωг)

3 Codex Vaticanus: akouōn logia T̄U epistamenos epistēmēn parausistou kai orasin T̄U idōn en upnō apokekalummenoi oi oftalmoi autou (ΑΚΟΥШΝ ΛΟΓΙΑ ΟΥ ΕΠΙϹΤΑΜΕΝΟϹ ΕΠΙϹΤΗΜΗΝ ΠΑΡΑΥϯΙϹΤΟΥ ΚΑΙ ΟΡΑϹΙΝ ΟΥ ΙΔШΝ ΕΝ ΥΠΝШ ΑΠΟΚΕΚΑΛΥΜΜΕΝΟΙΟΙΟΦΘΑΛΜΟΙΑΥΤΟΥ). Translation: hear (or listen, understand) words of god knows knowledge highest and sees god perceives in sleep (or trance) revealed the eyes his

- Septuagint manuscript 55: akoúōn lógia kuepistámenos epistēmēn usístou kai orasin teou eiden en upnō apokekalumménoi oi oftalmoi autou (ΔΚρϬοου λϪγιλ ιυϬπιϛ αллϻϼος Ϭπιϛρμιω υϯϕοτϖ ιωι ορϼσιν θϬου ϳιλον ον υπνοο ΔπολιϬκϼλυμμϙϯνϴ ϴ οϯϴλμϴ λυτϖ). Translation: hear (or listen, understand) words of lord knows knowledge highest and sees god perceives in sleep (or trance) revealed the eyes his

- Septuagint manuscript 551: akoúōn lógia teou epistámenos epistēmēn usístou kai orasin teou orōn en upnō apokekalumménoi oi oftalmoi autou (ΔΚρϬοου λϪγιλ θϬου Ϭπιϛ αллϻϼος Ϭπιϛρμιω υϯϕοτϖ ιωι ορϼσιν θϬου ορϣν ον υπνοο ΔπολιϬκϼ λυμμϙϯνϴ ϴ οϯϴλμϴ ἀυτῶ). Translation: hear (or listen, understand) words god knows knowledge god looks and sees god perceives in sleep (or trance) revealed the eyes his

• Septuagint manuscript 664: akoúōn lógia ṯeou epistámenos epistēmēn par' usístou kai orasin ṯeou idōn en upnō apokekalumménoi oi ofṯalmoi autou (ⲇⲕⲟⲑⲟⲟⲛ ⲗⲯⲅⲓⲇ ⲑⲟⲟⲩ ⲟ̄ⲡⲓⲥⲁⲅⲓⲙⲉⲟⲥ ⲟ̄ⲡⲓⲥⲣⲙⲗⲗ ⲡⲁⲣ' ⲩⲯⲫⲟ̄ⲧⲟ ⲗⲁⲓ ⲟⲣⲁⲥⲓⲛ ⲑⲟⲟⲩ ⲓⲇⲟⲟⲛ ⲟⲛ ⲩⲡⲛⲟⲟ ⲇⲡⲟⲗⲕⲟ̄ⲕⲁ ⲗⲩⲙⲙⲁⲅⲛⲟ̄ ⲑ ⲟⲑⲑⲇⲗⲙⲟ̄ ⲇⲩⲧⲟ). Translation: hear (or listen, understand) words god knows knowledge from the highest and sees god perceives in sleep (or trance) revealed the eyes his

• Septuagint manuscript 53: akoúōn lógia ṯeou epistámenos epistēmēn usístou kai orasin ṯeou idōn en upnō kekalummenoi oi ofṯalmoi autou (ⲇⲕⲟⲑⲟⲟⲛ ⲗⲯⲅⲓⲇ ⲑⲟⲟⲩ ⲟ̄ⲡⲓⲥ ⲁⲅⲓⲙⲉⲟⲥ ⲟ̄ⲡⲓⲥⲣⲙⲗⲗ ⲩⲯⲫⲟ̄ⲧⲟ ⲗⲁⲓ ⲟⲣⲁⲥⲓⲛ ⲑⲟⲟⲩ ⲓⲇⲟⲟⲛ ⲟⲛ ⲩⲡⲛⲟⲟ ⲗⲕⲟ̄ⲕⲁ ⲗⲩⲙⲙⲗ̄ⲯⲟ̄ ⲑ ⲟⲑⲑⲇⲗⲙⲟ̄ ⲇⲩⲧⲟ). Translation: hear (or listen, understand) words god knows knowledge highest and sees god perceives in sleep (or trance) covered the eyes his

• Leningrad Codex: nə'ūm šōmēa' 'imrê-'Ēl wəyōdēa' da'at 'Elyôn mahăzēh Šadday yeḥĕzeh nōpēl ûgəlûy 'ênāyim (נְאֻם שֹׁמֵעַ אִמְרֵי־אֵל וְיֹדֵעַ דַּעַת עֶלְיוֹן מַחֲזֵה שַׁדַּי יֶחֱזֶה נֹפֵל וּגְלוּי עֵינָיִם). Translation: declares hears pronouncement of El (or god) and knows mind Elyon (or highest) and sees Shaddai (or demonic) forecasts fall and manifest eyes

• Peshitta: åmr dšmó måmrå dålhå: wydó mdóå dmrymå: wḥzwå dålhå ḥzå: kd rmå wptyhn óynwhy (ܐܡܪ ܕܫܡܥ ܡܐܡܪܐ ܕܐܠܗܐ: ܘܝܕܥ ܡܕܥܐ ܕܡܪܝܡܐ: ܘܚܙܘܐ ܕܐܠܗܐ ܚܙܐ: ܟܕ ܪܡܐ ܘܦܬܝܚܢ ܥܝܢܘܗܝ,). Translation: declares hears commandment from god and knows the mind of the heights, and sees from god visions with wide open eyes

• Targum Onkelos: 'ēmar dišma' mêmar min qŏdām 'Ēl wîda' madda' min qŏdām 'illā'â ḥēzû min qŏdām Šadday ḥāzê šəkîb ûmitgəlê lÊh (אֲמַר דְּשָׁמַע מֵימַר מִן קֳדָם אֵל וְיִדַע מַדַּע מִן קֳדָם עִלָּאָה חֲזוּ)

מִן קֳדָם שַׁדַּי חֲזֵי שְׁכִיב וּמִתְגְּלֵי לֵיהּ). Translation: declares hears commandment proceeding from El (or god) and knows the intelligence proceeding from the highest and sees from Shaddai (or powerful) sees laying down from Yah

• Targum Jerusalem: 'āmar gabrā' dišma' mamlal min qŏdām Yəyā wîda' dē'â min qŏdām 'îlawêh dahăzê min qŏdām Šaday hăwâ hāzê wəkad hăwâ bā'ê hăwâ mištatah 'al 'appôy wərāzê nəbû'ătā' mitgalyāyn lÊh wahăwâ mitnabbē' 'al napšêh dəhû' Nāpîl bəharbā' wəsôp nəbiyûtÊh ləmitqayymā' (אָמַר גַּבְרָא דִשְׁמַע מַמְלַל מִן קֳדָם יְיָ וִידַע דַעְה מִן קֳדָם עִילָוֵיהּ דַחֲזֵי מִן קֳדָם שַׁדַּי הֲוָה חֲזֵי וְכַד הֲוָה בְּעֵי הֲוָה מִשְׁתַּטַּח עַל אַפּוֹי וְרָזֵי נְבוּאֲתָא מִתְגַּלְיָין לֵיהּ וַהֲוָה מִתְנַבֵּא עַל נַפְשֵׁיהּ דְּהוּא נְפִיל בְּחַרְבָּא וְסוֹף נְבִיוּתֵיהּ לְמִתְקַיְּימָא). Translation: spoke man the heard speech from before Yahweh, and perceived knowledge from before the highest who saw from before Shaddai. He himself saw it, and when he himself saw, he stretched out on his face and came to him revelation of Yah, and produced prophecies from the mind (or soul) from Orion's (or Napil's) sword (or dry gust). And he penned (or finished, wrote) his prophecy from Yh, and it will happen.

• Targum Pseudo-Jonathan: 'êmar dəšāma' mêmar min qŏdām 'ĕlāhā' wîda' ša'tā' dərātah bÊh 'ĕlāhā' 'ilā'â dəhêzû min qŏdām Šaday hāmê wəkad hăwâ bā'ê dəyitgəlê lÊh hăwâ mištatah ûnəpal 'al 'appôy wərazyā' sətîmayā' mah də'itkasê min nəbiyā' hăwâ mitgəlê lÊh (אֵימַר דִּשְׁמַע מֵימַר מִן קֳדָם אֱלָהָא וִידַע שַׁעְתָּא דְּרָתַח בֵּיהּ אֱלָהָא עִלָּאָה דְּחֵיזוּ מִן קֳדָם שַׁדַּי חָמֵי וְכַד הֲוָה בְּעֵי דְּיִתְגְּלֵי לֵיהּ הֲוָה מִשְׁתַּטַּח וּנְפַל עַל אַפּוֹי וְרַזְיָא סְתִימַיָא מַה דְּאִתְכַּסֵי מִן נְבִיָּא הֲוָה מִתְגְּלֵי לֵיהּ). Translation: spoke the heard command (or word) from before god and perceived the heat within Yah god highest, who saw before Shaddai's spectacle (or vision), when he himself saw the revelation of Yah, he himself bowed and lay down on his face, and strong (or powerful) storm (or winter storm) which from throne came, the prophet disclosed for Yah.

193

• Sahidic manuscript 2006: etcōtm enšaje mpnoute etsooun enousbō ebol hitm pjoeis eafnay etorasis mpnoute efobš erenefbal holp ebol (ⲉⲧⲥⲱⲧⲙ ⲉⲛϣⲁϫⲉ ⲙⲡⲛⲟⲩⲧⲉ ⲉⲧⲥⲟⲟⲩⲛ ⲉⲛⲟⲩⲥⲃⲱ ⲉⲃⲟⲗ ϩⲓⲧⲙ ⲡ︦ⲭⲟⲉⲓⲥ ⲉⲁϥⲛⲁⲩ ⲉⲑⲟⲣⲁⲥⲓⲥ ⲙⲡⲛⲟⲩⲧⲉ ⲉϥⲟⲃϣ ⲉⲣⲉⲛⲉϥⲃⲁⲗ ϭⲟⲗⲡ ⲉⲃⲟⲗ). Translation: when declares by saying of the god of knowledge of the doctrine by the Lord through seeing his vision from the god in his sleep while his eyes were uncovered

• Sahidic manuscript 2047: etsōtm enšaje mpnoute etsooutn nousbō ebol hitm petjose etnay euhorasis nte mpnoute hn ouhinēb erenefbal holp ebol (ⲉⲧⲥⲱⲧⲙ ⲉⲛϣⲁϫⲉ ⲙⲡⲛⲟⲩⲧⲉ ⲉⲧⲥⲟⲟⲩⲧⲛ ⲛⲟⲩⲥⲃⲱ ⲉⲃⲟⲗ ϩⲓⲧⲙ ⲡⲉⲧϫⲟⲥⲉ ⲉⲧⲛⲁⲩ ⲉⲩϩⲟⲣⲁⲥⲓⲥ ⲛⲧⲉ ⲡⲛⲟⲩⲧⲉ ϩⲛ ⲟⲩϩⲓⲛⲏⲃ ⲉⲣⲉⲛⲉϥⲃⲁⲗ ϭⲟⲗⲡ ⲉⲃⲟⲗ). Translation: when heard by saying of the god who is upright in the doctrine from the highest who sees a vision from the god in a sleep while his eyes were uncovered

• Sahidic manuscript 2169: efsōtm enšaje mpnoute efsooun nouepistēmē ebol hitm petjose auō torasis mpnoute afnau eros hn ouōbš erenefbal holp ebol (ⲉϥⲥⲱⲧⲙ ⲉⲛϣⲁϫⲉ ⲙⲡⲛⲟⲩⲧⲉ ⲉϥⲥⲟⲟⲩⲛ ⲛⲟⲩⲉⲡⲓⲥⲧⲏⲙⲏ ⲉⲃⲟⲗ ϩⲓⲧⲙ ⲡⲉⲧϫⲟⲥⲉ ⲁⲩⲱ ⲑⲟⲣⲁⲥⲓⲥ ⲙⲡⲛⲟⲩⲧⲉ ⲁϥⲛⲁⲩ ⲉⲣⲟⲥ ϩⲛ ⲟⲩⲱⲃϣ ⲉⲣⲉⲛⲉϥⲃⲁⲗ ϭⲟⲗⲡ ⲉⲃⲟⲗ). Translation: when heard by saying of the god of knowledge of the doctrine by the Lord through seeing his vision of the god of science of the highest doctrine and vision from the god in a vision within white in his sleep while his eyes were uncovered

The Aramaic text the Greeks translated could not have read exactly as the Masoretic text reads, as there are specifically Hebrew and Moabite words in the Masoretic version that the Aramaic translator would have translated. Nevertheless, the difference is significant beyond the language used, as all references to Shaddai are again missing from the Greek version, suggesting that the Aramaic translator as unwilling to refer to the 'demonic god.' For more information on the meaning of Shaddai in Aramaic see note 44. As the Deir Alla Inscription (KAI 312), which was carved in Moabite between 880 and 770 BCE confirms that Balaam was a prophet of several gods, including Šdyn (𐤔𐤃𐤉𐤍), generally anglicized as Shaddayin, the Moabite name of the god is restored in this translation, along with the names of El and Elyon from the Leningrad Codex.

4 Codex Vaticanus: Kenaion (ΚΕΝΑΙΟΝ)

- Codex Alexandrinus: Kaineon (ΚΑΙΝΕΟΝ)
- Codex Ambrosiano A 147: Kanaion (ΚΑΝΑΙΟΝ)
- Septuagint manuscript 509: Kananaion (Καναναιον)
- Septuagint manuscript 127: Keinaion (Κειναιον)
- Septuagint manuscript 318: Kananaion (Χαναναιον)
- Septuagint manuscript 707: Kainaion (Καιναιον)
- Septuagint manuscript 319: Keneōn (Κενεων)
- Septuagint manuscript 246: Kainion (Καινιον)
- Septuagint manuscript 71: Kaineōn (Καινεων)
- Septuagint manuscript 761: Ķettieim (Χεττιειμ)
- Septuagint manuscript 416: Kennaion (Κενναιον)
- Leningrad Codex: qênî (קֵינִי). Translation: smiths (or metalsmiths)
- Peshitta: qynyå (ܩܝܢܝܐ). Translation: smiths
- Targum Onkelos: Šalmā'â (שַׁלְמָאָה). Translation: Shalmites (an Arab tribe)
- Targum Jerusalem: Šalmayā' (שַׁלְמַיָא). Translation: Shalmites (an Arab tribe)
- Targum Pseudo-Jonathan: Yitrô (יִתְרוֹ). Translation: Jethro
- Sahidic manuscript 2006: Kinnaios (ΚΙΝΝΑΙΟΣ)
- Sahidic manuscript 2047: Kaineos (ΚΑΙΝΕΟΣ)

CHAPTER 24

5 Codex Alexandrinus: Kētiaiōn (ⲕⲏⲧⲓⲀⲓⲱⲚ)

- Septuagint manuscript 15: Kitieōn (ⲕⲓ̄ⲗⲓⲟⲟⲟⲛ)
- Septuagint manuscript 127: Tetteieim (ⲧⲟ̄ⲧⲧⲟⲩⲇⲇⲙ)
- Septuagint manuscript 318: Kētaiōn (ⲕⲗⲧⲁⲓⲟⲟⲛ)
- Septuagint manuscript 18: Kētieōn (ⲕⲗ̄ⲗⲓⲟⲟⲟⲛ)
- Septuagint manuscript 58: Kitēaiōn (ⲕⲓⲧⲗⲁⲓⲟⲟⲛ)
- Septuagint manuscript 75: Koitaiōn (ⲕⲑⲧⲁⲓⲟⲟⲛ)
- Septuagint manuscript 767: Kettaiōn (ⲭⲟ̄ⲧⲁⲓⲟⲟⲛ)
- Septuagint manuscript 416: Kitiaiōn (ⲕⲓ̄ⲗⲁⲓⲟⲟⲛ)
- Septuagint manuscript 610: Ketieim (ⲭⲟ̄ⲗⲓⲇⲙ)
- Leningrad Codex: Kittîm (כִּתִּים)
- Peshitta: Ktyå (ܟܬܝܐ)
- Targum Onkelos: Rômā'ê (רוֹמָאֵי). Translation: Roman
- Targum Jerusalem: Librānayā' min mədînətā' rabbətā' wəyiṣrəpûn 'imhôn ligyônîn sagyayn min dəRômā'ê (מְדִינְתָּא רַבְּתָא וְיִצְרְפוּן עִמְהוֹן לִגְיוֹנִין סַגִּיִין מִן דְרוֹמָאֵי לִבְרָנַיָּא מֶן). Translation: Liburnia from the province (or city), great and combining with the legions spreading from Rome
- Targum Pseudo-Jonathan: Lambarnəyā' ûmē'ara' 'Italyā' wəyistarpûn bəligyônîn dəyipqûn min Qûsətantînê (לְמְבַּרְנְיָא וּמֵאַרְע אַטַלְיָא וְיִצְטַרְפוּן בְּלִגְיוֹנִין דְּיִפְּקוּן מִן קוּסְטַנְטִינֵי). Translation: Lombardy and attack the land of Italy and combining with legions commanded by Constantine
- Vetus Latina manuscripts 403 and 1964: Citheorum (ⲥⲓⲧ̄ⲏⲉⲟⲣⲩⲙ)
- Codex Gothicus Legionensis (VL 91): Sethim (ⲥⲉⲧ̄ⲏⲓⲙ)
- Sahidic manuscript 2006: Hitios (ϩⲓⲧⲓⲟⲥ)
- Sahidic manuscript 2047: Hidreōs (ϩⲓⲁⲣⲉⲱⲥ)

Kittim was a kingdom in eastern Cyprus, founded in the 13th century BCE, and used by the Hebrews as the name of the island of Cyprus. The name was recorded during the Egyptian New

Kingdom as Kåtjåy (𐤊 𐤊𐤉𐤕 ᛕᛁ), Phoenician as Kty (𐤊𐤕𐤉), and ancient Greek as Kition (Κίτιον). It was also applied to the Aegean islands and Greece in later periods. The Leningrad Codex refers to a fleet coming from Kittim, and not a "hand."

6 Codex Vaticanus: Ebraious (ЄΒΡΑΙΟΥС). Translation: Hebrews

- Septuagint manuscript 82: Ebaious (Εὐαίου)

- Leningrad Codex: 'Ēber (עֵבֶר). Translation: Eber

- Peshitta: ôbr (ܥܒܪ). Translation: crosser (or Habiru, Eber)

- Targum Onkelos: lə'ēbar Pərāt (לְעֵבַר פְּרָת). Translation: those across the Euphrates

- Targum Jerusalem: bənê 'Ēber Nahărā' (בְּנֵי עֵבֶר נַהֲרָא). Translation: sons of Eber (or Eberites) in Syria (or Aram, rivers)

- Targum Pseudo-Jonathan: bənôy də'Ēber (בְּנוֹי דְעֵבֶר). Translation: sons of Eber

- Codex Gothicus Legionensis (VL 91): Heber (𐌷𐌴𐌱𐌴𐍂)

- Sahidic manuscript 2006: Eoraios (Єορⲁιος)

- Sahidic manuscript 2047: Ebraios (Єβρⲁιος)

If the Canaanite text of Numbers was based on an Akkadian Cuneiform source text, then this term must have been ḫabiru (𒄩𒁉𒊒), meaning "dusky," which was a word used to describe groups of marauders in the Middle East in the era. The term was in use from approximately 1800 to 1200 BCE, however, does not appear to have been an ethnic term, but was generally used to describe rebels, mercenaries, outlaws, raiders, servants, and slaves. The inclusion of the Habirus in the curse against the Assyrians, suggests the Israelites were not considered Habirus at the time, as Balaam was unable to curse the Israelites.

CHAPTER 24

7 The reference to Assyria implies it is a major nation at the time, which dates the composition of the text to either before the collapse of the Old Assyrian Empire, circa 1392 BCE, or during the era of the Neo-Assyrian Empire, between circa 911 and 612 BCE. As the Habirus disappeared from the historic records in the 1100s BCE, this indicates that the curse of Balaam dates to before 1392 BCE.

CHAPTER 25

Israel stayed in Shittim, and the people began going whoring after the daughters of Moab. They called them to the sacrifices of their idols, and the people ate from their sacrifices and worshiped their idols. Israel declared themselves sacred to Lord Peor,[1] and the Lord was very angry with Israel.

The Lord said to Moses, "Take all the heads of the people, and make them examples for the Lord against Shemesh,[2] and the anger of the Lord will be turned away from Israel."

Moses said to the tribes of Israel, "Everyone! Kill his friends who have been made sacred to Lord Peor!"

And a man of the children of Israel came and brought his brother and a Midianite woman before Moses, and before all the community of the children of Israel, and they were weeping at the door of the tabernacle of witness. Phinehas the son of Eleazar, the son of Aaron the priest, saw it, and rose out of the middle of the community, and took a dagger in his hand, and went in after the Israelite man into the furnace, and stabbed them both through, both the Israelite man, and the woman through her womb, and the violence was stopped among the children of Israel. Those that died in the violence were 24,000.

The Lord said to Moses, "Phinehas the son of Eleazar the son of Aaron the priest has caused my anger to cease from the children of Israel when I was exceedingly jealous with them, and so I did not consume the children of Israel in my jealousy. So say to him, 'Look, I give him a covenant of peace, and he and his seed after him have a perpetual covenant of the priesthood, because he was zealous for his God, and made atonement for the children of Israel.'"

The name of the murdered Israelite man, who was murdered with the Midianite woman, was Zambri the son of Salu, prince of a house of the tribe of Simeon. The name of the Midianite woman who was murdered, was Kozbi, daughter of Zur, a prince of the nation of Ommoth. It is a chief house among the people of Midian.

The Lord said to Moses, "Say to the children of Israel, "Attack the Midianites as enemies, and murder them, for they are enemies to you by the treachery in which they trap you through Peor and through Kozbi their sister, daughter of a prince of Midian, who was murdered in the day of the violence because of Peor."

CHAPTER 25 NOTES

1 Codex Vaticanus: Beelfegōr (ϐεελφεϲωρ)

• Septuagint manuscript 121: Belfegōr (ϐελϝεϲγωϐ)

• Septuagint manuscript 128: Beelfebōr (ϐϭϩϝϭϭμωϐ)

• Septuagint manuscript 618: Feelfegōr (φϭϩϝϭϭγωϐ)

• Septuagint manuscript 53: Beelgōr (ϐϭϩγϝωϐ)

• Leningrad Codex: Ba'al Pə'ôr (בַּעַל פְּעוֹר). Translation: Lord Peor.

• Peshitta: Bȯl Pȯwr (ܒܥܠ ܦܥܘܪ). Translation: Lord Peor

CHAPTER 25

- Targum Onkelos: Ba'ālā' Pə'ôr (בְּעֵלָא פְּעוֹר). Translation: Lord Peor
- Targum Jerusalem: ṭa'āwāwtā' dipPə'ôr (טָעֲוּותָא דִפְעוֹר). Translation: mistake of Peor
- Targum Pseudo-Jonathan: Ba'ālā' Pə'ôr (בְּעֵלָא פְּעוֹר). Translation: lord of Peor
- Sahidic manuscript 2006: Belfegōr (Ⲃⲉⲗⲫⲉⲅⲱⲣ)
- Sahidic manuscript 2047: Beelfegōr (Ⲃⲉⲉⲗⲫⲉⲅⲱⲣ)

Fagōr (Φαγωρ) was the name of a place that Joshua conquered in the Septuagint's version of the Book of Joshua. There are no known locations associated with the name Pə'ôr, which implies the location was abandoned after the events of Numbers Chapter 25, or perhaps shortly afterward when Joshua conquered the city in Joshua Chapter 13. Other Hebrew texts, such as Micah refer to the Lord of Peor in association with the Shittim Valley, however, this name appears to have been an insult directed towards Lord Hammon who was worshiped at Tell el-Hammam in the 800s BCE.

There is no clear link between Hammon and Pə'ôr, implying the worshipers of Pə'ôr disappeared around the time the Israelites traveled through the Shittim Valley. The major ruins in the Shittim Valley, are found at Tell el-Hammam, which was occupied from at least 3600 BCE until the beginning of the Late Bronze Age (circa 1500 BCE) when the site was abandoned for unknown reasons. It was rebuilt in the 900s BCE as a Samaritan city. As Tell el-Hammam is in the Shittim Valley, and was destroyed or abandoned when the Israelites moved through the region, using either the traditional Christian dating, or the Minoan Eruption and collapse of the Hyksos Dynasty from the Book of Exodus, the Bronze Age city was likely Fagōr (Φαγωρ). The exact dating of the abandonment of the Bronze Age city is unclear, and there is some evidence of occupation for a few decades after 1550 BCE, but the site does appear to have been abandoned around 1500 BCE.

2 Codex Vaticanus: Ēliou (ΗλΙΟΥ). Translation: Helios (or the sun)

- Codex Alexandrinus: laou (λλου). Translation: people
- Septuagint manuscript 71: K_x^y (ﭏ). Translation: lord
- Leningrad Codex: Šámeš (שֶׁמֶשׁ). Translation: Shemesh (or sun)
- Targum Onkelos: šimšā' (שִׁמְשָׁא). Translation: sun
- Targum Jerusalem: šimšā' (שִׁמְשָׁא). Translation: sun
- Targum Pseudo-Jonathan: šimšā' (שִׁמְשָׁא). Translation: sun
- Sahidic manuscript 2006: Rē (ΡΗ). Translation: Ra (or day, Sun)

Helios and Shemesh were the Greek and Canaanite gods of the sun. The Septuagint and Leningrad Codex have similar verses, however, the Hebrew version is generally translated differently, with translators adding various words, for example:

King James Edition:

> And the LORD said unto Moses, Take all the heads of the people, and hang them up before the LORD against the sun, that the fierce anger of the LORD may be turned away from Israel.

Tanakh (JPS 1985):

> The LORD said to Moses, "Take all the ringleaders and have them publicly impaled before the LORD, so that the LORD's wrath may turn away from Israel.

New American Standard Bible:

> The LORD said to Moses, "Take all the leaders of the people and execute them in broad daylight before the LORD, so that the fierce anger of the LORD may turn away from Israel.

CHAPTER 25

The term "sun" has also been phased out of modern translations since it has been documented that the Shemesh was a Canaanite god, which this verse is clearly referring to.

The Leningrad Codex verse is:

וַיֹּאמֶר יְהוָֹה אֶל־מֹשֶׁה קַח אֶת־כָּל־רָאשֵׁי הָעָם וְהוֹקַע אוֹתָם לַיהוָה נֶגֶד הַשָּׁמֶשׁ וְיָשֹׁב חֲרוֹן אַף־יְהוָה מִיִּשְׂרָאֵל

Which translates as:

And said Yahweh to Moses, "Take all the leaders of the people and denounce Yahweh against Shemesh, and bring and end the burning anger of Yahweh against Israel."

CHAPTER 26

After the plague, the Lord said to Moses and Eleazar the priest, "Take a count of all the community of the children of Israel, from twenty years old and up, according to the houses of their fathers' families; every one that went out to set himself in formation.

Moses and Eleazar the priest said in Araboth of Moab at the Jordan by Jericho, "This is the count of every one from twenty years old and up as the Lord commanded Moses." The sons of Israel that came out of Egypt are as follows:

Reuben was the firstborn of Israel, and the sons of Reuben: Enoch and the family of Enoch, to Phallu belongs the family of the Phalluites, to Hezron belongs the family of Hezronite, to Karmi belongs the family of Karmites. These are the families of Reuben, and their count was 43,730.

The sons of Phallu were Eliab, and the sons of Eliab, Namuel, and Dathan, and Abiram. These were renowned men of the community, these were those who rose up against Moses and Aaron in the gathering of Korah, in the rebellion against the Lord. Eretz opened her mouth and swallowed them up and Korah, when their assembly perished the fire devoured the 250, and they were for a sign. But the Sons of Korah did not die.

The sons of Simeon, both the family of the sons of Simeon: to Namuel belonged the family of the Namuelites, to Jamin belonged the family of the Jimnites, to Jakin belonged the family of the Jakinites, to Zerah belonged the family of the Zerahites, to Saul belonged the family of the Saulites. These are the families of Simeon according to their count, 22,200.

The sons of Judah: Er and Onan, and Er and Onan died in the land of Canaan. These were the sons of Judah, according to their families: to Shelah belonged the family of the Shelanites, to Pharez belonged the family of the Pharzites, to Zerah belonged the family of the Zerahites. The sons of Pharez were: to Hezron belonged the family of the Hezronites, to Hamul belonged the family of the Hamulites. These are the families of Judah according to their count, 76,500.

The sons of Issachar according to their families: to Tola belonged the family of the Tolaites, to Pua belonged the family of the Punites, to Jashub belonged the family of the Jashubites, to Shimron belonged the family of the Shimronites. These are the families of Issachar according to their count, 64,400.

The sons of Zebulun according to their families: to Sered belonged the family of the Sardites, to Helon belonged the family of the Elonites, to Jahleel belonged the family of the Jahleelites. These are the families of Zebulun according to their count, 60,500.

The sons of Gad according to their families: to Zephon belonged the family of the Zephonites, to Haggi belonged the family of the Haggites, to Shuni belonged the family of the Shunites, to Ozni belonged the family of the Oznites, to Eri belonged the family of the Erites, to Arodi belonged the family of the Arodites, to Areli belonged the family of the Arelites. These are the families of the children of Gad according to their count, 43,500.

The sons of Asher according to their families: to Imnah belonged the family of the Imnites, to Jesus belonged the family of the Jesusites, to Beriah belonged the family of the Beriites. To Eber belonged the family of the Heberites, to Malchiel belonged the family of the Malchielites. The name of the daughter of Asher: Serah. These are the families of Asher according to their count, 43,400.

The sons of Joseph according to their families: Manasseh and Ephraim. The sons of Manasseh. To Makir belonged the family of the Makirites. Makir fathered Gilead, and to Gilead belonged the family of the Gileadites. These are the sons of Gilead: to Jeezer belonged the family of the Jeezerites, to Helek belonged the family of the Helekites. To Asriel belonged the family of the Asrielites. To Shechem, the family of the Shechemites. To Shemida belonged the family of the Shemidaites. To Hepher belonged the family of the Hepherites. To Zelophehad the son of Hepher there were no sons, but daughters: and these were the names of the daughters of Zelophehad: Mahlah, Noah, Hoglah, Milkah, and Tirzah. These are the families of Manasseh according to their count, 52,700.

These are the children of Ephraim: to Shuthelah belonged the family of the Shuthelahites, to Tanach belonged the family of the Tanachites. These are the sons of Shuthelah: to Eden the family of the Edenites. These are the families of Ephraim according to their count, 32,500. These are the families of the children of Joseph according to their families.

The sons of Benjamin according to their families: to Bala belonged the family of the Belaites, to Ashbel belonged the family of the Ashbelites, to Ahiram belonged the family of the Ahiramites. To Shupham, the family of the Shuphamites. The sons of Bala were Ard and Naaman: to Ard belonged the family of the Ardites, and to Naaman belonged the family of the Naamites. These are the sons of Benjamin by their families according to their count, 35,500.

The sons of Dan according to their families: to Shupham belonged the family of the Shuphamites. These are the families of Dan according to their families. All the families of Shupham according to their count, 64,400.

The sons of Naphtali according to their families; to Jahzeel belonged the family of the Jahzeelites, to Guni belonging the family of the Gunites. To Jezer belonged the family of the Jezerites, and to Shillem belonged the family of the Shillemites. These are the families of Naphtali, according to their count, 40,300.

This is the count of the children of Israel, 601,730.

The Lord said to Moses, "The land will be divided, so that they may inherit according to the count of the names. To the greater number, you will give the greater inheritance, and to the smaller number, you will give the lesser inheritance. To each one, as they have been counted, will their inheritance be given. The land will be divided among the names by lot, they will inherit according to the tribes of their families. You will divide their inheritance by lot between the many and the few.

The sons of Levi according to their families: to Gershon and the family of the Gedsonites, to Kohath and the family of the Kohathites, to Merari and the family of the Merarites. These are the families of the sons of Levi: the family of the Libnites, the family of the Hebronites, the family of the Coreites, and the family of the Mushites, and Kohath fathered Amram. The name of his wife was Jochebed, daughter of Levi, who carried these for Levi in Egypt, and she gave birth to Amram, Aaron, Moses, and Mariam their sister. To Aaron were born Nadab, Abihu, Eleazar, and Ithamar. Nadab and Abihu died when they offered strange fire before the Lord in the Wilderness of Sinai. There were according to their count, 23,000, every male from a month old and up, for they were not counted among the children of Israel, because they have no inheritance among the children of Israel.

This is the count of Moses and Eleazar the priest, who counted the children of Israel in Araboth of Moab, at Jordan by Jericho. Among these people, there was not a man counted by Moses and Aaron, who the children of Israel counted in the Wilderness of Sinai. For the Lord had said to them, "They will surely die in the wilderness, and there was not even one of them left, except Caleb the son of Jephunneh, and Joshua the son of Nun.

CHAPTER 27

The daughters of Zelophehad the son of Hepher, the son of Gilead, the son of Makir, of the tribe of Manasseh, of the sons of Joseph, came near. These were their names: Maala, Noah, Hoglah, Milcah, and Tirzah. They stood before Moses, and before Eleazar the priest, and before the princes, and before all the community at the door of the tabernacle of witness, and said, "Our father died in the wilderness, and he was not among the community that rebelled against the Lord in the gathering of Korah. He died for his own sin, and he had no sons. Don't let the name of our father be blotted out from among his people, because he has no son. Give us an inheritance among our father's brothers."

Moses brought their case before the Lord. The Lord said to Moses, "The daughters of Zelophehad have spoken rightly. You will give them a possession of an inheritance among their father's brothers, and you will assign their father's inheritance to them. You will tell the children of Israel, 'If a man dies, and has no son, you will assign his inheritance to his daughter. If he has no daughter, you will give his inheritance to his brother. If he has no brothers, you will give his inheritance to his father's brother. If there be no brothers of his father, you will give the inheritance to his nearest relation of his tribe, to inherit his possessions."

This will be for the children of Israel an ordinance of judgment, as the Lord commanded Moses.

The Lord said to Moses, "Go up to the mountain that is in the country beyond Jordan (this is Mount Nebo),[1] and look at the land of Canaan, which I give to the sons of Israel for a possession. You will see it, and you also will be added to your people, like Aaron your brother was added to them in Mount Hor, because you transgressed my commandment in the Wilderness of Sin, when the community resisted and refused to sanctify me, you did not sanctify me at the water before them." (This is the water of Strife in Kadesh in the Wilderness of Sin.)

Moses said to the Lord, "Let the lord of the gods, spirits, and all flesh, appoint a man over this community. Who will go out before them? Who will come in before them? Who will lead them out? Who will bring them in? The community of the Lord will not be as sheep without a shepherd."

The Lord answered Moses, "Take with yourself Joshua the son of Nun, a man who has the Spirit in him, and you will lay your hands on him. You will set him before Eleazar the priest, and you will give him an order before all the community, and you will give an order concerning him before them. You will put your glory on him, that the children of Israel may listen to him. He will stand before Eleazar the priest, and consult for him the judgment of statements against the Lord, and they will go out at his word, and at his word they will come in, he and the children of Israel with one accord, and all the community."

Moses did as the Lord commanded him, and he took Joshua and set him before Eleazar the priest, and before all the community. He laid his hands on him and appointed him as the Lord ordered Moses.

CHAPTER 27 NOTES

1 Codex Vaticanus: oros Nabau (ΟΡΟC ΝΑΒΑΥ). Translation: Mount Nabau

• Septuagint manuscript 127: oros Nagau (ορος ΝΔγαυ). Translation: Mount Nagau

• Septuagint manuscript 128: oros Nabab (ορος ΝΔuΔu). Translation: Mount Nabab

• Septuagint manuscript 72: orous Naban (οβοσ ΝΔuⲇⲥ). Translation: Mount Naban

• Septuagint manuscript 528: aros Nauau (ορος ΝΔuΔu). Translation: Mount Nauau

• Septuagint manuscript 126: orous Nabōn (οβοσ ΝΔuⲟⲟⲛ). Translation: Mount Nabon

• Leningrad Codex: har hā'Ăbārîm (הַר הָעֲבָרִים). Translation: Mountain of Abarim

• Peshitta: dÔbryå (ܕܒܥܒܪܐ). Translation: in Obrya

• Targum Onkelos: da'Ăbārā'ê (דַעֲבָרָאֵי). Translation: in Abarae

• Targum Pseudo-Jonathan: tawwrā' də'Abrā'ê (טַוּוֹרָא דְעֲבָרָאֵי). Translation: hill of Abrae

• Sahidic manuscript 2006: ptoou Nabau (ⲡⲧⲟⲟⲩ ΝΑΒΑΥ). Translation: desert (or mountain) Nabau

Mount Nebo is not listed in this verse in the Leningrad Codex, Peshitta, or Targums, and appears to have been added to the Greek translation as a scribal note. It is mentioned in other verses of the Masoretic text regarding these mountains, and they seem consistent that Nebo was in the Abarim Mountains. Mount Nebo has been identified with the mountain now known as Mount Nebo, the highest mountain in the Abarim Mountains, since at least the 4th century CE when a Byzantine church was erected on the mountain. The church was abandoned sometime after the 6th century and rebuilt in the 20th century. There is some scholarly debate about whether this was the original Mount Nebo or not, however, at this time the Orthodox and Catholic churches accept it as the Mount Nebo from Numbers, as do Islamic scholars.

CHAPTER 28

The Lord said to Moses, "Command the children of Israel, 'You observe offerings to me at my feasts and my gifts, my presents and my burnt offerings as a sweet-smelling savor.' You will say to them, 'These are the burnt offerings that you will bring to the Lord: two year-old lambs without imperfection every day, for a whole burnt offering perpetually. You will offer one lamb in the morning, and you will offer the second lamb towards the evening. You will offer a tenth of an ephah of fine flour for a sacrifice, mixed with a quarter of a hin oil. It is a perpetual whole burnt offering, a sacrifice offered in Mount Sinai as a sweet-smelling savor to the Lord. Its drink offering will be a quarter of a hin for each lamb.'"

"In the holy place will you pour a strong drink as a drink offering to the Lord. The second lamb you will offer towards evening, and you will offer it according to its sacrifice and according to its drink offering for a smell of sweet savor to the Lord. On the sabbath day, you will offer two year-old lambs without imperfection, and two tenths of fine flour mixed with oil for a sacrifice, and a drink offering. It is a whole burnt offering of the sabbaths on the sabbath days, besides the continued whole burnt offering, and its drink offering.'"

"At the new moons, you will bring a whole burnt offering to the Lord. Two calves from the herd, and one ram, and seven year-old lambs without imperfection. Three tenths of fine flour mixed with oil for one calf, and two tenths of fine flour mixed with oil for one ram. A tenth of fine flour mixed with oil for each lamb, as a sacrifice. A sweet-smelling savor, a burnt offering to the Lord. Their drink offering will be half a hin per calf, and a third of a hin per ram, and a quarter of a hin of wine per lamb. This is the whole burnt offering monthly throughout the months of the year. He will offer one goat kid for a sin offering to the Lord. It will be offered beside the continual whole burnt offering and its drink offering."

"In the first month, on the fourteenth day of the month, is the Passover to the Lord. On the fifteenth day of this month is a feast, and for seven days you will eat unleavened bread. The first day will be for you a holiday, and you will do no servile work. You will bring whole burnt offerings, as a sacrifice to the Lord: two calves from the herd, one ram, and seven year old lambs, and they will without imperfection. Their sacrifice will be fine flour mixed with oil, three tenths for one calf, and two tenths for one ram. You will offer a tenth for each lamb, for the seven lambs. You will offer one goat kid for a sin offering, to make atonement for you. Besides the perpetual whole burnt offering in the morning, which is a whole burnt sacrifice for a continuance. These you will offer daily for seven days, a gift, a sacrifice for a sweet-smelling savor to the Lord, beside the continual whole burnt offering, you will offer its drink offering. The seventh day will be for you a holiday. You will do no servile work in it."

"On the day of the new grain, when you offer a new sacrifice at the festival of weeks, to the Lord, there will be for you a holiday, and you will do no servile work. You will bring whole burnt offerings for a sweet-smelling savor to the Lord, two calves from the herd, and one ram, and seven lambs without imperfection. Their sacrifice will be fine flour mixed with oil, and there will be three tenths per calf, and two tenths per ram. A tenth for each lamb separately, for the seven lambs, and a goat kid, for a sin offering, to make atonement for you, besides the perpetual whole burnt offering, and you will offer to me their sacrifice. They will be for you undamaged, and you will offer their drink offerings."

CHAPTER 29

"In the seventh month, on the first day of the month, there will be for you a holiday, and you will do no servile work. It will be for you a day of blowing the trumpets. You will offer whole burnt offerings for a sweet savor to the Lord, one calf from the herd, one ram, and seven year-old lambs without imperfection. Their sacrifice will be fine flour mingled with oil, three tenth amounts for one calf, and two tenth amounts for one ram. A tenth deal for each of the seven lambs. One goat kid for a sin offering, to make atonement for you. Besides the whole burnt offerings for the new moon, and their sacrifice, and their drink offerings, and their perpetual whole burnt offering, and their sacrifice and their drink offerings according to their ordinance for a sweet-smelling savor to the Lord. On the tenth of this month, there will be for you a holiday, and you will afflict your minds, and you will do no work."

"You will bring close the whole burnt offerings for a sweet-smelling savor to the Lord, burnt sacrifices to the Lord, one calf from the herd, one ram, seven year-old lambs, and they will be for you without imperfection. Their sacrifice will be fine flour mingled with oil, three tenth amounts for one calf, and two tenth amounts for one ram. A tenth deal for each lamb, for the seven lambs. One goat kid for a sin offering, to make atonement for you besides the sin offering for atonement, and the continual whole burnt offering, its

219

sacrifice, and its drink offering according to its ordinance for a smell of sweet savor, a burnt sacrifice to the Lord."

"On the fifteenth day of this seventh month you have a holiday and will do no servile work, and you will keep it a feast to the Lord seven days. You will bring close whole burnt offerings, as a sacrifice for a smell of sweet savor to the Lord, on the first day thirteen calves from the herd, two rams, and fourteen year-old lambs, and they will be without imperfection. Their sacrifice will be fine flour mingled with oil, and there will be three tenth amounts for one calf, for the thirteen calves, and two tenth amounts for one ram, for the two rams. A tenth deal for every lamb, for the fourteen lambs. One goat kid for a sin offering, besides the continual whole burnt offering there will be their sacrifice and their drink offerings."

"On the second day, twelve calves, two rams, fourteen year-old lambs without imperfection. Their sacrifice and their drink offering will be for the calves and the rams and the lambs according to their number, according to their ordinance. One goat kid for a sin offering, and besides the perpetual whole burnt offering, and their sacrifice and their drink offerings."

"On the third day, eleven calves, two rams, and fourteen year-old lambs without imperfection. Their sacrifice and their drink offering will be to the calves and the rams and the lambs according to their number, according to their ordinance. One goat kid for a sin offering, besides the continual whole burnt offering there will be their sacrifice and their drink offerings."

"On the fourth day, ten calves, two rams, and fourteen year-old lambs without imperfection. There will be their sacrifice and their drink offerings to the calves and the rams and the lambs according to their number, according to their ordinance. One goat kid for a sin offering, besides the continual whole burnt offering there will be their sacrifice and their drink offerings."

"On the fifth day, nine calves, two rams, and fourteen year-old lambs without imperfection. Their sacrifice and their drink offerings will be to the calves and the rams and the lambs according to their number, according to their ordinance. One goat kid for a sin offering, and beside the perpetual whole burnt offering there will be their sacrifice and their drink offerings."

"On the sixth day, eight calves, two rams, and fourteen year-old lambs without imperfection. There will be their sacrifice and their drink offerings to the calves and rams and lambs according to their number, according to their ordinance. One goat kid for a sin offering, besides the perpetual whole burnt offering there will be their sacrifice and their drink offerings."

"On the seventh day, seven calves, two rams, and fourteen year-old lambs without imperfection. Their sacrifice and their drink offerings will be to the calves and the rams and the lambs according to their number, according to their ordinance. One goat kid for a sin offering, besides the continual whole burnt offering, there will be their sacrifice and their drink offerings."

CHAPTER 29

"On the eighth day, there will be for you a release. You will do no servile work on it. You will offer whole burnt offerings as sacrifices to the Lord, one calf, one ram, and seven year-old lambs without imperfection. There will be their sacrifice and their drink offerings for the calf and the ram and the lambs according to their number, according to their ordinance. One goat kid for a sin offering, and in addition, the continual whole burnt offering, and there will be their sacrifice and their drink offerings. These sacrifices will you offer to the Lord in your feasts, besides your vows, and you will offer your free will offerings and your whole burnt offerings, and your sacrifice and your drink offerings, and your peace offerings."

CHAPTER 30

Moses told the children of Israel everything that the Lord commanded Moses.

Moses told the heads of the tribes of the children of Israel, "This is that which the Lord has commanded. Whatever man will vow a vow to the Lord, or swear an oath, or bind himself with an obligation in his mind, he will not profane his word, all that will come out of his mouth he will do. If a woman will vow a vow to the Lord, or bind herself with an obligation in her youth in her father's house, and her father should hear her vows and her obligations, where she has bound her mind, and her father should hold his peace at her, then all her vows will stand, and all the obligations with which she has bound her mind will remain to her. But if her father straightly forbids her in the day in which he will hear all her vows and her obligations, which she has contracted in her mind, they will not stand. The Lord will hold her guiltless because her father forbade her."

"If she should be indeed married, and her vows are on her according to the utterance of her lips, the obligations which she has contracted in her mind, and her husband should hear, and hold his peace at her in the day in which he should hear, then this will all her vows be binding, and her obligations, which she has contracted in her mind will stand. If her husband should in any way forbid her in the day in which he should hear her, none of her vows or obligations which she has contracted in her mind will stand, because her husband has disallowed her, and the Lord will hold her guiltless."

"The vow of a widow or her who is divorced, whatever she will vow in her mind, will remain with her. If her vow was made in the house of her husband, or the obligation in her mind with an oath, and her husband should hear, and hold his peace at her, and not disallow her, then all her vows will stand, and all the obligations which she contracted in her mind, will stand against her. But if her husband should completely forbid the vow on the day in which he heard it, none of the things which will proceed out of her lips in her vows, and in the obligations contracted in her mind will remain with her, her husband has canceled them, and the Lord will hold her guiltless."

"Every vow, and every binding oath to afflict her mind, her husband will confirm it to her, or her husband will cancel it. But if he is wholly silent at her from day to day, then will he bind on her all her vows, and he will confirm to her the obligations which she has bound on herself because he held his peace at her in the day in which he heard her. If her husband should completely in any way cancel them after the day in which he heard them, then he will carry his iniquity."

These are the ordinances that the Lord commanded Moses, between a man and his wife, and between a father and daughter in her youth in the house of her father.

CHAPTER 31

The Lord said to Moses, "Avenge the vengeance of the children of Israel on the Midianites, and then you will be added to your people."

Moses said to the people, "Arm men among yourselves, and set yourselves in array before the Lord against Midian, to inflict vengeance on Midian from the Lord. Send a thousand of each tribe from all the tribes of the children of Israel to set themselves in formation."

They counted out the thousands of Israel, a thousand of each tribe, twelve thousand, and armed them for war. Moses sent them away, a thousand from every tribe in their forces, and Phinehas the son of Eleazar the son of Aaron the priest, with the holy instruments, and the signal trumpets were in their hands. They set themselves in formation against Midian, as the Lord commanded Moses, and they killed every male. They killed the kings of Midian together with their subjects, including Evi, Rekem, Zur, Ur, and Reba, the five kings of Midian. They killed Balaam the son of Beor with their others slain. They took as captives the women of Midian, and their property, and their livestock, and all their possessions, and they plundered their people. They burnt with fire all their cities in the places of their habitation and they burnt their villages with fire. They took all their plunder, and all their spoils, both man and beast. They brought to Moses and Eleazar the priest, and all the children of Israel, the captives, and the spoils, and the plunder, to the camp to Araboth in Moab, which is by the Jordan near Jericho. Moses and Eleazar the priest and all the rulers of the community went out of the camp to meet them. Moses was angry with the captains of the army, the heads of thousands, and the heads of hundreds who came from the battle formation."

Moses asked them, "Why have you kept every female alive? For they were the cause of the children of Israel by the word of Balaam to revolt and despise the word of the Lord, because of Peor there was violence in the community of the Lord. Now then kill every male in all the spoils, kill every woman, who has been with a man. As for all the captive women, who have not been with men, keep them alive. You will camp outside the great camp seven days. Everyone who has killed and who touches a slain man, will purify himself on the third day, and you and your captives will purify yourselves on the seventh day. You will purify every garment and every leather utensil, and every work of goatskin, and every wooden vessel."

Eleazar the priest said to the men of the army that came from the battle formation, "This is the ordinance of the law which the Lord has commanded Moses. Besides the gold, and the silver, and the brass, and the iron, and lead, and tin, everything that will pass through the fire will be clean, nevertheless, it will be purified with the water of sanctification, and whatever will not pass through the fire will pass through water. On the seventh day, you will wash your garments, and be clean, and afterward, you may come into the camp."

The Lord said to Moses, "Count the captives both the humans and animals, you and Eleazar the priest, and the heads of the families of the community. You will divide the spoils between the warriors that went out to battle, and the whole community. You will take a tribute for the Lord from the warriors that went out to battle, one mind out of 500 from the men and the livestock, including the oxen, sheep, and donkeys, and you will take from their half. You will give them to Eleazar the priest as the first fruits of the Lord. From the half belonging to the children of Israel, you will take one per 50 from the men, and the oxen, sheep, donkeys, and all the livestock, and you will give them to the Levites that keep the orders in the tabernacle of the Lord."

Moses and Eleazar the priest did as the Lord commanded Moses. That which remained of the spoil which the warriors took, was 675,000 sheep, 72,000 oxen, and 61,000 donkeys, and 32,000 captured virgin girls. The half, the whole portion of those that went out to war, from the number of the sheep, was 337,500, and those sacrificed to the Lord from the sheep were 675. The oxen, 630,000, and those sacrificed to the Lord were 72. The donkeys, 30,500, and those sacrificed to the Lord were 61. Of the people, 16,000, and those sacrificed of them to the Lord were 32.[1] Moses gave the sacrifice to the Lord, the heave-offering to God. To Eleazar the priest, as the Lord commanded Moses, from the half belonging to the children of Israel, whom Moses separated from the warriors. The half taken from the sheep, belonging to the community was 337,500, the oxen were 36,000, the donkeys were 30,500, and the humans were 16,000. Moses took the half belonging to the children of Israel, the one out of 50 of men and livestock, and he gave them to the Levites who keep the orders of the tabernacle of the Lord as the Lord commanded Moses.

All those who were appointed to be officers of thousands of the army, captains of thousands and captains of hundreds, approached Moses, and said to Moses, "Your servants have counted the warriors with us and not one is missing. We have brought our sacrifice to the Lord, every man who has found an article of gold, whether an armlet, chain, ring, bracelet, or a hair-clasp, to make atonement for us before the Lord."

Moses and Eleazar the priest took the gold from them, including all the worked articles. All the worked gold, including the offering that they offered to the Lord, was 16,750 shekels from the captains of thousands and the captains of hundreds. The warriors took plunder, each one for himself. Moses and Eleazar the priest took the gold from the captains of thousands and captains of hundreds and brought them into the tabernacle of witness, a memorial of the children of Israel before the Lord.

CHAPTER 31

CHAPTER 31 NOTES

1 This verse about human sacrifice to the Lord is also found in the Leningrad Codex, but not always translated by modern translators:

וְנֶ֫פֶשׁ אָדָ֗ם שִׁשָּׁ֥ה עָשָׂ֖ר אָ֑לֶף וּמִכְסָם֙ לַֽיהֹוָ֔ה שְׁנַ֥יִם וּשְׁלֹשִׁ֖ים נָֽפֶשׁ

Compare translations:

King James Version (1769 revision):
> And the persons were sixteen thousand; of which the LORD'S tribute was thirty and two persons.

Tanakh (JPS 1985):
> and 16,000 human beings.

A direct translation of the Leningrad Codex verse would be:
> and people, men: 16,000; levy to Yahweh: 32 people.

CHAPTER 32

The children of Reuben and the children of Gad had vast herds of livestock, and they saw the land of Jazer, and the land of Gilead and the place was a good place for livestock. The children of Reuben and the children of Gad came and said to Moses, and Eleazar the priest, and the princes of the community, "Ataroth, Dibon, Jaazer, Nimrah, Heshbon, Elealeh, Shibmah, Nebo, and Beon, the land which the Lord has delivered up before the children of Israel, is pasture land, and your servants have livestock."

They said, "If we have found grace in your sight, let this land be given to your servants for a possession, and do not make us cross over Jordan."

Moses said to the sons of Gad and the sons of Reuben, "Will your brothers go to war, and will you sit here? Why do you pervert the minds of the children of Israel, that they should not cross over into the land, which the Lord gives them? Did your fathers not do this, when I sent them from Kadesh Barne to spy out the land? They went up to the valley of the cluster, and spied the land, and turned back the heart of the children of Israel, that they should not go into the land, which the Lord gave them. The Lord was very angry in that day and swore, saying, 'Surely these men who came up out of Egypt from twenty years old and up, who know good and evil, will not see the land which I swore to give to Abraham and Isaac and Jacob, for they have not closely followed after me,' except Caleb the son of Jephunneh, who was set apart, and Joshua the son of Nun, for they closely obeyed the Lord. The Lord was very angry with Israel, and for forty years he caused them to wander in the wilderness until all the generation which did evil in the sight of the Lord was dead. Look, you have risen in the place of your fathers, an evil race of sinful men, to increase yet farther the fierce anger of the Lord against Israel. For you will turn away from him to desert him yet once more in the wilderness, and you will sin against this whole community."

They came to him, and replied, "We will build corrals here for our livestock, and cities for our possessions, and we will arm ourselves and go as an advanced guard before the children of Israel, until we have brought them into their place, and our possessions will remain in walled cities because of the inhabitants of the land. We will not return to our houses until the children of Israel have been distributed, each to his own inheritance. We will no longer inherit with them from the other side of Jordan from now onward because we have our full inheritance on the east side of Jordan."

Moses said to them, "If you will do according to these words, if you will arm yourselves before the Lord for battle, and every one of you will pass over Jordan fully armed before the Lord until his enemy is destroyed from before his face, and the land will be subdued before the Lord, then afterward you will return, and be guiltless before the Lord, and as regards Israel, and this land will be for you for a possession before the Lord. But if you will not do so, you will sin against the Lord, and you will know your sin when afflictions will come on you. Build cities and storehouses for yourselves, and folds for your livestock, and that which you suggested."

The sons of Reuben and the sons of Gad said to Moses, "Your servants will do as our lord commands. Our storehouses, and our wives, and all our livestock will be in the cities of Gilead. But your servants will go over, all armed and set in order before the Lord to battle, as our lord says."

Moses appointed to them as judges Eleazar the priest, and Joshua the son of Nun, and the chiefs of the families of the tribes of Israel. Moses said to them, "If the sons of Reuben and the sons of Gad will pass over Jordan with you, everyone armed for war before the Lord, and you will subdue the land before you, then you will give to them the land of Gilead as a possession. But if they will not pass over armed with you to war before the Lord, then will you cause to pass over their possessions and their wives and their livestock before you into the land of Canaan, and they will inherit with you in the land of Canaan."

The sons of Reuben and the sons of Gad answered, "Whatever our lord says to his servants, that will we do. We will go over armed before the Lord into the land of Canaan, and you will give us our inheritance beyond Jordan."

Moses gave to them, to the sons of Gad and the sons of Reuben, and to the half-tribe of Manasseh of the sons of Joseph, the kingdom of Sihon king of the Amorites, and the kingdom of Og king of Bashan, the land and its cities with its frontiers, the cities of the land around it. The sons of Gad built Dibon, and Ataroth, and Aroer, and Shophan, and Jazer, they set them up, and Beth Nimrah, and Beth Haran, strong cities, and folds for sheep. The sons of Reuben built Heshbon, and Elealeh, and Kiriathaim, and Ba'al Meon, surrounded with walls, and Sibmah, and they called the names of the cities which they built, after their own names. A son of Makir the son of Manasseh went to Gilead, and took it, and destroyed the Amorites who lived in it. Moses gave Gilead to Makir the son of Manasseh, and he lived there. Jair the son of Manasseh went and took their folds, and renamed them the Villages of Jair. Nobah went and took Kenath and her villages, and renamed them Nobah after his name.

Chapter 33

These are the stages of the children of Israel, as they went out from the land of Egypt with their army by the hand of Moses and Aaron. Moses wrote their exodus and their stages, by the word of the Lord, and these are the stages of their travels. They departed from Ramesses[1] in the first month, on the fifteenth day of the first month. On the day after the Passover, the children of Israel went out defiantly in front of all the Egyptians. The Egyptians buried their dead, all that the Lord slaughtered, every firstborn in the land of Egypt, when the Lord executed vengeance on their gods.

The children of Israel departed from Ramesses and camped in the corrals,[2] and they departed from the corrals and camped in Etham,[3] which is a part of the wilderness.

They departed from Etham and camped at the mouth of the watercourse[4] which is opposite Ba'al Zephon,[5] and camped opposite Migdol.[6]

They departed from before the mouth of the river and crossed the middle of the sea into the wilderness, and they traveled three days through the wilderness and camped in the Bitter Lakes.[7]

They departed from the Bitter Lakes and went to Elim.[8] In Elim were twelve fountains of water and 70 palm trees, and they camped there by the water.

CHAPTER 33

They departed from Elim and camped by the Sea of Edom.

They departed from the Sea of Edom and camped in the Wilderness of Sin.

They departed from the Wilderness of Sin and camped in Raphaca.[9]

They departed from Raphaca and camped in Alush.

They departed from Alush and camped in Rephidim,[10] and there was no water there for the people to drink.

They departed from Rephidim and camped in the Wilderness of Sinai.

They departed from the Wilderness of Sinai and camped at the Graves of Desire.

They departed from the Graves of Desire and camped in Hazeroth.

They departed from Hazeroth and camped in Rithmah.

They departed from Rithmah and camped in Rimmon Perez.

They departed from Rimmon Perez and camped in Libnah.

They departed from Libnah and camped in Rissah.

They departed from Rissah and camped in Kehelathah.

They departed from Kehelathah and camped in Shepher.

They departed from Shepher and camped in Haradah.

They departed from Haradah and camped in Makheloth.

They departed from Makheloth and camped in Tahath.

They departed from Tahath and camped in Terah.

They departed from Terah and camped in Mithkah.

They departed from Mithkah and camped in Hashmonah.

They departed from Hashmonah and camped in Moseroth.

They departed from Moseroth and camped in Bene Jaakan.

They departed from Bene Jaakan and camped in the mountain Gudgodah.

They departed from the mountain Gudgodah and camped in Jotbathah.

They departed from Jotbathah and camped in Abronah.

They departed from Abronah and camped in Ezion Geber.

They departed from Ezion Geber and camped in the Wilderness of Sin.

They departed from the Wilderness of Sin and camped in the Wilderness of Paran. This is Kadesh.

They departed from Kadesh and camped at Mount Hor near the land of Edom.

Aaron the priest went up by the command of the Lord, and died there in the fortieth year since the departure of the children of Israel from the land of Egypt, in the fifth month, on the first day of the month. Aaron was 123 years old when he died on Mount Hor. Arad the Canaanite king, who lived in the land of Canaan, heard when the children of Israel were entering the land.

They departed from Mount Hor and camped in Hashmonah. They departed from Hashmonah and camped in Punon.

They departed from Punon and camped in Oboth.

They departed from Oboth and camped in Gai, on the other side of the Jordan on the border of Moab.

They departed from Gai and camped in Dibon Gad.

They departed from Dibon Gad and camped in Almon Diblathaim.

They departed from Almon Diblathaim and camped on the mountains of Abarim, near Nebo.

They departed from the mountains of Abarim and camped to the west of Moab, at the Jordan near Jericho.

They camped by the Jordan between Beth Jeshimoth as far as Belsa to the west of Moab.

The Lord spoke to Moses at the west of Moab by Jordan at Jericho, saying, "Speak to the children of Israel and say to them, "You are to pass over Jordan into the land of Canaan. You will destroy all that live in the land before your face, and you will abolish their high places, and all their molten images you will destroy, and you will demolish all their pillars."

CHAPTER 33

"You will destroy all the inhabitants of the land, and you will live in it, for I have given their land to you for an inheritance. You will inherit their land according to your tribes; to the greater number you will give the larger possession, and to the smaller, you will give the lesser possession. To whatever part his name will go out by lot, there will be his property. You will inherit according to the tribes of your families. But if you will not destroy the residents in the land from before you, then it will happen that whoever you spare will be thorns in your eyes, and darts in your sides and they will be enemies to you on the land on which you will live, and it will happen that as I had determined to do to them, I will also do to you."

CHAPTER 33 NOTES

1 Codex Vaticanus: Ramessōn (ρλмєccωɴ)

- Codex Alexandrinus (LXX A): Ramessē (ρλмєccн)
- Septuagint manuscript 624: Ramesē (ρλмλccн)
- Septuagint manuscript 509: Ramessō (ρλμ6σҀω)
- Septuagint manuscript 318: Ramesi (ρλμ6σ𝑞)
- Septuagint manuscript 319: Rammesē (ρλμμ6σλ)
- Septuagint manuscript 16: Ramesē (ρλμ6σλ)
- Septuagint manuscript 426: Ramessēs (ρλμ6σσλc)
- Septuagint manuscript 75: Ramesi (ρλμ6σι)
- Septuagint manuscript 82: Ramesēs (ρλμ6σλc)
- Septuagint manuscript 458: Remessē (ρ6μ6σσλ)
- Septuagint manuscript 527: Ramesōn (ρλμ6Ҁωɴ)

- Septuagint manuscript 53: Kramessē (Κϱαμϵ́σσϧ)
- Septuagint manuscript 619: Ramaisōn (Ῥαμαίϲⲱν)
- Leningrad Codex: Ra'məsēs (רַעְמְסֵס).
- Peshitta: Rȯmsys (ܪܥܡܣܝܣ)
- Targum Onkelos: Ra'məsēs (רַעְמְסֵס)
- Targum Pseudo-Jonathan: Pîlûsîn (פִּילוּסִין). Translation: Pelusium
- Sahidic manuscript 2006: Ramessē (ⲢⲀⲘⲈⲤⲤⲎ)

The location of Ramesses has been a matter of debate since before the Septuagint was translated, and the translators were not sure which ancient Egyptian city the name Ramesses was referring to. The historic city of Ramesses (𓇳𓌻𓋴) was built in the era of Pharaoh Shoshenq I (943 to 922 BCE) and was still a major city when the stories found in Numbers were most likely compiled into a book under King Josiah (640 to 609 BCE). The Late-Period city of Ramesses was a rebuilding of the New Kingdom era city of Pi-Ramesses (𓊪𓂋𓇳𓌻𓋴), and as the city of Pi-Ramesses was never called Ramesses during the New Kingdom era, it must be assumed that the name was updated when the stories were compiled under Josiah.

The city of Pi-Ramesses, which was founded in 1290 BCE, was itself a rebuilding of Avaris (𓉐𓅱𓃀𓊖), the Hyksos capital, which had been destroyed when the Hyksos were driven from Egypt in circa 1550 BCE, meaning it is not clear if the name Avaris or Pi-Ramesses was updated to Ramesses. Both Avaris and Pi-Ramesses had served as imperial capital cities when Egypt had ruled Canaan, and so either could be the city in the text, however, if one accepts that Pi-Ramesses was the city called Ramesses, then it dates the events in Exodus to the 1200s BCE, immediately before the Bronze Age Collapse, yet there are already reports from a century earlier of the Shasu (Nomads) of Yhw in the Seir Region of modern Jordan, which are generally accepted as a reference to the Israelites, meaning the original name was probably Avaris, which had become obscure by Josiah's time, and was updated to the contemporary name.

The city of Pelusium, mentioned in the Jerusalem and Jonathan Targums on Exodus and Numbers, was the easternmost major city in the Nile Delta during the Greco-Roman era. The city had existed since the Old Kingdom era, and therefore it is plausible that if was the original city in the text, however, that is unlikely.

The original name of the city was Sin (𓊖) in the Old Kingdom era, however, which continued to b used alongside later names that were applied to the city, and was the common name of the city in languages using the Akkadian Cuneiform script, commonly spelled as Sîn (𒌍𒉈𒊏), the name of the Akkadian moon-god, later spelled as Syån (ϷΝ^Ϡ), Saĩn (Σαῖν), Sîn (סִין), and Sin (ⲤⲓⲚ) during the Classical era. During the New Kingdom era, the name of the city was changed to Per-Amen (𓉐𓏤𓇋𓏠𓈖), meaning the "house of Amen,| which also continued to be used, resulting in the Coptic Peremoun (Ⲡⲉⲣⲉⲙⲟⲩⲛ). During the early Iron Age, the name Per-Sin (קֵאן) developed, which was later transliterated into Greek as Pelousion (Πηλουσιον), and then adopted into Hebrew and Judean-Aramaic as Pilusin (פִּילוּסִין), meaning the name could not have been in the early Aramaic translation of Exodus and Numbers. Nevertheless, it is clear that the city was not viewed as being the historic city of Ramesses by the Judeans in the early-Christian era.

2 Codex Vaticanus: Sŏkōṭ (ⲤⲞⲬⲰⲐ)

- Septuagint manuscript 15: Socōṭ (Σοⳑⲱⲑ)
- Septuagint manuscript 28: Okkŏṭ (ⲞⳑⲬⲱⲐ)
- Septuagint manuscript 82: Oṭom (ⲞⲐⲟμ)
- Septuagint manuscript 130: Okŏṭ (ⲞⲬⲱⲐ)

- Septuagint manuscript 72: Sokḵōṯ (Σοʟχοοθ)
- Septuagint manuscript 527: Aḵḵōṯ (ᴧχχοοθ)
- Leningrad Codex: sūkkōt (סֻכֹּת)
- Peshitta: skwt (ܣܟܘܬ)
- Targum Onkelos: sūkkōt (סֻכֹּת)
- Targum Pseudo-Jonathan: sūkkôt (סֻכּוֹת)
- Vetus Latina: Soccoth (Soccotʜ)
- Sahidic manuscript 2006: Soḵōṯ (Coxωθ)
- Sahidic manuscript 2044: Sogḵōṯ (Corxωθ)

The Septuagint and Leningrad Codex both treat Sukkot as a place name, however, this is also the word for "stables," or "corrals," which implies the original text was about the Israelites retrieving their animals before leaving Egypt.

3 Codex Vaticanus: Bouṯan (ʙoⲩⲑᴧⲛ)

- Septuagint manuscript 127: Souṯam (Σουθᴧμ)
- Septuagint manuscript 417: Mouṯan (Μουθᴧⲛ)
- Septuagint manuscript 58: Bouṯam (βουθᴧμ)
- Septuagint manuscript 426: Ouṯam (Oυθᴧμ)
- Septuagint manuscript 413: Bouṯa (βουθᴧ)
- Septuagint manuscript 71: Boṯan (βοθᴧⲛ)
- Septuagint manuscript 767: Biṯan (βιθᴧⲛ)
- Septuagint manuscript 799: Oṯam (Oθᴧμ)
- Leningrad Codex: 'Ētām (אֵתָם)
- Peshitta: Åtm (ܐܬܡ)
- Targum Onkelos: 'Ētām (אֵתָם)
- Targum Jerusalem: 'Êtān (אֵיתָן)
- Targum Pseudo-Jonathan: 'Êtām (אֵיתָם)
- Sahidic manuscript 2006: Bouṯan (ʙoⲩⲑᴧⲛ)

242

This is believed to represent "Khetam," one of the Egyptian fortresses that sat between the Mediterranean coast and the Gulf of Suez. In the Middle Kingdom's Tale of Sinhue, Sinhue reported sneaking past an Egyptian fort in the vicinity at night when he was escaping Egypt.

4 Codex Vaticanus: stoma Epirōṯ (ⲥⲧⲟⲙⲁ ⲉⲡⲓⲣⲱⲑ). Translation: mouth (or face, source) of Epiroth

• Septuagint manuscript 527: stoma Irōṯ (ⲥⲟⲙⲁ ⲓⲣⲱⲑ). Translation: mouth (or face, source) of Iroth

• Septuagint manuscript 318: stoma Ērōṯ (ⲥⲟⲙⲁ Ⲏⲣⲱⲑ). Translation: mouth (or face, source) of Eroth

• Septuagint manuscript 58: stoma epi Aeirōṯ (ⲥⲟⲙⲁ ⲉⲡⲓ Ⲁⲉⲣⲱⲑ). Translation: mouth (or face, source) at (or near, on, upon) Airoth

• Septuagint manuscript 120: stoma Eirōn (ⲥⲟⲙⲁ Ⲉⲓⲣⲱⲛ). Translation: mouth to Eiron

• Septuagint manuscript 529: stoma eis Rōṯ (ⲥⲟⲙⲁ ⲇⲥ Ⲣⲟⲟⲑ). Translation: mouth to Roth

• Septuagint manuscript 82: stoma Epeirōṯ (ⲥⲟⲙⲁ Ⲉⲡⲇⲣⲱⲑ). Translation: mouth of Epiroth

• Septuagint manuscript 126: stoma ei Rōṯ (ⲥⲟⲙⲁ ⲇ Ⲣⲟⲟⲑ). Translation: mouth (or face, source) if Roth

• Leningrad Codex: pî hahîrōt (פִּי הַחִירֹת). Translation: fold of the hirot

• Peshitta: pwm Hårytå (ܦܘܡ ܚܪܝܬܐ). Translation: mouth (or entrance, riverbank) of Haryta

• Targum Onkelos: pûm hîrātā' (פּוּם חִירָתָא). Translation: mouth (or entrance, riverbank) of the heir (or interior)

• Targum Jerusalem: pûnədəqê hêrātā' (פּוּנְדְּקֵי חִירָתָא). Translation: innkeepers of the heir (or interior)

CHAPTER 33

- Targum Pseudo-Jonathan: pûmê hîrātā' (פּוּמֵי חִירְתָא).
Translation: mouth of the heir (or interior)

- Sahidic manuscript 2006: tapro ntirōṯ (ⲧⲁⲡⲣⲟ ⲛⲧⲓⲣⲱⲑ).
Translation: mouth of Tirouth

- Sahidic manuscript 2044: tapro naeirōṯ (ⲧⲁⲡⲣⲟ ⲛⲁⲉⲓⲣⲱⲑ).
Translation: mouth of Aeirouth

The name "Hirot" is an ancient Egyptian word transliterated as hr-t, which meant both watercourse (𓉐𓏤𓈖) and Nile deposits (𓆰𓈖𓏥) depending on context. The term was generally used in the Nile Delta, where the watercourses moved regularly as sediment built up. This was most likely a reference to the mouth of the Pelusiac branch of the Nile River, the ancient eastern-most branch of the Nile.

5 Codex Vaticanus: Beelsepfōn (ⲃⲉⲉⲗⲥⲉⲡⲧⲫⲱⲛ)

- Septuagint manuscript 509: Belselfōn (βελσελφων)
- Septuagint manuscript 15: Beelseffōn (βεελσεββων)
- Septuagint manuscript 319: Beelsemfōr (βεελσεμφωρ)
- Septuagint manuscript 75: Beēlsepfōn (βεελσεμπβων)
- Septuagint manuscript 458: Beelsepfōr (βεελσεπβωρ)
- Septuagint manuscript 246: Beelsemfōn (βεελσεμβων)
- Septuagint manuscript 71: Beēlsepfōn (βελλοσπβων)
- Leningrad Codex: Ba'al Səpôn (בַּעַל צְפֹן)
- Peshitta: Bôlspwn (ܒܠܣܦܘܢ)
- Targum Onkelos: Bə'ēl Səpôn (בְּעֵל צְפוֹן)
- Targum Jerusalem: 'appê ta'ăwāwtā' (אַפֵּי טַעֲוָותָא). Translation: cast perversions (idols)
- Targum Pseudo-Jonathan: ta'ăwawt Səpôn (טַעֲוָות צְפוֹן).
Translation: perversion of Zephon
- Sahidic manuscript 2006: Bersefōn (ⲃⲉⲣⲥⲉⲫⲱⲛ)

CHAPTER 33

- Sahidic manuscript 2044: Belsepfōn (**Вєλсєпϥⲱⲛ**)

Ba'al Zephon was a Canaanite god mentioned in the Ugaritic Texts from circa 1300 BCE and considered to be the Canaanite version of Amen (Amun). The origin of the name appears to have been Mount Zephon on the modern Syrian-Turkish border at the northern-most frontier of Canaan. Its usage in Egypt appears to be based on a group of Canaanites settling in the area of Lake Bardawil on the north coast of the Sinai Peninsula, a shallow saline lake with a surface area of 147,000 acres (59,500 hectares). Ba'al Zephon continued to be worshiped in the region well into the Greek era.

The story of the sea being blown away so the Israelites could walk across it, only to return and drown the Egyptian army is reminiscent of the Greek story of the Serbonian Bog, also called Lake Serbonis, which had a deceptive appearance of looking solid but was a bog that swallowed people that tried to pass through it. The Serbonian Bog myth has been identified with Lake Bardawil since the Greeks ruled Egypt. In ancient Egyptian records, Lake Bardawil was described as a quagmire that whole armies had been swallowed up by. Given that Ba'al Zephon is identified in this chapter, and is known to refer to Lake Bardawil, it is clear that this unusual event took place in Lake Bardawil, and not in the Red Sea, as later writers assumed.

6 Codex Vaticanus: Magdōlou (**ⲙⲁⲅⲇⲱⲗⲟⲩ**)

- Septuagint manuscript 318: Magdolou (Μαγδολ/ου)

- Septuagint manuscript 129: Makdōlou (Μακδωλ/ου)

- Septuagint manuscript 426: Magdalou (Μαγδα/ου)

- Leningrad Codex: migdōl (מִגְדֹּל). Translation: tower, fortification, platform

- Peshitta: Mgdwl (ܡܓܕܘܠ)

- Targum Onkelos: Migdōl (מִגְדֹּל)

- Targum Pseudo-Jonathan: Migdôl (מִגְדּוֹל)
- Sahidic manuscript 2006: Magdōn (ⲘⲀⲅⲀⲱⲚ)
- Sahidic manuscript 2044: Magdōl (ⲘⲀⲅⲀⲱⲗ)

A Ptolemaic-era geographical text housed at the Cairo Museum lists four border fortresses along the Greek-era Arsinoe Canal, including Migdol and Ba'al Zephon. It seems likely these later fortresses were named after the fortresses in the Torah, which the Ptolemys had paid to have translated at the Library of Alexandria. Most scholars associate Migdol with El Qantara, a city that today lays along the Suez Canal, between the Mediterranean Port Said and the Bitter Lakes. This location is possible, however, the term is generic enough that any fortified tower may be indicated. In the Egyptian Middle Kingdom Era Tale of Sinhue, the hero Sinhue also described passing a fortification between the Nile and the Bitter Lakes as he fled Egypt, which suggests whatever the fortification was, it had been there for centuries by the time the Israelites passed it.

7 Codex Vaticanus: Pikriais (ⲠⲓⲕⲣⲓⲀⲓⲥ). Translation: bitter

- Septuagint manuscript 120: Pikrias (ⲡⲓⲕβⲓⲀⲥ)
- Leningrad Codex: mārâ (מָרָה). Translation: bile
- Peshitta: Mwrt (ܡܖܝܐ)
- Targum Onkelos: mārâ (מְרָה). Translation: bile
- Targum Jerusalem: mārâ (מְרָה). Translation: bile
- Targum Pseudo-Jonathan: mārâ (מְרָה). Translation: bile
- Sahidic manuscript 2006: siše (ⲥⲓϣⲉ). Translation: bitter
- Sahidic manuscript 2048: enetsaše (ⲉⲚⲉⲧⲥⲀϣⲉ). Translation: to god of bitter

The Greek translators of this locale in Exodus, both transliterated mrh (מרה) as Merra (Μερρα), and translated it as picria (πικρια). In Numbers, they just translated the word as pikriais (πικρίαις) meaning "bitter." The location of this bitter water has been debated and is largely dependent on where the events involving the Papyrus Sea and Mount Sinai took place. This list of locations does mention the Israelites crossing the sea after reaching Ba'al Zephon but does not name the sea. The "Erythrean Sea" was only mentioned later when it was mentioned the second time in Exodus.

Based on the "Papyrus Sea" event being at Lake Bardawil, the bitter waters would likely be the Bitter Lakes, halfway between the Mediterranean coast and the Gulf of Suez. The larger of the two Bitter Lakes, the Great Bitter Lake had dried out completely by the time the Suez Canal was constructed, which now connects these two lakes, as well as linking them to the Mediterranean and Gulf of Suez. The Pyramid Texts, which date back to the Old Kingdom era, mention the Great Bitter Lake, implying the existence of one or more Small Bitter Lake(s), and therefore the name is very ancient, long preceding the era of Moses.

It seems improbable that there would have been another area of bitter waters in the region that the Egyptians somehow never noticed through thousands of years of occupation, and therefore, the Bitter Lakes are almost certainly the place being described in this chapter. If this interpretation is correct, it would mean the Israelites started moving east along the coastal road to Canaan, and then turned back and headed south into the Sinai after leaving Lake Bardawil.

8 Codex Vaticanus: Ailim (ⲀⲓⲀⲓⲘ)

- Codex Colberto-Sarravianus: Eleim (Ελдμ)
- Septuagint manuscript 509: Salein (ΣдλдN)
- Septuagint manuscript 84: Ailēm (Ⲁⲓλⲏμ)
- Septuagint manuscript 318: Elim (Ελμ)
- Septuagint manuscript 82: Aleim (Ⲁλдμ)

- Septuagint manuscript 458: Seleim (Σℓϳϥμ)
- Septuagint manuscript 767: Selim (Σℓϳιμ)
- Septuagint manuscript 799: Elēm (Ελℓμ)
- Leningrad Codex: 'Êlim (אֵילִם)
- Peshitta: Åylm (ܐܝܠܡ)
- Targum Onkelos: 'Êlim (אֵילִם)
- Targum Jerusalem: 'Êlîmâ (אֵילִימָה)
- Targum Pseudo-Jonathan: 'Êlim (אֵילִם)
- Sahidic manuscript 2006: Elim (Ελιμ)
- Bohairic manuscript BnF Coptic 1: Elim (Ελιμ)
- Bohairic manuscript Vatican Coptic 1: Ulim (Υλιμ)

The location of Elim is debated, like the other stations along the route the Israelites took out of Egypt. Its location is largely based on the assumptions about the events of the Papyrus Sea, the location of the Bitter Waters, and ultimately the location of the Wilderness of Sin and Mount Sinai. It is traditionally identified by Muslims as the Oyun Musa (عيون موسى), meaning "Moses Spring" in the western Sinai Peninsula, where there are twelve ancient wells. It is not clear when the location was named, and it is plausible that this location was named after Moses by Emperor Constantine's mother, Helena Augusta, when she named Mount Sinai and the Sinai Peninsula in the 330s CE. As the Greek translators did not identify the town, it could not have been widely known as the 'Moses Spring' circa 250 BCE. Another theory is the Elim may have referred to the Wadi Gharandel in the Sinai Peninsula, again this is based on the theory that Exodus' Mount Sinai was the large mountain range named Sinai by Helena Augusta in the 330s CE.

If the Israelites were trying to leave Egypt, and one would assume Moses was leading them towards Midian, where he first encountered the fire-angel, then the logical direction was east following the southern road across the Sinai Peninsula, which runs east from the Bitter Lakes to the modern town of An-Nekhel in central Sinai, before continuing on to mountains of Hashem El Tarif in eastern Sinai. An-Nekhel is known to have been used as a watering hole along the southern road since Pharaonic times. It is postulated to have been a Canaanite town, founded during the Hyksos era, named after the Canaanite goddess Nikkal-wa-Ib, meaning "Great lady of the Fruitful," who was the goddess of orchards. If this theory is correct, then there must have been a settlement with orchards in the region, matching to some degree the Exodus' description of a place of wells and trees.

9 Codex Vaticanus: Rafaka (ρΑφΑκΑ)

- Codex Alexandrinus: Rafakan (ρΑφΑκΑΝ)
- Codex Venetus: Rafa (ρΑϨΑ)
- Septuagint manuscript 58: Rafakai (ρΑϨΑιια/)
- Septuagint manuscript 120: Rakafa (ρΑκαϨΑ)
- Septuagint manuscript 343: Rafak (ρΑϨΑιι)
- Septuagint manuscript 29: Rafain (ρΑϨΑιν)
- Septuagint manuscript 767: Dafaka (ΔΑϨΑκα)
- Septuagint manuscript 321: Rafek (ρΑϨᲒιι)
- Leningrad Codex: Dāpəqâ (דָּפְקָה). Generally transliterated as Dophkah
- Peshitta: Rpqâ (ܪܦܩܐ)
- Targum Onkelos: Dāpəqâ (דְּפְקָה)
- Targum Pseudo-Jonathan: Dāpəqâ (דְּפְקָה)
- Sahidic manuscript 2006: Rafaga (ρΑφΑκΑ)
- Sahidic manuscript 2044: Dafaga (ᲐΑφΑρΑ)

The town of Dophkah is believed to have been near modern Elat, on the coast of the Gulf of Aqaba. The difference in the spelling of the names found in the Greek and Syriac translations, versus the Hebrew and Coptic translations likely originated in either the Canaanite (Judahite, Samaritan, or Edomite) or early Aramaic translations, as both the Canaanite D (ᴧ) and R (ᕁ), and Aramaic D (ᆨ) and R (ᆨ) were similar in shape.

10 Codex Vaticanus: Rafidin (ⲢⲀⲪⲒⲆⲒⲚ)

- Septuagint manuscript 426: Rafidim (Ραφιδιμ)
- Septuagint manuscript 616: Rafadein (Ραφαδδειν)
- Septuagint manuscript 75: Rafidēn (Ραφιδηω)
- Septuagint manuscript 761: Rafideim (Ραφιδιμ)
- Septuagint manuscript 767: Rafiadein (Ραφιαδδειν)
- Septuagint manuscript 416: Rafēdin (Ραφηδιν)
- Leningrad Codex: Rəpîdim (רְפִידֹם)
- Peshitta: Rpydyn (ܪܦܝܕܝܢ)
- Targum Onkelos: Rəpîdim (רְפִידֹם)
- Targum Pseudo-Jonathan: Rəpîdîm (רְפִידִים)
- Sahidic manuscript 2006: Rafidin (Ραφιⲁⲓⲛ)
- Bohairic manuscripts: Rafazin (Ραⲯⲁⲍⲓⲛ)

This location is generally associated with the Wadi Feiran, or the Feiran Oasis within it. The Wadi Feiran is an 130 km (81 miles) long wadi (seasonal river) which runs down the Jebel Musa to the Gulf of Suez. The Feiran Oasis, also called El Hesweh, is approximately 4.8 km (3 miles) long, and generally habitable year-round. The Greek geographer and polymath Claudius Ptolemy identified this as the location of Paran from the Torah, which is likely where the Arabic name came from.

The assumption that Wadi Feiran is Rephidim is again predicated on Jebel Musa being Mount Sinai, or at least in the vicinity of Mount Sinai, however, if Horeb is Sinai, then Sinai would have to be near or in Midian, as that was where Moses first encountered the fire-messenger that sent him back to Egypt, and a location in southern Sinai seems highly improbable for a Midianite shepherd, especially one trying to avoid Egyptians, who were mining in the region.

If the Israelites had followed the southern road across the Sinai Peninsula en route to Mount Sinai / Horeb / Seir, they would have passed the An-Nekhel in central Sinai, and then proceeded east to the mountains of Hashem El Tarif in eastern Sinai, before following the Arabah north towards Jebel al-Madhbah. The likely location of this event along the route is at Hashem El Tarif, which did at one point have a spring flowing down from the top of the summit. The location of Rephidim at Hashem El Tarif is supported by the subsequent attack of the Amalekites, who, according to the Book of Numbers lived in the Negev, south of Judea, which is directly north of Hashem El Tarif.

CHAPTER 34

The Lord said to Moses, "Order the children of Israel, 'You are entering into the land of Canaan. It will be an inheritance for you, the land of Canaan with its boundaries. Your southern border will be from the Wilderness of Sin to the border of Edom, and your southern border will be on the edge of the Dead Sea[1] in the east. Your border will go around you from the south to the ascent of Akrabbim, and will proceed by Ennac, and will follow southward to Kadesh Barnea, and it will go out to the village of Arad and will proceed by Azmon. The border will span from Azmon to the river of Egypt,[2] and the sea will be the end. You have your border on the sea, the Mediterranean Sea[3] will be the boundary. This will be for you the border on the west."

"This will be your northern border. From the Mediterranean Sea, you will measure for yourselves, by the side of the mountain. You will measure for yourselves the mountain from Mount Nur at the entrance into Hama, and the termination of it will be the frontiers of Sarada.[4] The border will go out to As-Safira,[5] and its termination will be at Hazar-enan.[6] This will be your border from the north. You will measure for yourselves the eastern border from Hazar-enan to the treeless land.[7] The border will go down the treeless land to Rablah[8] eastward to the fountains, and the border will go down from Rablah behind the Sea of Galilee[9] in the east. The border will go down the Jordan, and the end will be the Dead Sea. This will be your land and its borders around it."

Moses ordered the children of Israel, "This is the land which you will inherit by lot, even as the Lord commanded us to give it to the nine tribes and the half-tribe of Manasseh. The tribe of the children of Reuben, and the tribe of the children of Gad have received their inheritance according to the houses of their families, and the half-tribe of Manasseh have received their inheritances. Two tribes and half a tribe have received their inheritance beyond Jordan by Jericho to the southeast."

The Lord said to Moses, "These are the names of the men who will assign the land before you as an inheritance: Eleazar the priest and Joshua the son of Nun. You will take one ruler from each tribe to divide the land to you by lot. These are the names of the men:"

"From the tribe of Judah: Caleb the son of Jephunneh."

"From the tribe of Simeon: Shelumiel the son of Ammihud."

"From the tribe of Benjamin: Elidad the son of Kislon."

"From the tribe of Dan, the prince was Bukki the son of Jogli."

"From the sons of Joseph, among the tribe of the sons of Manasseh, the prince was Hanniel the son of Oufi, and from the tribe of the sons of Ephraim, the prince was Kemuel the son of Shiphtan."

CHAPTER 34

"From the tribe of Zebulun, the prince was Elizaphan the son of Parnach."

"From the tribe of the sons of Issachar, the prince was Paltiel the son of Azzan."

"From the tribe of the children of Asher, the prince was Ahihud the son of Shelomi."

"From the tribe of Naphtali, the prince was Pedahel the son of Ammihud."

The Lord commanded these to distribute the inheritances to the children of Israel in the land of Canaan.

CHAPTER 34 NOTES

1 Codex Vaticanus: talassēs tēs alukēs (ⲐⲀⲀⲀⲤⲤⲎⳞ ⲦⲎⳞ ⲀⲀⲨⳞⲎⳞ). Translation: sea of salt (the modern Dead Sea)

• Septuagint manuscript 799: alukēs talassēs (ⲁⲗⲩⳡⳡⳡ ⲑⲁⲗⲗⲟⲟⳡ). Translation: Salt Sea (the modern Dead Sea)

• Septuagint manuscript 416: talattēs tēs alukēs (ⲑⲁⲗⲁⲧⲉ ⲉ ⲁⲗⲩⳡⳡ). Translation: sea of salt (the modern Dead Sea)

• Leningrad Codex: yām-hammelaḥ (יָם־הַמֶּלַח). Translation: sea of salt (the modern Dead Sea)

• Peshitta: ymå dmlḥå (ܝܡܐ ܕܡܠܚܐ). Translation: sea of salt (the modern Dead Sea)

• Targum Onkelos: yammā' dəmilḥā' (יַמָּא דְמִלְחָא). Translation: sea of salt (the modern Dead Sea)

• Targum Jerusalem: yamā' dəmilḥā' (יַמָּא דְמִלְחָא). Translation: sea of salt (the modern Dead Sea)

CHAPTER 34

• Sahidic manuscript 2006: talassa mmlh (ⲑⲁⲗⲁⲥⲥⲁ ⲙⲙⲗϩ). Translation: sea of salt

• Sahidic manuscript 2044: talassa nnehmoy (ⲑⲁⲗⲁⲥⲥⲁ ⲛⲛⲉϩⲙⲟⲩ). Translation: sea of salt

The Sea of Salt was an old name of the Dead Sea.

2 Codex Vaticanus: křeimarroun Aiguptou (ⲭⲉⲓⲙⲁⲣⲣⲟⲩⲛ ⲁⲓⲅⲩⲡⲧⲟⲩ). Translation: river of Egypt

• Codex Colberto-Sarravianus: kimarrou Aiguptou (ⲭⲉⲓⲙⲁⲣⲣⲟⲩ ⲁⲓⲅⲩⲡⲧⲟⲩ). Translation: river of Egypt

• Codex Alexandrinus: křeimarron Aiguptou (ⲭⲉⲓⲙⲁⲣⲣⲟⲛ ⲁⲓⲅⲩⲡⲧⲟⲩ). Translation: river of Egypt

• Septuagint manuscript 509: křeimarroun Aiguptoun (χϥμαρϙωυ Ἀιγυπτων)

• Septuagint manuscript 127: kimarrou Aiguptou (χιμαρϙου Ἀιγυπτω)

• Septuagint manuscript 392: kimarron Aiguptou (χιμαρϼ῀ Ἀιγυπτω)

• Septuagint manuscript 30: křeimaron Aiguptou (χϥμαρ῀ Ἀιγυπτω)

• Septuagint manuscript 58: křeimarrou Aiguptou (χϥμαρϙου Ἀιγυπτω). Translation: river of Egypt

• Septuagint manuscript 343: kimaron Aiguptou (χιμαρ῀ Ἀιγυπτω)

• Septuagint manuscript 72: křeimarou Aiguptou (χϥμαρου Ἀιγυπτω)

• Septuagint manuscript 19: křeimarroun ex Aiguptou (χϥμαρϙωυ ϭξ Ἀιγυπτω). Translation: river on Egypt

• Leningrad Codex: naḥlâ Miṣrāyim (נַחְלָה מִצְרָיִם). Translation: territory of Egyptians

- Peshitta: nḥlå dmṣryn (ܢܚܠܐ ܕܡܨܪܝܢ). Translation: river of the Egyptians
- Targum Onkelos: naḥălā' dəMiṣrāyim (נַחֲלָא דְמִצְרָיִם). Translation: river of Egyptians
- Jerusalem Targum: Nîlôs Miṣrayim (נִילוֹס מִצְרָיִם). Translation: Nile of Egypt
- Jonathan Targum: Nîlôs dəMiṣrā'ê (נִילוֹס דְמִצְרָאֵי). Translation: Nile of the Egyptians
- Sahidic manuscript 2006: peǩimarros nǩēme (ⲡⲉⲭⲓⲙⲁⲣⲣⲟⲥ ⲛⲕⲏⲙⲉ). Translation: wadi of black (or Egypt)

This river was accepted as the Nile in ancient Hebrew and Aramaic interpretations, including the Jerusalem and Jonathan Targums.

3 Codex Vaticanus: ṭalassēs tēs megalēs (ⲐⲀⲗⲀⲤⲤⲎⲤ ⲦⲎⲤ ⲘⲉⲄⲀⲗⲎⲤ). Translation: sea the great (or Mediterranean Sea)
- Leningrad Codex: hayyām haggādôl (הַיָּם הַגָּדוֹל). Translation: the sea the great
- Peshitta: ymå rbå (ܝܡܐ ܪܒܐ). Translation: sea great (or Mediterranean Sea)
- Targum Onkelos: yammā' rabbā' (יְמָא רַבָּא). Translation: sea great (or Mediterranean Sea)
- Targum Jerusalem: yamā' rabbā' (יְמָא רַבָּא). Translation: sea great (or Mediterranean Sea)
- Targum Pseudo-Jonathan: yamā' rabbā' (יְמָא רַבָּא). Translation: sea great (or Mediterranean Sea)
- Sahidic manuscript 2006: ṭalassa noh (ⲐⲀⲗⲀⲤⲤⲀ ⲚⲞϬ). Translation: sea great

This Great Sea is an old name of the Mediterranean Sea.

CHAPTER 34

4 Codex Vaticanus: Asadak (ܐܣܕܕܟ)

- Codex Colberto-Sarravianus: Sarada (ܣܪܕܐܐ)
- Codex Alexandrinus: Sadadak (ܣܕܕܕܟ)
- Codex Ambrosiano A 147: Saradak (ܣܪܕܕܟ)
- Codex Venetus: Sardǎk (Σαρδαχ)
- Septuagint manuscript 28: Sadak (Σλδαⱡ)
- Septuagint manuscript 121: Sasadak (ΣλⒶδαⱡ)
- Septuagint manuscript 127: Asaraddak (Ασαρλλδαⱡ)
- Septuagint manuscript 318: o Adadak (o Αδαδαⱡ). Translation: the Adadac.
- Septuagint manuscript 319: Aradak (Αρᵉαδαⱡ)
- Septuagint manuscript 30: Sardak (Σαρδαⱡ)
- Septuagint manuscript 343: Saddak (Σλλδαⱡ)
- Septuagint manuscript 56: Sadada (Σλδαδα)
- Septuagint manuscript 422 Sedak (Σϐδαⱡ)
- Septuagint manuscript 59: Kaddak (Κλλδαⱡ)
- Leningrad Codex: Sədādâ (צְדָדָה). Generally transliterated as Zedad.
- Peshitta: Ṣdd (ܨܕܕ)
- Targum Onkelos: Sədād (צְדָד)
- Jerusalem Targum: 'Awwlas dəCîləqā'ê (אַוְולָס דְקִילְקָאֵי). Translation: Awwlas of the Cilicians
- Jonathan Targum: 'Ābəlas dəQîləqā'ê (אָבְלָס דְקִילְקָאֵי). Translation: Abelas of the Cilicians
- Sahidic manuscript 2006: Sarak (Ⲥⲁⲣⲁⲕ)
- Sahidic manuscript 2044: Sadarak (Ⲥⲁⲗⲁⲣⲁⲕ)
- Bohairic manuscripts: Ararad (Ⲁ̅ⲣⲁⲣⲁⲗ)

This is theorized as being the inland Syrian town of Sedad (صدد), east of northern Lebanon, however, Sarada was listed as being

258

coastal, and therefore could not be Sedad. Based on the previous mention of Mount Nur and the city of Hama, Zedad was likely on the Mediterranean coast south of modern Samandagi, where both the Orontes River, which flows through Hama, and the Karusu River which flows down from the Nur mountains, empty in the Mediterranean. The interpretations found in the Targums generally placed it in Cilicia, northwest of the Nur Mountains.

5 Codex Vaticanus: Defrōna (ᴅⲉⳝⲣⲱⲛⲁ)

- Codex Ambrosiano A 147: Zefrōna (ⲍⲉⳝⲣⲱⲛⲁ)

- Codex Venetus: Frōna (ⳝⲣⲱⲛⲁ)

- Septuagint manuscript 121: Zebrōna (ⲍ�6ⲩⲣⲱⲛⲁ)

- Septuagint manuscript 318: Zefrona (ⲍ�6ⳝⲐⲁ)

- Septuagint manuscript 707: Efrōna (ⲉⳝⲣⲱⲛⲁ)

- Septuagint manuscript 58: Sefrōna (Ⲋ�6ⳝⲣⲱⲛⲁ)

- Septuagint manuscript 107: Efōnna (ⲉⳝ∞ⲛⲛⲁ)

- Septuagint manuscript 59: Ezefrōna (ⲉⲌ�6ⳝⲣⲱⲛⲁ)

- Septuagint manuscript 376: Efrōn (ⲉⳝⲣⲱⲛ)

- Septuagint manuscript 610: Efrōnna (ⲉⳝⲣⲱⲛⲛⲁ)

- Leningrad Codex: Ziprōnâ (זִפְרֹנָה)

- Peshitta: Zprwn (ܙܦܪܘܢ)

- Targum Onkelos: Ziprôn (זִפְרוֹן)

- Jerusalem Targum: Zāpêrîn (זָפֵירִין)

- Jonathan Targum: qeren Zəkûtā' (קֶרֶן זְכוּתָא). Translation: town of Zekuta

- Sahidic manuscript 2006: Sepfamar (Ⲥⲉⲡⳝⲁⲙⲁⲣ)

- Sahidic manuscript 2044: Efrōna (Ⲉⳝⲣⲱⲛⲁ)

- Bohairic manuscripts: Sefrōna (Ⲥⲉⳝⲣⲱⲛⲁ)

CHAPTER 34

According to the Talmud, Rabbi Akiva ben Yosef lived in a Syrian town named As-Safira in the 1st century, which has subsequently been identified as the town of As-Safira (السفيرة) in northern Syria. Jerome called this town Zephyrium in the 4th century, and also identified it as the northern boundary of Canaan. It is unclear when As-Safira was founded, however, in 750 BCE, a treaty was signed there now known as Sfire Treaty I, which listed a number of gods, including El Elyon (Highest God). This seems to confirm it is the town the Hebrews at the time called Ziphron, and therefore the name As-Safira is used.

6 Codex Vaticanus: Arsenaeim (ΑⲣⲤⲉⲚΑⲉⲒⲘ)

- Codex Colberto-Sarravianus: Asernaein (ΑⲤⲉⲣⲚΑⲉⲒⲚ)
- Codex Venetus: Arsenaein (Αρσυλϟν)
- Septuagint manuscript 407: Asernaeim (Αοϝνλϟμ)
- Septuagint manuscript 527: Asernain (Αοϝναϟν)
- Septuagint manuscript 64: Arsenain (Αρσυναϟν)
- Septuagint manuscript 707: Asenaeim (Ασυλϟμ)
- Septuagint manuscript 127: Arernaein (Αρϝνλϟν)
- Septuagint manuscript 58: Asernaēn (Αοϝνλω)
- Septuagint manuscript 73: Arsernaein (Αρσϝνλϟν)
- Septuagint manuscript 426: Asarēnan (Ασαρλωϙν)
- Septuagint manuscript 500: Sernaein (Σϝνλϟν)
- Septuagint manuscript 56: Asernaam (Αοϝνλλμ)
- Septuagint manuscript 29: Arsenasi (Αρσυλσι)
- Septuagint manuscript 72: Asernaē (Αοϝνλⳑ)
- Septuagint manuscript 82: Aserena (Αοϝαλ)
- Septuagint manuscript 618: Arsenai (Αρσυναϟ)
- Septuagint manuscript 528: Sernaeim (Σϝνλϟμ)
- Septuagint manuscript 68: Asenaein (Ασυλϟν)

CHAPTER 34

- Septuagint manuscript 610: Aserain (ⲁⲟⲣⲁⲓⲛ)
- Septuagint manuscript 619: Arsernain (ⲁⲣⲟⲣⲛⲁⲓⲛ)
- Leningrad Codex: Ḥăsar 'ênān (חֲצַר עֵינָן). Generally
Transliterated as Hazar-enan.
- Peshitta: Ḥsr ȯynn (ܣܝܪ ܚܣܢ)
- Targum Onkelos: Ḥăsar 'ênān (חֲצַר עֵינָן)
- Targum Jerusalem: yrat 'Ayynûtā' (ירת עיינותא). Translation:
gift (or dowry) of Ayynutah
- Targum Pseudo-Jonathan: Kîrayā' dəbêt Sākāl wəlimsî'ût dārātā'
rabbətā' dimMiṣ'ā' bên ṭîrat 'Înəwəwtā' ləbêt Darmāšeq (כִּירְיָא דְבֵית
סָכָל וְלִמְצִיעוּת דָּרָתָא רַבְּתָא דְמִמְצָעָא בֵּין טִירַת עִינְוָותָא לְבֵית דַרְמָשֶׁק).
Translation: Kiraya of house of Sakal and to the middle of the great
court which is Misah, between the tower of Inewwtah and the
house of Darmaseq
- Sahidic manuscript 2006: Arsenein (ⲁⲣⲥⲉⲛⲁⲉⲓⲛ)
- Sahidic manuscript 2044: Asernaein (ⲁⲥⲉⲣⲛⲁⲉⲓⲛ)

The location of this settlement is unknown, however, may be
Hazarin (حزارين), in the Dead Cities (المدن الميتة) in northwest Syria.
The settlement seems to have been abandoned between the 6th and
10th centuries, and re-inhabited during the Ottoman era. The 2nd
century Targum Jonathan rendered Hazar-enan as 'walled suburb
of the springs,' meaning the rabbi Jonathan ben Uzziel, believed the
location was simply a settlement on the edge of the wilderness in
northern Syria.

7 Codex Vaticanus: Semfamar (ⲥⲉⲙⲫⲁⲙⲁⲣ)
- Codex Colberto-Sarravianus: Sefama (ⲥⲉⲫⲁⲙⲁ)
- Codex Ambrosiano A 147: Sepfama (ⲥⲉⲡⲧⲫⲁⲙⲁ)
- Septuagint manuscript 407: Sempfamar (Σεμπφαμαρ)
- Septuagint manuscript 127: Sefamar (Σεφαμαρ)

CHAPTER 34

- Septuagint manuscript 630: Sepfamar (Σόπϕᾰμαρ)
- Septuagint manuscript 18: Sefamar (Σόϕᾰμαρ)
- Septuagint manuscript 56: Semfama (Σόμϕᾰμα)
- Septuagint manuscript 82: Asefama (Ασόϕᾰμα)
- Septuagint manuscript 416: Emfamar (Εμϕᾰμαρ)
- Septuagint manuscript 53: Sepfagma (Σόπϕᾰγμα)
- Leningrad Codex: Šəpāmâ (שְׁפָמָה)
- Peshitta: Špm (ܫܦܡ)
- Targum Onkelos: Šəpām (שְׁפָם)
- Targum Jerusalem: not mentioned in the verse
- Targum Pseudo-Jonathan: 'Apmî'â (אַפְמִיאָה)
- Sahidic Manuscript 2006: Sefaraman (Сеϕараман)
- Sahidic Manuscript 2044: Sepfamar (Сепϕамар)

The Greek translation reads like the name of a town, which has shaped how the Masoretic Text are interpreted by both Christians and Jews, however, the Hebrew term שפמ simply means treeless land, which means the eastern border was the border of the Syrian Desert (Syrian Steppe, Jordanian Steppe, Badia), much as the western border was the Mediterranean Sea. The original meaning of the term שפמ is imported from the Leningrad Codex in this translation.

8 Codex Vaticanus: Arbēla (Αρβηλα)
- Septuagint manuscript 319: Arnaein (Αρναϵιν)
- Septuagint manuscript 509: Bēla (Βηλα)
- Septuagint manuscript 129: Arbēl (Αρβηλ)
- Septuagint manuscript 82: Arbala (Αρβαλα)
- Septuagint manuscript 799: Arbola (Αρβολα)
- Leningrad Codex: Riblâ (רִבְלָה). Generally Transliterated as Riblah

CHAPTER 34

- Peshitta: Dblt (ܪܒܠܐ)
- Targum Onkelos: Riblâ (רִבְלָה)
- Targum Jerusalem: not mentioned in the verse
- Targum Pseudo-Jonathan: Dəpanê (דְּפַנֵי)
- Sahidic manuscript 2006: Bēra (ⲂⲎⲢⲀ)
- Sahidic manuscript 2044: Bēla (ⲂⲎⲖⲀ)

The town of Rablah (ربلة) continues to exist rear the Syrian-Lebanese border. It was a significant site throughout the history of Canaan, as it sat along the main route between the Nile and Euphrates. Pharaoh Necho II established a camp in Rablah after defeating King Josiah's army in 609 BCE, en route to his battle with the Assyrians. King Nebuchadnezzar of Babylon also set up a camp there during his invasion of Judah a few decades later. As the name of the town continues to be essentially the same, the modern name Rablah is used.

9 Codex Vaticanus: talassēs tēs alukēs (ⲐⲀⲖⲀⲤⲤⲎⲤⲦⲎⲤⲀⲖⲨⲔⲎⲤ). Translation: sea of salt (the modern Dead Sea)

- Septuagint manuscript 799: alukēs talassēs (ἀλυκῆς θαλάσσης). Translation: Salt Sea (the modern Dead Sea)
- Septuagint manuscript 416: talattēs tēs alukēs (θαλάττης ῆ ἀλυκῆς). Translation: sea of salt (the modern Dead Sea)
- Leningrad Codex: yām-hammelaḥ (יָם־הַמֶּלַח). Translation: sea of salt (the modern Dead Sea)
- Peshitta: ymå dmlḥå (ܝܡܐ ܕܡܠܚܐ). Translation: sea of salt (the modern Dead Sea)
- Targum Onkelos: yammā' dəmilḥā' (יַמָּא דְמִלְחָא). Translation: sea of salt (the modern Dead Sea)
- Targum Jerusalem: yamā' dəmilḥā' (יַמָא דְמִלְחָא). Translation: sea of salt (the modern Dead Sea)

Chapter 34

- Sahidic manuscript 2006: ṯalassa nǨerana (ⲑⲁⲗⲁⲥⲥⲁ ⲛ̄Ⲭⲉⲣⲁⲛⲁ). Translation: sea of Kherana

- Sahidic manuscript 2044: ṯalassa nǨennara (ⲑⲁⲗⲁⲥⲥⲁ ⲛ̄Ⲭⲉⲛⲛⲁⲣⲁ). Translation: sea of Khennara

CHAPTER 35

The Lord said to Moses to the west of Moab by Jordan near Jericho, "Give orders to the children of Israel, and they will give to the Levites cities to live in from the lots of their possession, and they will give to the Levites the suburbs of the cities around them. The cities will be for them to live in, and their districts will be for their livestock and all their beasts. The suburbs of the cities which you will give to the Levites will be from the wall of the city and out 2000 cubits around it. You will measure outside the city on the east side 2000 cubits, and on the south side 2000 cubits, and on the west side 2000 cubits, and on the north side 2000 cubits, and your city will be among this, and the suburbs of the cities as described."

"You will give the cities to the Levites, the six cities of refuge which you will give for the slayer to flee there, and in addition to these, forty-two cities. You will give to the Levites in all forty-eight cities, them and their suburbs. As for the cities which you will give out of the possession of the children of Israel, from those that have much you will give much, and from those that have less you will give less: they will give of their cities to the Levites each one according to his inheritance which they will inherit."

The Lord said to Moses, "Speak to the children of Israel, and you will tell them, 'You are to cross over Jordan into the land of Canaan. You will appoint to yourselves cities: they will be for you cities of refuge for the slayer to flee to, everyone who has struck a life unintentionally. The cities will be for you places of refuge from him that as relative represents the blood, and the slayer will not die until he stands before the community for judgment. The cities which you will assign, including the six cities, will be places of refuge for you."

"You will assign three cities on the other side of Jordan, and you will assign three cities in the land of Canaan. It will be a place of refuge for the children of Israel, and the stranger, and he that travels among you. These cities will be as a place of refuge for everyone to flee there who has unintentionally killed a man. If he should hit him with an iron instrument, and the man should die, he is a murderer, let the murderer be put to death. If he hits him with a stone thrown by his hand, which can kill a man, and he dies, he is a murderer, let the murderer be put to death. If he should hit him with an instrument of wood from his hand, which can kill a man, and he dies, he is a murderer, let the murderer be put to death."

"The avenger of blood himself will kill the murderer when he will meet him he will kill him. If he stabs him viciously or throws anything on him from an ambuscade, and the man dies, or if he hits him with his hand in anger, and the man dies, let the man that hit him be put to death, he is a murderer. Let the murderer be put to death. The avenger of blood will kill the murderer when he meets him. But if he should stab him suddenly, not viciously, or throw any vessel or weapon at him, not from an ambuscade, or hit him with any stone accidentally, and he dies, but he was not his enemy, nor wanted to hurt him, then the assembly will judge between the hitter and the avenger of blood, according to these judgments. The community will rescue the slayer from the avenger of blood, and the community will restore him to his city of refuge, to what place he fled for refuge, and he will live there until the death of the high priest, whom they anointed with the holy oil. But if the slayer should in any way go outside the limits of the city to which he fled for refuge, and the avenger of blood finds him, and the avenger of blood should kill the slayer, and he is not guilty."

"Let him remain in the city of refuge until the high priest dies, and after the death of the high priest, the slayer will return to his own land. These things will be for you for an ordinance of judgment throughout your generations in all your dwellings. Whoever takes a life, you will kill the murderer by the testimony of witnesses, and one witness will not testify against a mind that he should die. You will not accept ransoms for life from a murderer who is worthy of death, and he will be certainly put to death. You will not accept a ransom to excuse his fleeing to the city of refuge, so that he should again live in the land, until the death of the high priest. So will you not pollute the land in which you live with murder. This blood pollutes the land, and the land will not be purged from the bloodshed on it, but by the blood of he that shed it. You will not defile the land on which you live, on which I live among you. I am the Lord living among the children of Israel."

CHAPTER 36

The heads of the tribe of the sons of Gilead the son of Makir the son of Manasseh, of the tribe of the sons of Joseph, came near and spoke to Moses and before Eleazar the priest, and before the heads of the houses of the families of the children of Israel: and they said, "The Lord commanded our lord to render the land of inheritance by lot to the children of Israel, and the Lord appointed our lord to give the inheritance of Zelophehad our brother to his daughters. They will become wives in one of the tribes of the children of Israel, so their inheritance will be taken away from the possession of our fathers, and will be added to the inheritance of the tribe into which the women will marry, and will be taken away from the portion of our inheritance. If there will be a release of the children of Israel, then will their inheritance be added to the inheritance of the tribe into which the women marry, and their inheritance will be taken away from the inheritance of our family's tribe."

Moses ordered the children of Israel by the commandment of the Lord, "The tribe of the children of Joseph says this. 'This is the thing which the Lord has appointed the daughters of Zelophehad, when he said, 'Let them be wives where they please,' only let them marry men of their father's tribe. So the inheritance will not go among the children of Israel from tribe to tribe, for the children of Israel will be cemented each in the inheritance of his family's tribe. Whatever daughter is an heiress to a property of the tribes of the children Israel, such women will be married each to one of her father's tribe, that the sons of Israel may each inherit the property of his father's tribe. The inheritance will not go about from one tribe to another, but the children of Israel will steadfastly continue each in his own inheritance.'"

As the Lord commanded Moses, so they did to the daughters of Zelophehad. So Tirzah, and Hoglah, and Milcah, and Noah, and Malaa, the daughters of Zelophehad, married their cousins, and they were married to men of the tribe of Manasseh of the sons of Joseph, and their inheritance was attached to the tribe of their father's family. These are the commandments, and the ordinances, and the judgments, which the Lord commanded by the hand of Moses, at the west of Moab, at Jordan by Jericho.

MAP

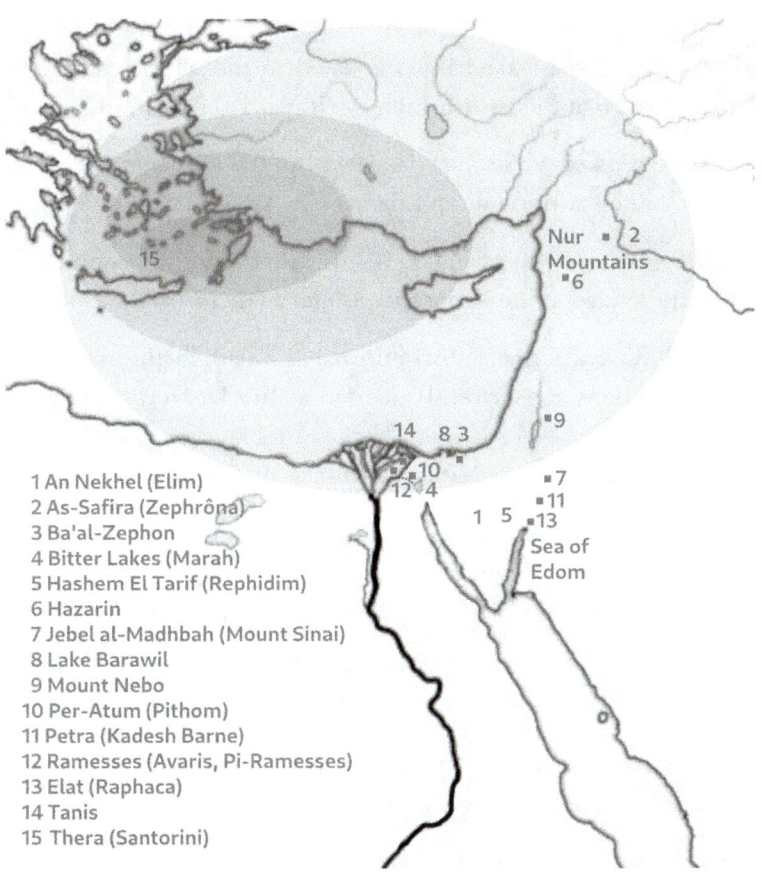

1 An Nekhel (Elim)
2 As-Safira (Zephrôna)
3 Ba'al-Zephon
4 Bitter Lakes (Marah)
5 Hashem El Tarif (Rephidim)
6 Hazarin
7 Jebel al-Madhbah (Mount Sinai)
8 Lake Barawil
9 Mount Nebo
10 Per-Atum (Pithom)
11 Petra (Kadesh Barne)
12 Ramesses (Avaris, Pi-Ramesses)
13 Elat (Raphaca)
14 Tanis
15 Thera (Santorini)

Egypt and Canaan at the time of the Minoan eruption. The gray regions denote the range and severity of the ash fall.

Septuagint Manuscripts

The following is a list of the Septuagint manuscripts referenced in the notes for this book.

LXX A (Codex Alexandrinus) is dated to the 5th century. It is currently located at the British Library (Royal 1 D. VIII) in London.

LXX B (Codex Vaticanus) is dated to the 4th century. It is currently located at the Vatican Library (Gr. 1209) in Vatican City.

LXX F (Codex Ambrosiano A 147) is dated to the 5th century. It is currently located at the Ambrosian Library (A. 147 inf.) in Milan.

LXX G (Codex Colberto-Sarravianus) is dated to the 4th or 5th centuries. Sections are currently located at the University Library (Voss. Graec. in qu. 8) in Leiden, National Library of France (Coisl. Gr. 17) in Paris, and the National Library of Russia (Gr. 3) in St. Petersburg.

LXX V (Codex Venetus) is dated to the 8th century. It is currently located at the Marciana Library (Gr. 1) in Venice.

LXX 15 is dated to the 10th century. It is currently located at the National Library of France (Coisl. Gr. 2) in Paris.

LXX 16 is dated to the 11th century. It is currently located at the Laurentian Library (v. 38) in Florence.

LXX 18 is dated to the 11th century. It is currently located at the Laurentian Library (Pal. 242) in Florence.

LXX 19 is dated to the 12th century. It is currently located at the Chigi Palace (R. VI. 38) in Rome.

LXX 28 is dated to the 10th or 11th centuries. It is currently located at the Vatican Library (Vat. gr. 2122) in Vatican City.

LXX 29 is dated to the 14th century. It is currently located at the Marciana Library (Gr. 2) in Venice.

LXX 30 is dated to the 11th or 12th centuries. It is currently located at the Casanatense Library (1444) in Rome.

LXX 44 is dated to the 15th century. It is currently located at the Stadtbibliothek (A 1) in Zittau.

LXX 46 is dated to the 15th century. It is currently located at the National Library of France (Coisl. Gr. 4) in Paris.

LXX 53 is dated to 1439. It is currently located at the National Library of France (Gr. 17 A) in Paris.

LXX 54 is dated to the 13th or 14th century. It is currently located at the National Library of France (Gr. 5) in Paris.

LXX 55 is dated to the 10th century. It is currently located at the Vatican Library (Regin. Gr. 1) in Vatican City.

LXX 56 is dated to 1093. It is currently located at the National Library of France (Gr. 3) in Paris.

LXX 58 is dated to the 11th century. It is currently located at the Vatican Library (Regin. gr. 10) in Vatican City.

LXX 59 is dated to the 15th century. It is currently located at the University Library (BE 7^b. 10) in Glasgow.

LXX 64 is dated to the 10th century. It is currently located at the National Library of France (Gr. 2) in Paris.

LXX 68 is dated to the 15th century. It is currently located at the Marciana Library (Gr. 5) in Venice.

LXX 71 is dated to the 13th century. It is currently located at the National Library of France (Coisl. Gr. 1) in Paris.

LXX 72 is dated to the 13th century. It is currently located at the Bodleian Library (Canonic. Gr. 35) in Oxford.

SEPTUAGINT MANUSCRIPTS

LXX 73 is dated to the 11th and 12th century. It is currently located at the Vatican Library (Vat. gr. 746) in Vatican City.

LXX 75 is dated to 1125. It is currently located at University College (52) in Oxford.

LXX 78 is dated to the 12th century. It is currently located at the Vatican Library (Gr. 383) in Vatican City.

LXX 82 is dated to the 12th century. It is currently located at the National Library of France (Coisl. Gr. 3) in Paris.

LXX 84 is dated to the 10th and 11th centuries. It is currently located at the Vatican Library (Gr. 1901) in Vatican City.

LXX 107 is dated to 1334. It is currently located at the Biblioteca Comunale Ariostea (188 I) in Ferrara.

LXX 118 is dated to the 11th or 12th century. It is currently located at the National Library of France (Gr. 6) in Paris.

LXX 120 is dated to the 12th or 13th centuries. It is currently located at the Biblioteca Marciana (Gr. 23) in Venice.

LXX 121 is dated to the 10th century. It is currently located at the Biblioteca Marciana (Gr. 3) in Venice.

LXX 125 is dated to the 14th century. It is currently located at the State Historical Museum (Gr. 30) in Moscow.

LXX 126 is dated to the 1475. It is currently located at the State Historical Museum (Gr. 19) in Moscow.

LXX 127 is dated to the 10th century. It is currently located at the State Historical Museum (Gr. 31) in Moscow.

LXX 128 is dated to the 11th century. It is currently located at the Vatican Library (Gr. 1657) in Vatican City.

LXX 129 is dated to the 11th or 12th centuries. It is currently located at the Vatican Library (Gr. 1252) in Vatican City.

LXX 130 is dated to the 12th or 13th centuries. It is currently located at the Austrian National Library (Theol. Gr. 23) in Vienna.

LXX 131 is dated to the 10th century. It is currently located at the Austrian National Library (Theol. Gr. 57) in Vienna.

LXX 246 is dated to 1195 CE. It is currently located at the Vatican Library (Gr. 1238) in Vatican City.

LXX 313 is dated to the 11th century. It is currently located at the National Library of Greece (43) in Athens.

LXX 318 is dated to the 10th or 11th centuries. It is currently located at the Vatopedi (598) on Mount Athos.

LXX 319 is dated to 1021. It is currently located at the Vatopedi (600) on Mount Athos.

LXX 320 is dated to the 12th century. It is currently located at the Vatopedi (602) on Mount Athos.

LXX 321 is dated to the 14th century. It is currently located at the Vatopedi (603) on Mount Athos.

LXX 343 is dated to the 11th century. It is currently located at the Great Lavra (352) on Mount Athos.

LXX 376 is dated to the 15th century. It is currently located at the Royal Library (Y-II-5) in El Escorial.

LXX 381 is dated to the 11th century. It is currently located at the Royal Library (Ω-1-13) in El Escorial.

LXX 392 is dated to the 10th century. It is currently located at the Abbey of Saint Mary of Grottaferrata (A. γ. I) in Grottaferrata.

LXX 407 is dated to the 9th century. It is currently located at the Patriarchal Library (Τάφου 2) in Jerusalem.

LXX 413 is dated to the 13th century. It is currently located at the Library of the Topkapı Palace (8) in Istanbul.

LXX 416 is dated to the 14th century. It is currently located at the University Library (Gr. 16, Bl 150-253) in Leipzig.

LXX 417 is dated to 1103. It is currently located at the Archiepiscopal. Library (1214) in London.

LXX 422 is dated to the 12th century. It is currently located at the British Library (Add. 35123) in London.

LXX 426 is dated to the 11th century. It is currently located at the British Library (Add. 39585) in London.

LXX 458 is dated to the 12th century. It is currently located at the University Library (62) in Messina.

LXX 500 is dated to the 11th or 12th centuries. It is currently located at the Austrian National Library (Suppl. Gr. 176) in Vienna.

LXX 509 is dated to the 9th or 10th centuries. Sections are currently located at the Bodleian Library (Auct. T. inf. 2. 1) in Oxford, University Library (Add. 1879. 7) in Cambridge, British Library (Add. 20002) in London, and the National Library of Russia (Gr. 62) in St. Petersburg.

LXX 527 is dated to the 14th century. It is currently located at the Bibliothèque de l'Arsenal (Gr. 8415) in Paris.

LXX 528 is dated to 1264. It is currently located at the National Library of France (Coisl. Gr. 5) in Paris.

LXX 529 is dated to the 13th century. It is currently located at the National Library of France (Coisl. Gr. 6) in Paris.

LXX 550 is dated to the 12th century. It is currently located at the National Library of France (Gr. 128) in Paris.

LXX 551 is dated to the 13th century. It is currently located at the National Library of France (Gr. 129) in Paris.

LXX 610 is dated to the 14th century. It is currently located at the National Library of France (Suppl. gr. 609) in Paris.

LXX 616 is dated to the 11th century. It is currently located at the Pelekete monastery (217) on Patmos Island.

LXX 618 is dated to the 13th century. It is currently located at the Pelekete monastery (410) on Patmos Island.

LXX 619 is dated to the 15th century. It is currently located at the Pelekete monastery (411) on Patmos Island.

LXX 624 is dated to the 5th or 6th centuries. It is currently located at the National Library of Russia (Gr. 5) in St. Petersburg.

LXX 630 is dated to the 10th century. It is currently located at the National Library of Russia (Gr. 673) in St. Petersburg.

LXX 646 is dated to the 12th century. It is currently located at the Vatican Library (Barber. gr. 474) in Vatican City.

LXX 664 is dated to the 14th century. It is currently located at the Vatican Library (Pii. II. gr. 20) in Vatican City.

LXX 707 is dated to the 10th or 11th centuries. Sections are currently located at Saint Catherine's Monastery (Codex Gr. 1) in the Sinai, and the National Library of Russia (Gr. 260) in St. Petersburg.

LXX 761 is dated to the 13th century. It is currently located at the Zentralbibliothek (C 11) in Zürich.

LXX 767 is dated to the 13th or 14th centuries. It is currently located at the Great Lavra (603) on Mount Athos.

LXX 799 is dated to 1280. It is currently located at the National Library of Greece (2491) in Athens.

LXX 803 (4QLXXNum) is dated to the 1st century BCE. It is currently located at the Rockefeller Museum (4Q121) in Jerusalem. This document is also known as DSS 4Q121.

LXX 833 is dated to the 8th or 9th centuries. It is currently located at the University Library (S. Salv. 140+126) in Messina.

LXX 963 is dated to the 2nd century. Sections are currently located at the Chester Beatty Library (P. Ch. Beatty VI) in Dublin, and the University of Michigan (P. Mich. Inv. 5554) in Ann Arbor.

ALTERNATIVE SOURCES

The following is a list of alternative translations that were used for comparative analysis. Both the Peshitta and Coptic translations are believed to have been heavily based on the Septuagint, although do inherit relics of older Imperial Aramaic translations, or imports from the Hebrew translation.

The Leningrad Codex is dated to 1008 (or 1009) CE. It is currently located at the National Library of Russia (Firkovich B 19 A) in St. Petersburg. The Leningrad Codex is the oldest complete copy of the Hebrew scriptures used within Judaism.

The Peshitta is the Syriac translation of the Christian bible. The Old Testament was translated from older Aramaic and Hebrew sources during the late 2nd century CE.

The Targum Onkelos is generally accepted as having been compiled by Aquila (Onkelos) of Sinope between 100 and 120 CE, although the surviving copies are all in Babylonian Aramaic, and the text appears to have been updated linguistically in Babylon in the 4th or 5th centuries CE. Some scholars believe Aquila was reworking a now lost, older Judean-Aramaic targum from the 1st century. The Megillah (3a) tractate of the Babylonian Torah claims that the Onkelos Targum is a restoration of a version of the Torah in use before the time of Ezra the scribe in the 4th century BCE. While the idea that Aquila and Onkelos were the same person is debated, the Talmuds mention both of them doing the same thing, creating a targum in the same era, but do not confirm they are the same person. Therefore, the Onkelos is sometimes viewed as being a continuation of an older Babylonian Aramaic translation from the Neo-Babylonian, Persian, or Greek eras.

The Targum Pseudo-Jonathan has historically been misidentified as the Targum Jonathan, and is also called the Targum Jerusalem in some literature, although this is not the same document as the

ALTERNATIVE SOURCES

Targum Jerusalem listed below. It is written in Palestinian-Aramaic, and generally dated to sometime between the 4th and 11th centuries. Some scholars believe it originated in the 4th century and was modified after the Islamic conquest of Palestine, as it includes some Arabic names generally found in Islamic sources. It existed before the crusades, as it was documented at the time.

The Targum Jerusalem, sometimes called the Targum Jerusalem II or the Fragments Targum, is a collection of fragments from one or more targums written in Judean Aramaic that surfaced in Italy during the medieval era. It contains a number of heretical concepts, such as Judean-polytheism, suggesting some are a relic of a polytheist Israelite sect from before the Maccabean Revolt. The oldest Targum Jerusalem fragments date to the medieval period or later, and are copies of a manuscript reworked in the 5th century CE. However, the Targum is written in a form of Judeo-Aramaic that supports its origin in the Persian, Hellenistic, or Hasmonean eras.

The Vetus Latina are the old Latin translations of the Septuagint and other Israelite texts that predate Jerome's Latin Orthodox Bible in the 5th century. Some of the texts appear to have been translated directly from Aramaic or Hebrew source texts, however, most appear to have been translations from the Greek translations.

The Codex Gothicus Legionensis (VL 91) is a 10th century Vulgate manuscript currently located at the Basilica of San Isidoro, in León. The original Vulgate was the Latin translation created by Jerome in the 5th century. Jerome's translation used both the Greek and Hebrew text for sources. It was used along side the Vetus Latina texts in Latin speaking regions until the Roman Catholic church adopted a formal form of it in 1590 known as the Sixtine Vulgate.

Sahidic manuscripts are translations of the Septuagint into Sahidic (also known as Thebaic), one of the six dialects of Coptic, the classical era form of the Egyptian language. Sahidic was the dominant form of Coptic used before the 11th century, and is believed to have originated in the region around Hermopolis, at the boundary between Upper and Lower Egypt. Translations of the Septuagint into Sahidic are known to have existed by the 4th century, however, early non-dialect specific translations are generally accepted as having been made as early as the 1st century CE, with some scholars suggesting the 1st century BCE. The early non-dialect specific forms of Coptic are generally grouped with Sahidic, as Sahidic did not have a standardized spelling until the 6th century.

Bohairic manuscripts are translations of the Septuagint into Bohairic (also known as Memphitic), one of the six dialects of Coptic, the classical era form of the Egyptian language. These dialects were written slightly differently, and therefore words transliterated into Coptic retain slightly different pronunciations, reflecting the different source texts used. Bohairic originated in the western Nile Delta of northern Egypt. The earliest Bohairic manuscripts date to the 4th century, however, the majority of texts come from the 9th century or later. Bohairic is the dialect used today as the liturgical language of the Coptic Orthodox Church, although Sahidic was used before the 11th century. Translations of the Septuagint were made into at least five of the Coptic dialects, however, complete copies only survive in Bohairic and Sahidic.

Bohairic manuscript Vatican Coptic 1 is dated to the 9th century. It is currently located at the Vatican Library (Copto 1) in Vatican City.

Bohairic manuscript BnF Coptic 1 is dated to 1356 to 1359. It is currently located at the National Library of France (1675: 520).

DEAD SEA SCROLLS

The following is a list of the Dead Sea Scrolls mentioned in the notes for this book. Most are held by the Israel Museum in Jerusalem.

DSS 2Q6 (2QNum^a) is dated to the Herodian Dynasty in Judea (37 BCE to 6 CE).

DSS 2Q7 (2QNum^b) is dated to the Herodian Dynasty in Judea (37 BCE to 6 CE).

DSS 4Q23 (4QLev-Num^a) is dated to the Hasmonean Dynasty in Judea (140 to 37 BCE).

DSS 4Q27 (4QNum^b) is dated to the Herodian Dynasty in Judea (37 BCE to 6 CE).

DSS 4Q121 (4QLXXNum) is dated to the Hasmonean Dynasty in Judea (140 to 37 BCE). This document is also known as LXX 803.

KETEF HINNOM SCROLLS

The Ketef Hinnom scrolls are two very damaged Judahite or Samaritan silver scrolls discovered during an archaeological dig into a Persian era pile of refuse in the Hinnom valley near Jerusalem. The first (KH1) contains a prayer or hymn that bears similarity to several verses from various books of the Tanakh (Old Testament), however, doesn't actually match any.

The second (KH2) is very similar to a verse from Numbers chapter 6 which is generally reconstructed as: "-hbrw. May be blessed he by Yhw[h], the warrior and the rebuker of [E]vil, may bless you, Yhwh keep you. May shine, Yh[w]h, his face [on] you and grant you p[ea]ce."

They are generally considered to be magical amulets created sometime between the 7th and 4th centuries BCE. It is unclear if it was a paraphrase of this verse in *Numbers*, or simply a similar phrase, however, if it was a paraphrase from *Numbers*, it would mean the text of *Numbers* was different at the time, as Yhwh is not referred to as "the warrior," in *Numbers*. They are currently on display in the Israel Museum in Jerusalem.

ALSO AVAILABLE

ALSO AVAILABLE

- Octateuch: The Original Orit

ENOCH AND METATRON SERIES:

- Books of Enoch Collection

- Books of Enoch and Metatron Collection

- Books of Metatron Collection

- Secrets of Enoch

OTHER TRANSLATIONS:

- Apocalypses of Ezra

- Arabic Maccabees

- Hebrew Maccabees

- Life of Adam and Eve

- Memories of the New Kingdom

- Septuagint's Esther and the Vetus Latina Esther

- Septuagint's Ezekiel and the Ba'al Cycle

- Septuagint's Job and the Testament of Job

- Septuagint's Proverbs and the Wisdom of Amenemope

- The Amarna Letters

- Testaments of the Patriarchs Collection

- Tobit and Ahikar

- Ugaritic Texts: Ba'al Cycle

- Wisdom of Ahikar